HIDDEN TREASURE

A map to the child's inner self

HIDDEN TREASURE

A map to the child's inner self

Violet Oaklander, PhD

KARNAC

First published in 2007 by
Karnac Books
118 Finchley Road, London NW3 5HT

British Library Cataloguing in Publication Data

A C.I.P. for this book is available from the British Library

ISBN-10: 1 85575 490 8
ISBN-13: 978 1 85575 490 4

Typeset by RefineCatch Limited, Bungay, Suffolk
Printed in Great Britain

www.karnacbooks.com

I would like to dedicate this book to Mollie Filler Solomon and Joseph Solomon, my wonderful parents who gave me the kind of childhood which I would wish for all children.

CONTENTS

ACKNOWLEDGEMENTS

I would like, in particular, to acknowledge my dear son and daughter: Mha Atma Khalsa and Sara Oaklander, who encouraged me and urged me and lovingly did whatever they could to make sure I wrote this book.

My daughter-in-law, Martha Oaklander, especially helped me in more ways than she knows.

HIDDEN TREASURE

A map to the child's inner self

CHAPTER ONE

Introduction

A s I write this, it has been twenty-eight years since my first book, *Windows To Our Children*, was published, but actually nothing much has changed. Oh sure, there have been many technological advances (I wrote *Windows* on a tiny Hermes portable typewriter and now have a fancy computer) and so much has happened in the world in these almost thirty years. But nothing much in terms of what children need has changed. They still suffer from child abuse and molestation, divorce, loss and separation and much, much more. Those of us who work with children are still desperate for tools to help children survive, cope and become whole enough to live in our stressful society. In these years I have continued to apply my work and have found that the Gestalt therapy approach to children and adolescents is still effective.

Because I did not have the time to write another book, I made audio tapes, one at a time, describing some of the advances and new ideas I utilized. I wrote articles here and there, and chapters for other people's books. I gave talks and presentations at numerous workshops. I realized that I needed to put all these new (since *Windows To Our Children*) ideas, thoughts, discoveries and developments in my work into one book. The beauty of this work for me is that as time goes by we are offered an opportunity to grow and develop even as we age.

At this time in my life (I turned 79 this past April), I consider myself "semi-retired." Seven years ago I gave up my private practice and now do some supervision, teaching and my two-week summer training programme. I still do some travelling in the US and out of the country giving workshops and keynote talks, but am trying very hard to limit these. In the past few years I worked in South Africa, Ireland, Austria, Mexico and England, as well as in a few cities in the US People come to my training programme from all over the world. Just when I think I will stop doing this intensive programme, I am getting enquiries from Brazil, Argentina, Taiwan, New Zealand and other far away places—from people fiercely eager to learn my method of working with children and adolescents. The hunger for good work with children is astounding.

A group of people have started a foundation, "The Violet Solomon Oaklander Foundation," to make sure my work will be carried on in the event of my total retirement. This group is at its beginning stages as I write this, and I feel so fortunate that I can be in on this from these beginning stages. These people are committed and passionate about the work I have espoused. Needless to say they are the cream of the crop and swell my heart with pride and gratitude.

My work has given me great joy. I hope that those of you who are doing this work will be helped by this book and will reap the same gifts that I have been given, the gift of helping children toward their rightful path of life and growth.

CHAPTER TWO

What brings children into therapy
A developmental perspective

What brings children into therapy? In answer to this question you would probably say well they are disturbed in some way; they are not getting along in school; they are aggressive or withdrawn; they have suffered trauma; they are reacting badly to the divorce of their parents; and on and on. These are all symptoms and reactions. What is it that is causing all these reactions and symptoms?

I have given this matter a lot of thought and would like to present my thesis. What I will say may seem very basic and elementary to you. Actually I am looking at the obvious, which we tend to overlook. Sometimes we need to just bring ourselves back to this obvious place.

Most of the children I have seen in therapy over the years have had two basic problems. For one, they have difficulty making good contact: contact with teachers, parents, peers, books. Secondly, they generally have a poor sense of self.

The expression "self-concept" is more often used to describe how children feel about themselves. I like to use "sense of self" since it avoids a judgmental stance and is a more integrated concept.

In order to make good contact with the world, one needs to have good use of those contact functions we label as looking, listening, touching, tasting, smelling, moving, expressing feelings, ideas, thoughts, curiosities and so forth (Polster and Polster, 1973). These happen to be the very same modalities that make up one's self. Children who are emotionally disturbed due to some trauma or other reason, tend to cut themselves off in some way; they will anaesthetize their senses, restrict the body, block their emotions and close down their minds. These acts deeply affect the healthful growth of children and further exacerbate their problems. They cannot make good contact when any of this happens, and further, the self is inhibited.

What I realized is that it is not only trauma and other problematic life situations that cause children to engage in these unhealthy practices. Various developmental factors contribute to this!

I believe that the healthy infant comes into the world with the capacity to make full use of her senses, her body, her emotional expressions, her intellect. The infant comes into the world as a *sensory* being: she needs to suck to live; she must be touched to thrive. As she grows she actively uses all of her senses. She looks intently at everything, she touches whatever she can reach, she tastes whatever she can get to her mouth.

Her *body* is in constant motion. Suddenly, it seems, awareness is evident. She may accidentally drop the rattle she has been clutching. She will cry and someone will pick it up and put it in her hand. But she does not want to hold it—she wants to drop it. She does this over and over until she has mastered this new skill. She will look at her hands over and over and suddenly, it seems she will realize she can reach for something. As she grows she does not restrict her body movements. When she crawls, walks, climbs, runs, she does so exuberantly and zestfully.

The baby expresses *emotions* right from the beginning. She smiles. She laughs. She appears to lie in her crib contentedly. But then she begins to cry. It is difficult for even the most perceptive mother to determine what her child wants. Is she hungry? Wet? Frightened? Angry? Lonely? As she develops gesture and sound and facial expression and particularly language, her emotional expression becomes quite clear. The young child is congruent with her feelings. You *know* it, for example, when a 2-year-old is frightened, or sad, or happy or angry. She does not hide her emotions as she may learn to do later in life.

And what about the *intellect*? We are in awe at how much a baby and a toddler can learn. She learns language, she is inquisitive, she explores and she asks a myriad of questions. She wants to know everything. She tries her best to make sense of the world. Her mind is a wonderful thing.

The organism, made up of the senses, the body, the intellect and the ability to express emotions is functioning in a beautiful, integrated way, just as it should as the child grows.

BUT—something begins to happen to every child—some more than others—to interfere with healthful growth. The senses become anaesthetized, the body is restricted, emotions are blocked and the intellect is not what it could be.

Why does this happen? Certainly various traumas such as abuse, divorce, rejection, abandonment, illness, to name a few, can cause the child to cut himself off in some way. He does this instinctively to protect himself. But there are a variety of developmental stages and social factors in the child's life that also cause children to restrict, block, inhibit themselves.

These developmental factors consist of: confluence and separation, egocentricity, introjects, getting needs met, setting boundaries and limits, the effect of a variety of systems, cultural expectations and the parent's responses to him, particularly his expressions of anger. There are undoubtedly many other factors. The child is a social animal and does not (and should not) live in isolation. How he engages in his world and the response of others to him affects him greatly. Many believe that the child is pre-destined by biology. To a certain extent this may be true. But every child, regardless of temperament and personality, is affected by these developmental factors to a greater or lesser extent.

Confluence

The child comes into the world confluent with mother: he is very much one with mother. He gets his sense of self from the mother: the mother's voice, gesture, look, touch. This confluence is very important to the child's well-being. The first task of the child is to separate and without this bonding there is really nothing to separate from and it can cause a great deal of anxiety on the part of the growing child. The child may struggle to separate, and at the same time needs to have that feeling of oneness with his parent. This is crucial. The struggle for separation begins in these infant years, not at adolescence as we generally believe. It goes on periodically as the child develops—in and out—back and forth—throughout the child's life. It is essential for the child to feel himself as a separate being. Yet this is a dilemma for the child as he has very little support of his own. The response to this struggle can help or hinder this task.

Egocentricity

Egocentricity always sounds bad when you say, "that person is so egocentric—he only thinks about himself. He thinks the whole world revolves around him." Children, however, are normally egocentric. Basically, they do not understand separate experience. They are puzzled by the fact that I may experience the world differently from how they are experiencing it. They imagine that everyone's experience is the same as their experience, and their experience is the same as mine. It is quite a learning process to understand separate experience, and children do experiment with this at early ages. For example, a 3½-year-old girl said to her grandmother, "Grandma, do you live alone?" When she replied that she did, the child said, "I'm sorry," and tears came into her eyes. Since Grandma was not happy living alone, she felt her granddaughter was extremely perceptive and compassionate. Actually, the child was projecting her feelings about herself. She couldn't imagine living alone without her parents. Piaget wrote extensively about egocentricity and believed that by the time the child is seven or eight, he is cognitively able to understand separate experience (Phillips, 1969). In my work I discovered that emotionally egocentricity persists much longer. In fact, emotionally many adults revert to an egocentricity state. For example, when something terrible happens, we say, "Oh, what did I do!" or "How could I have prevented this?" or "It's all my fault!" And this is what happens to children. Children blame themselves for everything bad that happens to them because of their ego-centricity and difficulty to separate out individual experience. Young children blame themselves if there is an illness, if they are abandoned, if they are rejected in some way, if the parent has a headache, if the parent is angry and grumpy, if they are molested and if there is some kind of trauma. They secretly feel that whatever bad thing that has happened is their fault. I always knew this about young children since I studied Piaget's writing for my Master's degree in special education with disturbed children. But I realized at some point through my work as a psychotherapist with children and adolescents that age made no difference. Children of all ages blame themselves for all sorts of terrible things.

An example: a 12-year-old boy was referred to me for an evaluation by the courts because his parents were going through a very angry divorce and custody battle. His grades were falling, he spent more and more time alone in his room and he evidenced a variety of physical symptoms. In session with me he totally denied caring about what his parents were doing. "It's their thing. I don't pay any attention." As he looked around my room, his interest focused on the sand trays and he asked me what they were for. I explained that people chose miniatures from the variety on the shelves and placed them in one of the trays in some kind of scene. I suggested that he try it. He scanned the many miniatures and selected three surfers (cake decorations) and, after moving the sand somewhat with his hands, he set them in. "I'm done," he said. I asked him to tell me what was happening. "Well, these are three surfers and they're surfing." It is typical of many children to give a very brief sentence describing their scene. We began a sort of dialogue to enhance and build a story.

Me: I would like you to be one of the surfers. Point to the one you will be.

Zack points to one of them.

Me: Hi surfer. What are the waves like?
Z: They are great.

And so we begin to talk about surfing, the waves, the ocean in general, whatever I can think of. As he talks one of the surfers falls over.

Me: Oh! What happened to him?

Z: He fell off his board.

Me: What will happen to him?

Z: He will drown because his board hits him on the head before he can get up.

Me: What does this other surfer do?

Z: He just surfs away.

Me: What about you (*pointing to the one he had chosen*)?

Z: Well, I guess I could have helped him, but I didn't so he drowned.

At that point Zack closed down, broke contact, and began to move away from the sand tray.

Me: Before we stop, I just want to ask you if your scene and story remind you of anything in your life.

Z: Well, I like to surf.

Me: Yes, and you know a lot about surfing. In your story the surfer you chose feels responsible for the other guy drowning. Do you ever feel responsible for anything in your life? Think that something is your fault?

Zach begins to sob.

Z: It's all my fault! They're always fighting about me. I don't know what to do!

The sand tray offers an opportunity for a very powerful projective technique. The child's story is often a powerful metaphor for some aspect of the child's life. Generally, a 12-year-old boy, if asked how he is, will answer, "fine" with little awareness of his true feelings. He is adept at ignoring and denying (like the surfer who just surfed away) and does not allow himself to see that he may be "drowning." When these hidden feelings are brought to the surface, it is then that healing can begin and he can learn that his parents' anger at each other is not his fault. He can learn to express his feelings in healthful ways. He can learn ways to cope with the situation. I can give him the support he needs. In a subsequent session with his parents, he was able to tell them what he was feeling.

(*Note*: I don't know where we would have gone with the story if one of the surfers hadn't fallen over, but I'm sure something would have come up.)

Therapists who work with children and adolescents need to understand the phenomenon of egocentricity and how it affects their lives.

Introjects

An introject is a message that we hear about ourselves and make part of who we are. Very young children are unable to discriminate the validity of these messages. They do not have the cognitive ability to say, "Yes, this fits for me," or "No, this doesn't fit me at all." She believes everything she hears about herself, in spite of any contrary evidence. Some of these messages are covert. If the child spills milk, the parent may not say, "Oh, you are so clumsy," but her facial expression may give that message. Since children are egocentric and take blame for everything, she feels she is a bad girl when her mother, for example, is grumpy or has a headache. We carry these negative messages throughout life. (We are actually operating on the belief system of a 4-year-old.) Even when we have spent years of therapy dealing with those messages, and feel that they are gone, we find that under stress, they emerge again. A therapist I know told me once, "I have spent years in therapy working on my relationship with my parents and feel that I have worked it through. But last week I went to visit them and all those bad feelings I had as a kid— bad feelings about myself—popped up again!" I believe that we never actually rid ourselves of these negative introjects. The best we can do is be aware of them and learn to manage them.

Even positive statements can be harmful. Global statements as, "You are the best boy in the whole world," are confusing to a child. He knows he is not the best—deep down he knows he was "bad" the other day. And so he transforms the message into a negative one. These global statements actually tend to fragment the child since a part of him loves hearing it, while the other part knows it isn't true. He may grow up to feel like a phony.

I tell parents they need to be specific, such as, "I like the way you picked up your toys," or, "I love the colours you used in your paint-ing—they make me feel good." Such statements are not introjects, but are messages that strengthen the self of the child.

Getting needs met

The young child will do anything to get her needs met. She knows she cannot meet them herself. She can't get a job, drive a car, buy food and so forth. Mastery is an essential ingredient of child devel-opment since it gives the child some feeling of control and power. Basically, though, she is completely dependent on the adults in her life for survival. She will not risk the wrath, abandonment or rejec-tion of her parents and will do anything to keep this from happen-ing. Besides her basic needs, the young child thrives on love and approval. The problem is that the child doesn't always know what to do to get what she needs, and sometimes her process in life can be inappropriate and cause further difficulties. Or she will develop a way of being that is meant to protect, but instead cuts off aspects of the self. For example, a child who is sexually molested will usually anaesthetize herself to keep from feeling anything, and this will stay with her throughout life without the proper intervention to give her back to herself.

Organismic self-regulation

The organism regulates itself in its attempt to keep us healthy (Perls, 1969). We understand this idea from a physical point of view: the organism tells us when to eat and when to stop eating, when to go to the bathroom, when to sleep and so forth. We don't always listen, but the organism persists. When I am talking at a seminar, I hate to stop to take a drink of water since I might lose my train of thought. But if I don't heed this need, my throat becomes raspy and I could eventually lose my voice. So I take a drink—and can feel that moment of homeostasis, a feeling of equilibrium. That need has been met and can now make room for new needs to be attended to. This phenomenon is true emotionally, psychologically, cognitively, spiritually. We feel various needs nagging at us, and when we pay attention and do what we need to do, closure is made for that particular need allowing new ones to emerge. This is the process of life and growth, and is never ending.

Anger

Here is an example of what happens to a child: He feels angry at his father who tells him to be quiet and stop pestering him. He has learned earlier that to express his anger is unacceptable and will only make matters worse. It could even be dangerous. So the child stuffs the feeling. However, the organism, in its everlasting quest for health, strives to get this feeling out—expressed in some way. Unfortunately, it is generally expressed in inappropriate or even harmful ways, harmful to his own well-being.

The child may retroflect the feeling, that is, he may push it back inside himself to make sure it is not expressed. He pushes it down so far, he is not aware of it at all. This is the child who gets headaches, stomach-aches, or is very quiet and withdrawn. Another child may deflect the feeling—turn away from it. But the organism needs to rid itself of this energy. This is the child who fights and kicks and acts out in general. I asked an 8-year-old client of mine what makes him fight so much with other children on the playground when he had never done that before. His answer was, "I have to do it because the kids are mean." He did not say, "because my father left us and I guess he doesn't care about me and my mother is crying all the time and maybe it's my fault." It was only after a good amount of project-ive work with him that he was able to articulate his authentic feelings. His behaviour changed drastically after that.

Children will become hyper, space out, wet the bed, become encropetic, become fearful and even phobic rather than express feeling directly. They generally split off from the feelings and are usually unaware of them. It takes a bit of work to uncover these buried feelings and often we find that the anger is mixed in with sadness or shame.

I could speculate about why one child chooses to deflect feelings and another something else, but it would require some controlled studies to find the answer. It is probably based on a variety of factors as early development, family dynamics, innate personality, etc.

Most of these behaviours are manifested without the child's awareness; but there are times when the decision is consciously made. An adult client of mine told me that she remembers, at age 4, deciding to always be very, very quiet. At that age as a lively, energetic, active little girl, she was playing with a favourite uncle, wrestling with him on the floor, and suddenly he made terrible noises, became stiff and died. (This she found out later.) She screamed in terror and her mother came running. The mother became hysterical but managed to call 9–1–1. The paramedics came and attempted to revive him but he was gone. They carried him out. Meanwhile my client kept pulling at her mother asking about her uncle. Her mother, crying hard, told her to be quiet and not to bother her. Since she was only four, she was sure she had done something terrible to her uncle and that her mother was very angry at her. It was then that she made the decision to withdraw as much as possible. She said she would have liked to disappear if she only knew how. She received a lot of reinforcement for being a very quiet little girl and when she was 16 she joined a convent, became a nun and took many vows of silence. When, at the age of 45, she made a decision to leave, she was totally unprepared for the world and decided to seek therapy. She felt that her quietness was interfering with her life and her ability to make friends. The memory of the incident with her uncle emerged when I asked her to go back to a time when she was not so quiet. (I asked her to go back to a time when she felt most alive as a little girl.) She had totally forgotten this incident until I had made this particular request.

Paradoxically, most of the behaviours occur as a result of organismic self-regulation and the organism's quest for health. The troublesome behaviours are seen as "resistances" or "contact-boundary disturbances", though they are the child's way to protect the self, to survive, to cope, to grow up. But instead the behaviours get the child into trouble, cause concern, affect physical health, use up a lot of energy, and most of all, generalize. With any stress, the child will become hyper, or get a stomach ache, or whatever their particular process is. If we say to the child, "Stop doing that" and lecture and punish, it is fruitless since the child is powerless to have control over these responses. If they do stop, another inappropriate behaviour will take its place. A 13-year-old girl told me something at the end of our time together that I will always remember with gratitude and warmth. When I asked her what stood out for her in our work together, she said, "I'll never forget our first session together. You took me on a fantasy trip and had me draw the place I came to. You never, ever lectured me like everyone else did. You never told me to shape up. I'll never forget that." This child came into therapy as part of an experimental programme to give children who were very emotionally disturbed some therapy. She had been in seven foster homes when I saw her and was about to be placed in an adolescent unit of a psychiatric hospital, a unit for "incorrigible" adolescents. In four months (the time I was given) of once a week work, she transformed to the point where she was not placed in the hospital, was going to school and feeling very proud of herself. The truth is that she didn't transform—instead she found herself.

When we are restricted and blocked, the self is greatly diminished. For some children the loss of self is so intense that they will do anything to find that self. Some will seek it by becoming confluent with another, that is, getting a feeling of self from someone else. They literally hang on to someone, constantly try to please, are unable to make a choice or commitment, or complete a task for fear of failure. Others try to find that self by exerting all the power they can muster, as with temper tantrums, fighting, setting fires and general power struggles.

Social aspects that affect the child's development

Setting limits

Of course we need to set limits to keep the child safe. The child learns at a very early age about the dangers of running across the street, jumping off too high a place and so forth. It's how we do it that makes the difference. Parents sometimes expect the child to remember the dangers. Actually, it is the parent's job to monitor the activities of the young child at all times until she has more maturity and cognitive awareness. It is not uncommon to see a parent harshly scold a child for something she was told once not to do. The child learns from gentle, loving repetition. It is just as important to stretch the limits as the child grows to allow for experimentation. I still remember when my son, Michael, then a 4-year-old, loved to leave the safety of his front door to explore further and further up the street. My neighbours and I would often sit outside with our small children, often waiting for an older child to come home from school. Leaving my baby with the neighbours, I would furtively follow after him at a great distance, hoping he didn't see me. I watched as he examined bushes, things he saw on the sidewalk, holes in the ground, various bugs and so forth. My neighbours would admonish me for not just grabbing him and making him come back. But I wanted to nurture his independence and exploratory nature as long as he was safe. At some distance he would turn around and I would pretend to be looking intently at the leaves of a bush. He would joyfully call to me and come running, anxious to tell me about some amazing thing he had discovered. My son, Michael, died when he was almost 15 years old and this is one of my many memories that fills me with joy and somehow diminishes my grief.

Cultural expectations

Children learn from their particular cultural group what is expected of them. In some cultures, we must be very quiet in church, for example. In others we can shout out in response to express our feelings. In some cultures, the child learns to keep his feelings inside. In others, there is more room for expression. In some cultures the child learns not to look at an adult when addressed. In other cultures the child is scolded for not making eye contact. It is important for therapists to learn about and respect these varied cultural considerations, beliefs, values and experiences. Difficulties often arise when the child finds herself in between two cultures. I have a personal experience of my own regarding this phenomenon. My parents were Russian-Jewish immigrants who had come to America in their late teenage years. Although they later learned how to read and write English and became US citizens, they mostly spoke Yiddish at home and Jewish culture was important to them. I was raised in this warm, expressive atmosphere, surrounded by books (Yiddish), music and political discussions. My life in Cambridge,

Massachusetts outside my home was drastically different. I loved my parents fiercely, but I admit I was embarrassed by their accents and Eastern European ways. One day, when I was 10 years old, I was invited to a classmate's birthday party. I had never been to such a party and had grand visualizations of what must take place. In my family, my mother generally made a special dinner and dessert for my birthday. I usually received a book from them and my older brothers for a gift. I was very excited by this invitation. My mother, who was a seamstress, made me a beautiful red velvet dress to wear, a dress worthy of a coronation. So off I went. As soon as I arrived at the girl's house, I knew something was wrong. I stood by as I watched the other children in their nice play clothes, each one carrying a gaily-wrapped present. I had no idea that one brings presents to such a party. I was tempted to turn and run home, but the mother of the birthday girl noticed me and came over, welcomed me, put her arm around me and led me into the room. I think she must have sized up the situation and tried to put me at ease. She sat me down in the middle of a long table. At each place was a party hat, a paper cup full of candy, a small gift, a noise maker and various other birthday paraphernalia. I had never in my life seen any of these things—and 65 years later, as I write this, I still see everything in my mind's eye clearly, and I still feel the same feeling of humiliation. I remember wishing the floor would open up and swallow me. There was a cake with candles (new to me), games like Pin The Tail On the Donkey and other festivities. I probably acted as if I were having a good time regardless of how different and out-of-place I felt since I had had plenty of practice doing that at school. At school I was very adept about acting "American" like everyone else. The main thing about the birthday event is that I never, ever told my mother about it. I knew, even at age 10, that she would be devastated. I often think about what could have happened to make this a better experience for me. Maybe we are more aware of differences now and schools are addressing cultural differences. Yes, I think that if we had had these discussions in school, I would have had a much better experience.

Systems that affect the child's development

We tend to blame the family system for everything. However, there are a variety of other systems in our social structure that affect children. Some I think of are: the school system, the court system, the church system, the welfare system, the social service system and of course our political system. One more is the medical system. When I was 5 years old I was badly burned and was in the hospital for a long time, resulting in skin grafts and a long recovery. The experiences I had there deeply affected my whole life. I can still remember the doctors and nurses admonishing me, "Be a good girl and stop that crying," despite my terrible pain, my tender years, my obvious confusion and feelings of abandonment. I heard those words many times, particularly when they were attending to the burns. This is a long story fraught with many terrible experiences in that hospital. Today, in spite of working on this experience at great length in therapy, I have trouble admitting that I have any pain. Somehow I still have a deep feeling that I am a bad person to have any pain. I talk to my little girl self and tell her that she was entitled to cry, that she is a good girl. But that uneasy, deep feeling persists. When I cried in front of my parents, I was comforted and loved, but I could not, as a 5-year-old, articulate and convey to them my deeper feelings. I sometimes imagine what it would have been like to have a therapist, such as myself, come to my bedside to help me uncover these hidden, buried thoughts and feelings through drawings or puppets or stories.

Children react to trauma in many different ways. I chose to keep my pain hidden as much as I could to be a good girl. Children will do whatever they can to achieve some kind of equilibrium to counteract a feeling of disintegration.

What do we do about all this?

When a child comes into therapy I know that she has lost what she once had, was entitled to have, as a tiny baby: the full and joyful use of her senses, her body, her intellect and the expression of her emotions. My job is to help her find and regain those missing parts of herself. To do this I have used a variety of creative, expressive techniques. These techniques are powerful projections and provide a bridge to the inner life of the child. They can help the child express buried emotions where words are insufficient. They are techniques that have been used for thousands of years as modes of expression by early cultures. They can provide experiences to help the child become familiar with those lost parts of self and provide opportunities for new, healthy ways of being, and last, but not least, they are fun.

In my book, *Windows To Our Children* (Oaklander, 1978, 1988), I have discussed these techniques at length. The chapter that follows here, "The Therapeutic Process", describes the specific use of these techniques. It is important to note that before any of them can be used, a relationship between the therapist and the child must be established, even if it is only a beginning of one. If a child is unable to establish one, the focus of the therapy must then be to help the child achieve this most basic form of trust.

CHAPTER THREE

The therapeutic process with children and adolescents

I have noticed that there appears to be a natural progression in my therapeutic work with children that I call "the therapy process". From a certain perspective, it may look as if nothing much is going on, that we're playing around when in actuality there is a very definite process, a sequence, if you will, in the therapy encounter with children. In spite of the fact that the word sequence implies a progression from one thing to another, this process is not always linear, though the relationship does come first. However, with subsequent aspects of the therapeutic process, I tend to go back and forth as I assess the child's needs. Most people assume that my work consists of using a variety of expressive, projective techniques. Although this is true to some extent, there is much more that requires attention before these techniques are used.

Relationship

Nothing happens without at least a thread of a relationship. The relationship is a tenuous thing which takes careful nurturing. It is the foundation of the therapeutic process and can, in itself, be powerfully therapeutic. This I/Thou relationship, based on the writings of Martin Buber (1958), has certain fundamental principles that are highly significant in work with children. We meet each other as two separate individuals, one not more superior than the other. It is my responsibility to hold this stance. I am as authentic as I know how to be—I am myself. I don't use a teacher voice or a patronizing voice. I will not manipulate nor judge. Although I am perpetually optimistic regarding the healthy potential of the child that I meet in my office, I will not place expectations upon her. I will accept her as she is, in whatever way she presents herself to me. I will respect her rhythm and, in fact, attempt to join her in that rhythm; I will be present and contactful. In this way our relationship flourishes.

Transference generally enters into any relationship; however, I do not encourage it. The child may react to me as a parent figure; however, I am not her parent. I have my own point of view, my own limits and boundaries, my own way of responding. In relating to my client as a separate being, I give her the opportunity to experience her own SELF, her own boundaries—to perhaps experience herself in a new way. I am not hopelessly enmeshed with her, as a parent might be. As I maintain my own integrity as a separate person, I give the client the opportunity to experience more of her own self, thus enhancing her sense of self and improving and strengthening her contact skills.

Further, I have a responsibility to be aware of any "buttons" pressed in me that may not be genuine emotional responses to the contextual situation, and to explore these counter-transference responses to eliminate their detriment to the client. I am true to myself as well. I am not afraid of my own feelings and responses, and I know my own limits. I honour what's important to me. We begin on time and end on time. I pace the session so that there is time for the child to help me clean up (except sand tray scenes). In this way closure is clearly evident.

Once the initial resistance is overcome, I can begin to feel that thread of relationship with most children. However, there are some children who cannot form a relationship, at least for some time. These are children who have been severely injured emotionally at a very early age, or perhaps at birth. Trust eludes them. For these children, the focus of the therapy becomes the relationship. Of course honouring and respecting the child's resistance is vital, for it is the one way that the child has learned to protect herself. Finding creative, non-threatening ways to reach the child is the task of the therapist.

Contact

The next issue that I address in the therapeutic process is that of contact. Is the child able to make and sustain good contact? Or does he move in and out of contact, or have difficulty making contact at all? In every session together, contact is a vital, existential issue. Nothing much happens without some contact present. What happens outside the session may be similar or different, and I can only work with what we have together. Sometimes a child has so much difficulty sustaining contact with me that the focus of the therapy becomes one of helping the child feel comfortable with making and sustaining contact. Contact involves having the ability to be fully present in a particular situation with all of the aspects of the organism—senses, body, emotional expression, intellect—ready and available for use. Children who have troubles, who are worried and anxious, frightened, grieving, or angry, will armour and restrict themselves, pull themselves in, cut parts of themselves off, inhibit healthful expression. When the senses and the body are restricted, emotional expression and a strong sense of self will be negligible.

Good contact also involves the ability to withdraw appropriately rather than to become rigidified in a supposedly contactful space. When this happens it is no longer contact, but a phony attempt to stay in contact. An example of this is the child who never stops talking, or who can never play alone and needs to be with people at all times.

We speak of contact skills—the how of contact. These skills involve touching, looking and seeing, listening and hearing, tasting, smelling, speaking, sound, gesture and language, moving in the environment. Sometimes in our therapeutic journey it is necessary to give children many experiences to open the pathways to contact. Children who have been abused particularly desensitize themselves, as do most children who have experienced some kind of trauma.

Sometimes I will notice that a child, who generally has the capacity to make good contact, will come into the session and appear to be distracted. I will know immediately that something has gone amiss prior to this time. I might casually ask the child to tell me something that happened at school that he didn't like, or something that happened on the way to my office. I need to assess the child's contact level at each meeting.

Resistance

Children evidence a variety of behavioural manifestations, often called resistances, as their way of attempting to cope and survive and make contact with the world as best as they can. Sometimes it works—but more often children do not get what they need as they engage in these behaviours. They are considered inappropriate by others, and only make things worse. Since they have little awareness of cause and effect, they try harder, generally by accelerating the behaviours, but their efforts fail them, and life is far from satisfying. As they gain more self-support through a stronger sense of self, the unsuccessful behaviours drop away and are replaced by more satisfying, effective ways of contacting the world.

Almost every child will be resistant—self-protecting—to some degree. If there is no resistance whatsoever, I know that this child's self is so fragile that she must do whatever she is told to do in order to feel that she can survive. I want to help this child strengthen herself so that she can feel some resistance, to have enough support to pause and consider.

Resistance is the child's ally; it is the way she takes care of herself. I expect resistance and I respect that resistance. I am more often surprised when it is not there than when it is. In some situations, I articulate it for the child, "I know you probably don't want to do this drawing, but I want you to do it anyway. Whatever you do, I don't want you to do your best. We just don't have time for that." I want to help the child soften somewhat, and go through the resistance to some degree for a little while. The very fact that I will accept the child's resistance often helps her take the risk to do something new. As the child begins to feel safe in our sessions, she will drop the resistance for a time. However, when she has experienced or divulged as much as she can handle, as much as she has inside support for, the resistance will come up again. In this way, resistance surfaces over and over again, and each time it must be honoured. We cannot force the child to go beyond her capabilities. Resistance is also a sign that beyond this place of defense, there is highly significant material to be explored and worked through. The child seems to know on some intuitive, visceral level when she can handle such material and I have learned to trust this process. As we work with self-expression and emotional expression activities, the issues emerge again and again. The therapeutic work with the child is accomplished in small segments.

I see resistance as a manifestation of energy as well as an indication of the contact level of the child. As the child engages with me or some activity or technique, there suddenly may be a perceivable drop in energy, and contact shifts away from me or the task at hand. I can often see this manifestation before the child's own awareness, by observing his body response at that moment. I may say, "Let's stop this for now and play a game" to the great relief of the child (obvious through the body). He is back in contact with me. Some children show their resistance in passive ways; that is, they will ignore, act distracted, seemingly not hear what I say, or begin, without response, to do something other than what I have suggested. If that child finally comes to a place where she can say clearly, "No, I don't want to do that," I will quickly reinforce that direct, contactful statement by immediately honouring it.

Senses

To enhance tactile sensation I might encourage the child to finger-paint or work with pottery clay, using lots of water. We might sit at the sand tray running our hands through the sand as we talk. I might bring in a variety of textures to touch and compare, or we might examine various textures right in the office. We might listen to sounds in and outside the office or the sounds of music or drum. We might look at flowers, colours, pictures, light, shadow, objects, each other. Books on early childhood education provide a wealth of ideas for activities to enhance the senses, and are effective with people of all ages. In my book, *Windows To Our Children* (1978, 1988), I describe how I made use of the Orange Exercise, originally described in *Human Teaching for Human Learning* (Brown, 1972, 1990), to open and enhance the senses. I gave each child in a group an orange. Slowly we investigated every aspect of the orange—examining it, smelling it, weighing it, feeling its temperature and texture, licking it. We peeled off the skin and examined it very carefully, biting and tasting it. We peeled the fibrous layer and examined this. We marvelled at the shiny, protective layer over the orange, noting that it had no taste. We divided each orange into segments, took a segment and very carefully went through the examination procedure. We then traded segments with everyone in the group, discovering in amazement that each segment was different in taste and texture, though all delicious. One 12-year-old girl remarked later, "I can never eat an orange, or any fruit, the way I used to anymore. Now I really know it." This child was referring to her enhanced awareness and sharpened sensory capabilities.

When children feel safe in my office, they will often regress and allow themselves to have experiences which one may deem more appropriate for a younger child. When this happens, I celebrate inside myself. Children who live in dysfunctional families, or have been traumatized in some way, tend to grow up too fast. They skip over many important developmental steps. Some children will pour lots of water on the clay, unconsciously replicating mud play. Others will use water in fairly creative ways. A 12-year-old boy, after learning that he had to help me clean up, insisted on washing all the clay tools. I told him that I usually don't wash them but he insisted. As I watched him at the sink, I was reminded of my 3-year-old daughter standing on a stool at the sink washing her toy dishes. This boy did not need a stool but he was involved in the washing much as my daughter had been. He was giving himself an experience that he needed; this was evident by his relaxed body and smiling face.

The body

Our next focus is the body. Every emotion has a body connection. Notice how your body reacts the next time you feel angry or joyous.

Notice the constriction of your head when you hold in your anger. Notice the tightening of the throat and chest as you fend off tears, the hunching of the shoulders when you feel anxious or frightened. Children develop body patterns at an early age, often creating at that time the defects in posture that we usually see more clearly in adolescents and adulthood.

Children who are troubled restrict their bodies and become disconnected from them. I want to help them unblock, loosen up, breathe deeply, know their own bodies, feel proud of that body, feel the power that lies within that body. Often we begin with the breath. Children, and adults, when anxious and fearful, restrict the breath, thus cutting themselves off further from themselves. We invent games that involve breathing. We do breathing exercises. We blow up balloons and move them through the air with our breath to see who can keep the balloon up the longest. We do relaxation, meditative exercises involving the breath. We blow cotton balls across a table to see whose will reach the end first. We play games involving making sounds, singing and screaming. Adolescents in particular are fascinated by the power of the breath. Over and over again they will tell me how they remembered to breathe deeply, imagining the breath bathing the body and the brain, during school examinations and how helpful this was to them. The secondary gain of feeling power over one's life, rather than a victim of it, is immeasurable.

We do many exercises involving the body. We might dance around the room, throw a Nerf ball, fall on pillows, have a fight with Encounter bats (made of thick foam rubber) or rolled up newspaper swords, play a hand wrestling game. Hyperactive children particularly benefit from controlled body experiments such as yoga, or body movement games when they can experience body control with movement. Bed-wetters benefit greatly from body work since they are generally quite disconnected from their bodies. Creative dramatics, particularly pantomime, is a tremendous aid for helping children know their bodies. Each movement must be exaggerated in order to get the idea across. We play many games involving mime.

We don't necessarily spend a whole session doing sensory, breathing and body activities. If it appears indicated, I will suggest an activity that the child may or may not be willing to do. Much depends on my own enthusiasm and willingness to involve myself in these activities with the child, as well as my skill in presenting them. We may spend five minutes or a whole session with these activities. We may need to negotiate and compromise, spending part of the time with what the child wants to do, and part with what I suggest. Once the child allows himself to be involved in these experiences, he generally enjoys them greatly. Therapy with children is like a dance: sometimes I lead and sometimes the child leads.

Strengthening the self

Helping the child develop a strong sense of self is a major prerequisite in helping him express buried emotions. Further, the child begins to feel a sense of well-being as well as a positive feeling about himself. Let me remind you that these steps as outlined in this discussion of the therapeutic process are not at all consecutive. We go back and forth as needed. We may be focusing on sensory work, and while the child is enjoying the tactile sensation of wet clay, for example, along with the kinesthetic experience inherent in working with pottery clay, he may feel an increased sense of self. This heightened feeling of self will often spontaneously evoke emotional expression.

Strengthening the self involves, besides sensory and body experiences:

defining the self
making choices
experiencing mastery
owning projections
the setting of boundaries and limits
having the ability to be playful and use the imagination
experiencing some power and control
contacting one's own aggressive energy.

Defining the self

To empower the self one must know the self. Many experiences are provided to help children make "self" statements. The child is encouraged to talk about herself through drawing, collage, clay, puppets, creative dramatics, music, metaphors, dreams—any technique that will help the child focus on herself. "This is who I am" and "This is who I am not" is what the child is learning and integrating into her awareness. I make lists that the child dictates to me, of foods she likes and foods she hates, things she doesn't like about school and things she does like, if any. The child might draw a picture of all the things she wishes for, or what makes her happy or sad or angry or afraid, or all the things she likes to do. Or I might ask the child to make, out of clay, figures or abstract shapes to represent herself when she feels good and when she feels bad. Honouring the child's thoughts, opinions, ideas, suggestions is an important aspect of strengthening the self. Sometimes, with adolescents, I will use an astrology book, or the manual after giving them a projective test. I will read various sentences pertaining to their birth sign, or the manual's interpretation of the test and will then ask, "Does this fit for you?" Each time the child can say, "Yes, this is how I am" or "No, I'm not like that" or even "Well, sometimes I'm like that and sometimes I'm not," she is establishing more of who she is. The more the child can be assisted to define herself, the stronger the self becomes and the more opportunity there is for healthful growth.

Choices

Giving the child many opportunities to make choices is another way to provide inner strength. Many children are fearful of making even the most insignificant choices for fear of making a wrong one. So I will provide as many non-threatening choices as I can: "Do you want to sit on the couch or at the table? Do you want markers or pastels?" Later the choices become a bit more complicated: "Which size paper would you like? (3 choices) What would you like to do today?" A typical response may be, "I don't know," or "I don't care," or "Whatever you want me to." I smile and patiently insist that they make the choice, unless, of course, I see that it is just too painful to make such a decision at this time. I encourage parents to give their children the opportunity to make choices whenever possible.

Mastery

Children who live in dysfunctional families, alcoholic families, who have been abused, neglected or molested, often grow up too fast and skip over many important mastery experiences vital to healthy development. In some cases the parents may do too much for the child, thwarting his need to struggle; other parents are so rigid they don't allow the child to explore and experiment. Some parents have the belief that frustration improves staying power. Children *never* learn to accomplish tasks through frustration. There is a fine line between struggle and frustration and it is important to be sensitive to that point. The baby struggles to put the smaller size box into the larger one, but when frustration sets in he begins to cry. The older child loses energy—cuts off contact. Mastery experiences come in many forms. Some are planned as bringing in a new game and figuring it out together, building a structure out of Lego or Lincoln Logs, or figuring out a puzzle. Some children, as they begin to feel safe with the therapist, create their own experiences, as drowning the clay with water, or intently washing clay tools. These kinds of experiences are closely related to regression. The child herself creates opportunities to relive the kinds of experiences she may have missed, or needed more of. A 14-year-old girl noticed a toy cash register with toy money in it and decided that we would play store. She put objects on the table, priced them with post-it notes and announced gleefully that she was the storekeeper and I would be the customer. This was a true regression for this tough, street-smart girl, telling me that she felt safe enough with me to do this. When she left, she whispered, "Don't tell anyone we did this!"

Of course children who use many of the projective techniques experience mastery, not by my saying, "That's a beautiful picture, or a wonderful sand scene," but by their own intrinsic satisfaction. I caution parents to avoid overblown, general statements such as "That's a beautiful drawing," or "You are a musical genius." Children generally turn such statements into negative introjects. More effective are statements such as, "I like the colours of that picture," or "I like the way you cleaned your room," staying with the "I" message.

Owning projections

Many of the techniques we use are projective in nature. When a child makes a sand scene, draws a picture, tells a story, he is tapping into his own individuality and experience. Often these expressions are metaphorical representations of his life. When he can own aspects of these projections, he is making a statement about himself and his process in life. His awareness of himself and his boundaries intensifies. When the child describes his safe place drawing to me, he feels heard and respected as I listen carefully. When I ask him to give me a statement about his place that I can write on his picture, he feels further validated. When we connect his statement to his life today, he begins to feel his own significance in the world. From a 14-year-old's safe place drawing of an ice cave, I write as he dictates, "I am walking through my ice cave and I am thinking." I ask him what he is thinking about. "I am thinking about everything—school, my life." I ask if anyone else is there. "No, no one knows how to get here—I'm the only one that knows the way in and the way out." I ask how this place relates to the reality of his life. "I need a place like that. It's hard for me to think about anything when my brother is around." (He is an identical twin!) He expands a bit about this situation and draws a picture representing how he feels when his brother is around—a tight mass of dark coloured lines. He admits that he doesn't know how to feel free without finding an ice cave in which to hide. We have come one step further toward helping this boy find and own himself.

Boundaries and limits

Good parenting involves clear limit setting appropriate for the child's age level so that the child can know, experiment and test her boundaries. When a boundary is not available, the child tends to feel anxious and may flail around in search of this boundary. Her sense of self becomes amorphous. The parents need to know when it is appropriate to stretch the boundaries so that the child, at each developmental level, can find new areas of exploration. In our sessions my limits and boundaries are clear. We begin on time; we end on time. I do not answer the phone—in fact they notice that I generally turn it off. My desk is off-limits and we don't flick paint around the room. At the end of each session the child helps me clean up (except for sand tray scenes.) Closure of the session is made clear by this activity. I don't articulate these "rules"; they are dealt with naturally as they come up. I believe that my respect for me and my limits frees children to become more acquainted with themselves.

Further, I am aware of my own limits in another way—I know, and sometimes learn in the process, what I can do or cannot do. If I am recovering from the flu, I will not engage in an Encounter bat fight with a child, for example. If I am required in a game to jump 100 times, I inform the child when I reach my limit. I can also respect the child's need to limit itself at times, and I need to be aware of my own unrealistic expectations.

Playfulness, imagination and humour

Young children naturally have a flair for playfulness and imagination and love to laugh at funny things. The have not restricted or inhibited themselves as yet. Imaginative play is an integral part of child development. Often these natural resources are stifled in children who are traumatized in some way. Providing many opportunities for imaginative play is a necessary component of child therapy and serves to free and enhance the self. The therapist needs to know how to play with the child; if this quality of life is obscured or lost, the therapist herself must find a way to regain this joyful behaviour. Fortunately, I have never lost the capacity for play and this attribute has served me well with my own children and with the many children with whom I've worked. Because there is so little opportunity in life to experience playfulness and imagination as an adult, I am very fortunate to have found my own avenues for these expressions. Many parents have difficulty allowing themselves to play joyfully with their children. When I am aware of this, we spend some time in my office just playing. I can be a good model for this activity.

Power and control

As children begin to trust me and feel at home in my office, they begin to take over the sessions. This step is one of the most exciting parts of the therapy for me. When I see this happen, I know that there is progress. The children I work with (and actually most children) have no power over their lives. They might fight for control, engaging in power struggles, but actually these children feel a terrible lack of power. The kind of control that happens in the sessions is not the same as a fighting for power—it is a contactful interaction, but one where the child, in the play (and the child always knows it's play), has the experience of control. It is one of the most self-affirming actions that takes place in our sessions. Here is an example with a little bit of the child's story.

(In child work it is essential for me to know the child's "story"— his history, the life he comes from, the life he is in now. Without this understanding of the child's field, the experience lacks connection and substance.)

Joey was found in an abandoned car when he was about 5 years old. He was tied to the seat with ropes, and it was concluded that he had been tied often and not allowed to move much, since his body showed evidence of rope burns, and his muscles were quite atrophied. He was close to death when found. After a time in the hospital, and two foster homes, he was adopted. (His birth parents were never found.) His adoptive parents brought him to therapy when he was 10 years old due to his extremely hyperactive behaviour (in spite of medication), as well as severe bouts of explosive and destructive anger.

Joey spent the first four sessions running around the room, picking things up and throwing them down. In these sessions my focus was to establish a relationship and help Joey sustain contact with me or something in the room and so I attempted to join him by running around the room with him, picking up the object he threw down, making a brief comment about it and chasing after him to the next item. I noticed that at the second session he paused for a second as I made my comment and by the fourth session he had slowed down considerably and was actually responding and interacting with me. The relationship flourished and we participated together in a number of sensory, contact enhancing activities. The musical instruments were a great favourite with Joey and we spent some time communicating without words through the drums and other percussion instruments. He spent one whole session looking through a kaleidoscope, finding interesting designs, inviting me to look at them and then waiting for me to find something he could look at. (A contactful episode par excellence.) Suddenly everything changed and he began to take control of the sessions in a new way. He spotted a set of handcuffs and set the stage for an enactment. "You are a robber and I am the policeman. You steal this wallet" (an old one on the shelf) "and I come after you and catch you." So we played this game with great gusto with various new directions from Joey. He was clearly in charge. At the second session as we played out the scenario, he said, "I wish I had some rope so I could tie you up." I brought in some rope at the next session and he gleefully tied me up. Once or twice I came out of my role to tell him the rope was too tight for me, and he quickly loosened it. We enacted this scene—me grabbing the wallet, he chasing me and grabbing me, putting on the handcuffs and tying me up—for several sessions. Joey added various elements and new dialogue at each session. When he tired of this game, Joey decided to play "principal's office". He surrounded himself with the staple machine, toy telephone and various office-like items. He directed me to be the therapist in my own office who called him for advice about various children in his school. Joey delighted in this game as well, and we played it many sessions. During this time his mother reported that he was a transformed child—happy, no longer destructive, calm.

We began to work on various other aspects of the therapy process in between other play scenes Joey invented, engaging in self-defining activities and focusing on emotional expression, particularly anger. He was quite responsive, and in fact often advised me, when we played principal's office, to tell my troubled child (usually a large teddy bear) to draw pictures of his angry feelings as well as other activities he himself had attempted. I saw Joey weekly for about one and a half years, including his parents every few sessions. At our last session Joey brought in a music tape he liked and, at his request, we danced to it the whole session with much abandon and laughter!

It is tempting to interpret Joey's dramatic play—much of it is quite obvious. Interpretive words seem superficial in comparison with the depth of his experience. A final note about Joey: He asked his mother why he was seeing me. She replied, "When you were little, you never had a chance to play. Violet is giving you that chance now."

Aggressive energy

The term "aggressive energy" offends some people for it reminds them of hostile and destructive behaviour. One of the definitions given in my dictionary for the word "aggressive" is "marked by driving forceful energy or initiative". It is this definition that I refer to when I use this term. It is the energy one uses to bite an apple. It is the energy one needs to express a strong feeling. It is an energy that gives one a feeling of power. It is an energy that gives one the self-support needed to take action. Children are confused about this kind of energy, equating it with trouble for themselves. Children who are fearful, timid, withdrawn and appear to have a fragile self are obviously lacking aggressive energy. Children who hit, punch, have overt power struggles and generally act "aggressive" lack this kind of energy as well. They are acting beyond their boundaries and not from a solid place within themselves.

I provide many experiences for a child to experience aggressive energy and to feel comfortable with it. The self-support she gains from these activities is a pre-requisite for expression of suppressed emotions. The child who has been traumatized needs help in expressing buried emotions in order to work through that trauma, be it illness, the death of a loved one, a loss of a pet, a divorce, abuse, a witness to violence, or molestation. Since the child takes everything personally as part of her normal developmental process, when she undergoes trauma she feels responsible and blames herself for that trauma. This self-blame severely diminishes the self and makes it very difficult for the child to fully express the emotions that need to be expressed to promote healing. Further, the child developmentally takes in many negative introjects, faulty beliefs about herself. These negative messages fragment the child, inhibit healthy growth and integration, and are the roots of her self-deprecating attitude, low self-esteem and feelings of shame. A beginning in turning this disheartening process around is to help the child develop a strong sense of self, which in itself gives one a sense of well-being and positive feeling of self. Self-support activities are essential for this task.

The aggressive energy activities have several requirements to be effective. First, they must take place in contact with the therapist. Having the child engage in these experiences by herself at home, or as the therapist passively looks on, does not have the same impact as when the therapist is actively engaged with the child. This engagement is required in order for the child to feel comfortable with the internal force she may have feared. Second, these activities take place in a safe container. The child know that the therapist is in charge and will not allow any harm to interfere with the experience. Third, there is a spirit of fun and playfulness in the interaction. Fourth, the play is exaggerated. Since the child has avoided this kind of energy (whether retroflecting or deflecting), she must go beyond the centre point before she can come back to balance.

Aggressive energy activities can involve smashing clay, shooting dart guns, pounding drums, smashing figures or cars together, puppets eating each other, having an Encounter bat fight and so forth. There are some games that promote this kind of energy, though unfortunately there aren't too many. Two games I have that were excellent aggressive energy games, but are no longer manufactured, are *Hawaiian Punch* and *Whack Attack* (try E-Bay). A game called *Splat*, where play-dough bugs are smashed, comes close. *Don't Break the Ice* is a game suitable for children who are fearful of demonstrating this energy at first. Hitting the "ice" with a small mallet is quite mild. Let me emphasize again that to experience aggressive energy in a therapeutic context requires involvement of the therapist with the child.

Janine was a 10-year-old girl who had suffered much trauma including physical and sexual abuse, and abandonment. She had been in several group and foster home placements, and finally was adopted into a new family. Her process was to be as good as possible and smile at all times. Before I could begin to help Janine express outwardly her myriad of feelings, including anger and grief, I knew that she needed to gain a stronger sense of self and to feel her aggressive energy. The turning point came with the puppets. One day I asked her to pick any puppet, and uncharacteristically she picked an alligator with a big mouth—(her usual choice would be a cute kitten or bunny). I picked up another alligator and said, "Hello. You sure have a big mouth and lots of teeth. I bet you're going to bite me." "Oh, no!" Janine's puppet answered. "I am your friend. We can play together." "Oh yeah?" I said, as I inched my puppet closer to her mouth. "I know you're going to bite me." Janine backed her puppet away as I came closer, but soon my puppet was directly into her puppet's mouth. Almost involuntarily, Janine's alligator lightly closed onto my puppet. "Ow! Ow! You bit me!!!" I yelled as my puppet dramatically dropped to the floor. "Do that again! Do that again!" Janine shouted. And so we did, over and over, bringing in other "bad" puppets as the shark and the wolf for her to bite. Not quite midway into this play, Janine was biting my various puppets with great force and our puppets engaged in a great struggle before mine dropped to the floor. At the end of this session Janine was smiling broadly (not her usual forced smile), stood up straight and left with a flourish. In subsequent sessions we successfully began to deal with her suppressed emotions.

Danny, 8 years old, had been witness to violence in his home until his mother fled, taking him with her and leaving behind all that he was familiar with, including his father. Danny appeared to have difficulty adjusting to his new environment: he was disruptive at school, bullied other children and physically and verbally abused his mother. In my office Danny was terrified of any aggressive energy activities. He refused to have an Encounter bat fight with me, and would command me to cease and desist if my puppet spoke aggressively to his.

As Danny felt safer and more comfortable with me, he began tentatively to suggest some of the more energetic actions. Eventually he initiated games of attack with me involving He-Man figures, shooting at a target with a rubber dart gun and other similar games. Simultaneously his behaviour at school and at home dramatically improved.

Many therapists have argued that children who have witnessed violence, particularly in the home, should not be introduced to "violent" play in the therapist's office. These children are particularly restricted and cut off from themselves. They blame themselves for the chaos and family disruption. They feel guilty if they are angry at having to leave their homes, or feel sad to leave their fathers. At the same time, they want to protect their mothers. They are so confused that the only recourse is to restrain themselves and push down their emotions. As with Danny, the organism, in its quest for health, broke through his boundaries in unacceptable aggressive behaviour. I believe that these children need opportunities to find the power within themselves in order that they may be freed from the constraints that inhibit their ability to accept and express their varied emotions, and to live freely and joyfully.

Emotional expression

To help children unlock buried emotions and to learn healthy ways to express their emotions in daily life is not a simple matter. A variety of creative, expressive, projective techniques assist in this work. These techniques involve drawings, collage, clay, fantasy and imagery, creative dramatics, music, movement, storytelling, the sand tray, photography, the use of metaphors and a variety of games. Many of these techniques have been used for hundreds of years by people of all cultures to communicate and express themselves. You might say we are giving back to children modes of expression that are inherently theirs. These modalities lend themselves to powerful projections that can evoke strong feelings. Everything the child creates is a projection of something inside of her, or at the very least, something that interests her. So if a child tells a story you can be sure that there is material in that story that reflects the child's life or who she is, and expresses some need, wish, want or feeling that the child has.

If a child creates a sand tray scene with the varied miniatures that are displayed on shelves, the very act of projecting this symbolic material is in itself therapeutic. Something within the child has been expressed. If the child tells a story about his scene, even more of himself is expressed on perhaps another level. If the child can own various aspects of the scene, integration takes place at a much quicker pace.

For example, Jimmy who is seven is very absorbed in making a sand scene. I can see as I watch him that all of his energy is devoted to his task. He is fully present and contactful with his task. I do not interrupt or talk, unless he asks me to help him find a certain object. I watch the clock so that I can pace the session in order to make sure he can make some kind of closure before the time is up. I may say, "You need to finish now," (although most children announce, "I'm done," with plenty of time to spare). If we don't have time to talk about his scene, that will be fine. I can see by his energy level that whatever he is doing is very important to him and needs to be done. Now Jimmy looks at me and tells me he is finished. There are ten minutes left to the session. He says, "This is the best I've ever done!" Jimmy, who loves to do sand scenes, says this each time he does one, indicating to me his satisfaction and pleasure. Jimmy describes the scene to me. There are numerous monster-type figures in conflict encounters with each other. There is a cave with some crystals in it. There are many, many trees and hidden among the trees is a tiny green caterpillar. Jimmy looks at his scene with perspective and articulates what makes sense to him. (Most children will look at their scenes and attempt to make sense out of them, an important part of the integrative process. Children always try to make sense of what goes on in their lives, and feel frustrated and confused most of the time. They need to experience the satisfaction and power of making sense of their own creations, at least.) Jimmy says that the monsters are fighting each other over the treasure in the cave, that he put lots of trees in because he likes trees so much, and that one can't always see things that are under them like the hidden caterpillar. I ask why the monsters are fighting and he answers that he doesn't know but maybe to get the treasure. "None of them will get the treasure because they are too busy fighting. But the caterpillar is safe because the monsters don't see him." (He is now developing a story/metaphor.) I then ask which figure or object is him, and after careful consideration he says that he is the caterpillar. (If we had had more time I might have had a dialogue with the caterpillar.) "What about the caterpillar makes you want to be it?" I ask. Without hesitation he says, "Because it is hidden and safe." I then ask in a very soft voice, "Jimmy, do you wish you had a safe place like that in your life?" He lowers his head, looks at his feet, and says softly, "Yes, I need one." He then begins to chatter about my Polaroid camera and the picture I will take of his scene. I know that his resistance has surfaced, and he has turned his attention elsewhere. Whatever has happened is just about enough for him at this time.

There are many therapeutic levels in this piece of work. Jimmy has expressed his actual life metaphorically in this scene, something he would never be able to articulate at his age—the conflict, the danger, the goodness and the hope that is inaccessible, the feeling of being small and powerless, the need to be safe and hidden, his fears and his anger. Of course these are my interpretations, though probably fairly accurate since I know about Jimmy and his life. My interpretations are not therapeutic, however. What is healing is Jimmy's expression of what he needed to express in his scene—understood by him perhaps on a very deep intuitive level, the feeling of safety in my office, the easy relationship that we have developed, the acceptance and respect he feels from me, the knowledge that there are limits and boundaries that I set and take responsibility for (as, for example, time), and his feeling of control and power within those limits to do what he needed to do without interruption. What is also therapeutic is our interaction regarding his scene, my interest in it and my acceptance of it as a serious piece of work. I ask questions, but I do not push for more than he will give me. For me the most therapeutic aspect of this session was Jimmy's statement about needing a safe place of his own. His expression, which surfaced from deep within, is now fertile ground for us to explore at a later time, rather than a hidden feeling blocking healthy organismic functioning. The resistance that came up, evidenced by Jimmy changing the subject, told me that Jimmy reached his limit in this piece of work, and that he did not have enough support to go further. Time, too, may have added to this resistance, since he knew our time was just about up. In a sense he grounded himself.

Often when the time is up I may need to help children ground themselves by asking superficial questions, such as, "What do you think you're having for dinner tonight?" It is essential to help children come back to earth if they become excited and high in the course of our sessions.

Assisting children in emotional expression often has a sequence of its own. Sometimes children have pushed their feelings down so far that they are completely disconnected from the whole concept. So when this becomes evident, we begin talking ABOUT feelings. What are feelings anyway? We explore, cognitively, all of the aspects of anger, grief, fear, joy. One can feel mild annoyance, for example, or, at the other end of the continuum, blind rage. Then there are body states that are often labelled as feelings such as frustration, boredom, confusion, anxiety, impatience, loneliness. We examine these states as well. We look at pictures, play games, make faces, move our bodies to drum beats, act out various feelings, use puppets, draw pictures, use clay, make lists, tell stories, read stories—all related to feelings and body states. Language plays an important role too. As children grow and develop mastery in language, they are much more able to be aware of and express the nuances of their feelings in a more satisfying way.

An 8-year-old girl who had been severely physically abused by her father was unable to express any feelings at all. It was as if she had no understanding of what feelings were. A game we played called The Happy Face Game mystified her. It consisted of cards with various faces and no matter which card she picked, she said the same thing. "I feel happy when it's my birthday. I feel mad when it's my birthday. I feel sad when it's my birthday." Even though she listened with some interest to my statements when I picked a card, she continued her birthday statements. We played many games about feelings, as indicated above. One day we were playing school at her request, and as the teacher she told me to write something that made me sad, mad and happy. While I did this I noticed that she was busy writing her own sentences on the chalkboard on the wall. She wrote, "I am sad because my cat ran away and I don't know where she is. I am mad because my mother wouldn't let me watch TV last night. I am happy because my father doesn't hit me now."

Children don't always move from talking about feelings to expressing their own feelings. We may use projections as a forum for expression. The drawings, the stories, the sand tray scenes will be replete with material to draw from in helping the child own her own feelings. For example, Terri, a 13-year-old girl, drew a snake in a desert after a fantasy exercise. I asked her to be the snake and describe her existence as that snake. Naturally, there was some resistance to this request. I said, "I know it's crazy but just say 'I'm a snake.' Imagine the snake is a puppet and you have to speak for it, give it a voice." So she said, "I'm a snake" (rolling her eyes). I immediately engaged the snake in a dialogue, asking it questions as "Where do you live? What do you do all day?" and so forth. Finally I said, "What's it like being out there in the desert by yourself, snake?" After some pause, she answered in a very low voice, head down, "Lonely." The change in her energy, body posture and voice quality told me that something was going on inside of her, that perhaps she was connecting in some way to the snake. So I said very softly, "Do you, as a girl, ever feel that way?" She looked up at me and as I held her gaze, she burst into tears. She continued at that point to describe her feelings of isolation and desperation.

I'd like to emphasize a few points here. First, it is very important for me to ask important questions in a very soft, almost casual manner. Second, I have learned that when children cry it is mortifying for them (especially for a 13-year-old). If I focus on the tears, as I might with an adult, I will probably facilitate the closing down process. So I keep on talking. "Tell me about your loneliness, Terri," and she did. When the session was over, Terri drew a quick figure next to the snake. "That snake is really me, isn't it?" she said. Not all children will identify so readily with their projections. Often I need to say, "Is there anything about your story that fits for you?" or "Do you ever feel like you want to attack someone like the lion in your scene?"

Since emotions often have a body counterpart, we spend some time helping children become more aware of their own body reactions. As children become attuned to their bodies, they can often use these responses as clues. For example, 16-year-old Susan stated that she never felt angry. We did a fantasy experience where I asked her to imagine something that could make her or someone angry and to notice what she felt in her body. She then drew a picture of a cloud over a head. She labelled this "The cloud of confusion." I suggested that she use this as a clue—that whenever she felt confused she would check to see if something was happening that she didn't like. ("Don't like" is a watered down, less threatening expression for some children.) If she could know she was angry, she could then choose an appropriate way of expressing it.

The child and I discuss at length various ways she might express angry feelings privately without bringing further trouble to herself. By this time I have hopefully convinced them of the organism's need to rid itself of this negative energy, rather than push it down. We make a list of these activities and practise them in the office. Some of the more popular methods include tearing magazines, drawing a face and jumping on it, hitting a designated pillow, screaming into a pillow, running or some other physical activity while focusing on the angry feeling, writing an unmailed letter to the object of the anger and so forth. It is necessary for children to have outlets such as these. Direct expression is certainly ideal, but difficult for all of us and especially for children. When they attempt to directly tell a teacher or a parent what is making them angry, they are accused of having a bad attitude and often punished. Children do tend to speak in a louder voice when angry; they have not yet learned the art of diplomacy.

The child generally will go to great lengths to avoid dealing with deep feelings—feelings that are kept hidden, and interfere with healthy development. He very rarely says, "Today I'd like to work on my father." The child has so little support to deal with the intensity and weight of these feelings that he will suppress them to the extent that he actually has little awareness of them. However, his behaviour and life process are greatly affected by these feelings, and helping children uncover them and express them is essential in therapeutic work. Eleven-year-old John exhibited behaviours and symptoms that were interfering with his life. His grades were falling, he became forgetful, often had headaches and stomach-aches. When I asked his mother when he began to have these symptoms, she vaguely stated that it had been going on for a couple of years, but actually had worsened lately. When I asked if anything had happened 2 years before, she said his brother had died, but she felt that they had all handled their grief quite well. I know that children need a lot of assistance to go through grief, and they are so good at pushing feelings down that they are often seen as doing well. Further, I know that changes in behaviour and new symptoms appear gradually, and become accelerated as time goes by.

A child does not say, "This is not working for me. I'll try something else." The behaviours and symptoms intensify and increase. At one of our sessions, I asked John to make a clay figure of his brother and to talk to him. He became quite agitated and refused. I gently asked, "What are you thinking about, John?" (I rarely ask children what they are feeling, since they usually say "fine" or "I don't know.") John shouted, "I hate those doctors!" I quickly put a lump of clay in front of him and handed him a clay mallet. "Give it to those doctors," I said. John began to smash the clay with the mallet. I became a sort of cheerleader, urging him on. (This is not a time for the therapist to stay quiet.) He smashed with lots of energy. "Yeah. Give it to them. Tell them why you're mad at them. " John began shouting, "I hate you. You wouldn't let me see my brother. I never saw him again. I hate you." After a while I asked John to make a figure of his brother. He made a figure in the hospital bed. "If you could say anything you wanted to him, what would you say?" Tears came down his face as he told his brother how much he missed him. There was silence as he intently looked at his clay brother. He said softly, "Goodbye," picked up the figure and kissed it, gently laid it down and said to me, "Do we have time for a game of Connect–4?" We spent a few more sessions focusing on his brother, and John's behaviour dramatically changed. He is now a happy, productive, well-adjusted boy.

Self-nurturing

A vital step in the therapeutic process is what I call self-nurturing work. In essence my goal is to help children be more accepting, caring and actively nurturing to themselves. This is a difficult task since children are brought up with the idea that it is selfish and wrong to care about the self. If a child says, "I'm very good at this," she may be accused of bragging. The children I work with have introjected, swallowed whole, taken in many faulty messages about themselves from a very early age at a time they did not have the maturity and cognitive ability to discriminate what fit for them or did not fit. These introjects cause children to restrict and inhibit aspects of the self and interfere with healthful growth. These negative self-messages tend to remain with them throughout life, and particularly emerge under stress. Children developmentally, in their egocentricity, blame themselves for the traumas that occur in their lives.

I find that even if parents change their manner of relating to and communicating with their children, their faulty belief system persists, often going underground to emerge at times of tension and pressure.

Even a young child, particularly the disturbed child, has a very well-developed critical self. He develops powerful negative introjects and often does a better job of criticizing himself than his parents do. This judgmental stance, often well hidden from others, is detrimental to healthful growth. The child may say to himself, "I should be a better boy," but the enactment of this wish is beyond his power and comprehension. The will to "be better" enhances his despair. Self-acceptance of all of one's parts, even the most hateful, is a vital component of unimpaired, sound development.

Fragmentation is a disastrous result of self-deprecation. Integration begins to take place when we can help the child begin to learn to accept the parts of herself that she hates, and to understand the function and purpose of those parts. Through this process, children acquire skills for treating themselves well.

This is a revolutionary concept for most children, since, as indicated above, they have learned that it is egotistical, self-centred and frowned upon to treat oneself well. They will then look to others to do this job, and feel let down when it doesn't happen, further reinforcing the negative introject. Adolescents feel guilty when they do nice things for themselves, which debilitates rather than strengthens.

The first part of the self-nurturing process involves digging out those hateful parts of self. Though fragmentation prevails, the child tends to identify herself totally with each hateful part. If the message is, "I'm stupid," then she feels that stupidity is her whole identity. Comprehending that the hateful part is only one aspect of herself is usually a new concept. Once a part is identified, the child may be asked to draw it, make it out of clay, or find a puppet that represents that part. The part is fully described, portrayed and exaggerated. The child is encouraged to talk to that part, and often critical, angry statements are directed at the hateful demon. In this way, she expresses her aggression outwardly, rather than turning it in toward the self. With this kind of outpouring of energy, she gains self-support for the next step that involves finding a nurturing component within the self. Sometimes the hateful part becomes a younger child, about 4 or 5 years old, an age when children absorb many negative self-messages. The child then dialogues with this younger self. Realizing that the part is actually a belief from a much younger age often helps the child to develop a nurturing stance. Sometimes we use a projective technique such as a fairy godmother puppet who is loving, accepting and nurturing to the hateful part. The child is then encouraged to repeat the fairy godmother's words to see how it feels to say them to himself. Ten-year-old Andrew expressed much anger and disgust at a drawing of the clumsy part of himself that he named "Mr. Klutz." Mr. Klutz couldn't do anything right and fell down and bumped into things all the time. As the fairy godmother puppet, he told Mr. Klutz after a while, "At least you try things!" Joseph turned to me in wonderment and said, "That's right, I do try things!" A piece of integration took place at that moment right before my eyes. I suggested to Joseph that he imagine his fairy godmother sitting on his shoulder each time he did something klutzy, and she told him that she liked him even when he fell or bumped into things, and she was glad he tried. Joseph reported in later sessions that he really wasn't as clumsy as he originally thought.

Seven-year-old Lisa thought she was stupid because she had trouble learning to read. Her fairy godmother puppet said, "You're pretty good in math so you're not so dumb as you think." (These were Lisa's own projected words.) Lisa was able to say these words to the drawing of her dumb self, without the use of the puppet, with sincerity. She reported later that she was reading pretty well now.

Twelve-year-old Zachary admitted that deep down he felt he was a very bad person and deserved his abuse and abandonment. He made a figure of a 4-year-old Zach, the age when he remembered his first beating. It was not difficult for him to see that this small figure of a small child had not deserved such treatment, and he was able to talk to his little boy self in a nurturing way. I asked Zachary to find something at home to represent this young child part of him, a pillow, a stuffed animal, a ball and to talk to him every night before he went to sleep, telling him what a nice kid he was and that he did not deserve the beatings. I especially wanted him to tell this part that he would always be with him, that he would never leave him. We practised this in the office after I explained that, even though this exercise seemed strange and weird, it was extremely important that he follow these directions. He did as directed, and exhibited a decided improvement in his demeanour.

Persistent inappropriate process

Generally the inappropriate behaviours that have brought children into therapy have diminished or completely disappeared by the time we have worked through the various components of the therapy process. After several months of therapy, Janine gradually grew to trust others and develop a strong sense of self. She began to express her emotions clearly and transformed herself from a meek, timid child into one who could comfortably stand up for herself. Joseph, who had presented himself as severely hyperactive, no longer needed to move incessantly in order to avoid contact. He now had good contact skills, and was calm and present in most situations. We were able to focus on the deeper emotions of anger and grief that lay within him.

There are times, however, when certain behaviours tend to persist, and it is at this time I focus on them. When a child initially comes into therapy, I do not confront the behaviours. I don't say, "Let's talk about your fighting." I might ask the child to describe the experience of fighting, paint his feelings during the fighting, or draw a picture of one of his fights. But we don't discuss the fighting with the intent of changing his behaviour at that time. (I do confront trauma fairly early on, however.) I see the behaviour as a symptom of something deeper. When the child does not appear to be happier, stronger and functioning well in his life, I need to first evaluate my work carefully. If the child and I have a good relationship, he is able to sustain contact, has been responsive and has shown a fairly healthy process during our time together, then I know I need to focus on that behaviour that is still causing concern and distress.

Since Gestalt Therapy is a process-oriented therapy, rather than a content-focused therapy, helping children become aware of their particular process takes precedence over modifying the behaviour through specific problem solving, rewards, lectures, or other types of interventions. It is through the awareness and experience of their actions that change begins to take place. Change within this context is often paradoxical in nature. Arnold Beiser (1970) states, "Change occurs when one becomes what he is, not when he tries to become what he is not." Following this principle I will devise activities and experiments to direct the child's awareness toward his behaviour. Prerequisite to these experiments are the child's new feelings of self-worth and self-support, as well as skills for appropriately expressing his feelings. Twelve-year-old James was very shy. He lived in a large, chaotic family and somehow had been lost in this atmosphere. I worked with the family as well as James individually, and though much good work was accomplished, James remained painfully shy with other children. A therapeutic group would have been helpful, but one was not available. Together we delved deeper into his shyness. He made a clay sculpture representing his shy self, and one for the self he wished for. He discovered that his shy self was quite young and had some poignant dialogues with his little boy self. He discovered that he had had very good reason to be shy at that time as a way of coping and protecting himself. I devised an experiment whereby he would approach a group of children at school at lunchtime, and pay full attention to the feelings in his body and the thoughts in his head. This was a painful experiment, but with his newly developed sense of self, he agreed to carry it through. At the next session he drew a picture of his feelings using different colours, and listed his thoughts: "They don't like me. I'm not good enough." James was surprised to recognize these thoughts as old messages about himself. A further experiment was suggested involving taking the younger James by the hand (figuratively) and talking to one boy in his class about an assignment. We talked about rejection, something he usually expected. And so with my support and with the idea that this was an experiment, James carried out the assignment with great success. Further such experiments along with their successes helped him realize that he could discard that old, shy self.

Ending of therapy

I am often asked about how I know when it is time to stop the therapy. If the child is doing well in his life, and our work has taken on an aura of just hanging out together, it's time to stop. If the child, who once couldn't wait to come to the sessions, becomes very busy in her life with friends and activities and says she doesn't have time to come, it's probably time to stop. If the child is doing well in life and our sessions are still fruitful, it is NOT time to stop. If nothing much is happening in our sessions and symptoms persist at home, it is time for me to take a good hard look at what I'm doing or not doing. If resistance comes up and persists, even though I know there is more work to be done, we sometimes have to stop for a while. This often happens with children who have undergone severe trauma, particularly molestation. The child can only work through certain aspects of the trauma at her specific developmental level. If a 4-year-old has been traumatized in some way, she may work through her anxieties and feelings over that trauma, but only to the extent of her 4-year-old cognitive and emotional abilities. At various stages of her life, issues may present themselves related to that early trauma, causing inappropriate behaviours or symptoms to emerge, calling for further therapy suitable for her current developmental level. Further, children often reach a plateau in their work and need time to integrate what has been accomplished. Sometimes parents take their children out of therapy for a variety of reasons, as financial and time constraints or insurance company limitations. When this happens I must respect the parents' wishes and leave the door open for subsequent work.

The length of time of therapy with a child is quite variable depending on many factors. Sometimes we work for a few sessions, sometimes three or four months or a school year and sometimes for

2 years. Regardless of the length of time or the reason for ending, special attention is given to closure. Closure is not taken lightly—it is an important aspect of the therapeutic process. In a sense, therapy has been the foreground, a vital figure in the child's life, and the completion of this gestalt allows the child to move on to a new place. As needs are met, new masteries achieved, new discoveries made, blocked feelings expressed, there is a period of homeostasis and satisfaction. This is closure, and from this place, the child can grow and develop in healthy ways.

Our last session can represent a rite of passage. To honour this event, we pay homage to our sessions. We talk about all the various activities that have taken place. The child and I look at her folder together much as a photograph album, remembering the various drawings and sand scene photos. Depending on the child's age we decide on the final event. We may make goodbye cards for each other, or the child might choose a favourite game to play. We talk about endings and beginnings. I have asked adolescents to create a sand scene representing our time together, or the feelings accompanying the ending or one thing that stands out for them from our time together. Some children will draw pictures of their mixed feelings: sad to be leaving and happy to be leaving. Such drawings can relieve the confusion they feel over having opposing feelings. What we do to honour our final meeting is a cooperative decision.

Parents and families

The focus of this chapter has been the therapeutic process with children and adolescents. Working with parents and the family is certainly part of that process, though at a different level. I do, as a general rule, see the parents with the child at least every four to six weeks, if I am seeing the child individually. I will bring in other members of the family as necessary, sometimes seeing the child and his siblings without the parents. Occasionally I have seen a child alone every other week, and with her mother or both parents the alternate week.

Educating parents about the therapy process is essential. Unless parents understand and know what I am doing, they can easily sabotage the work. Parent education becomes a vital part of the therapy process and most parents are grateful for it. If the parents are hostile and angry, I must honour that resistance, offer my support and continue my attempt to establish a working relationship with them. I know that often the hostility is a mask for their own pain, anxiety and feelings of failure as parents. If parents refuse to participate at all, but continue to bring in their child because they must, as by court order, I will continue to work with the child, often addressing the issue of their parents' attitude with the child. Every session can give that child inner strength to cope with his family.

Even when parents willingly participate in sessions, there is a decided difference in family work and individual child work. Children are certainly relieved and happy when parents change dysfunctional ways of relating to them, but often the negative introjects are just buried deeper only to surface at a later time. The child does not automatically become emotionally healthy when his family begins to make changes. He still needs to gain a stronger sense of self, express buried emotions, learn how to get his needs met or to meet his own needs appropriately, learn to be self-accepting and self-nurturing and begin to learn how to manage faulty messages of the self that have already become ingrained as part of his belief system about himself.

Note

This chapter appeared in *The Gestalt Review*, 1(4) (1997), and *The Heart of Development*, Volume 1: Childhood.

CHAPTER FOUR

Enhancing the sense of self of children and adolescents

Children need support within the self in order to express
blocked emotions. Children who have experienced trauma,
be it molestation, abuse, the death of a loved one, or the
divorce of their parents, block their emotions relating to the trauma
and have little experience in knowing how to express them. Because
children are basically egocentric and take everything personally
as part of their normal developmental process, they take responsibility and blame themselves for whatever trauma occurs. This
phenomenon causes children to push emotions down even further
since they do not have the ego strength to own them, much less
express them. Children, too, take in many negative introjects—faulty
beliefs about themselves—because they do not have the cognitive
ability to discriminate between the accurate and the inaccurate. These
negative messages cause fragmentation, inhibit healthy growth and
integration and are the roots of a self-deprecating attitude and low
self-esteem.

Helping the child develop a strong sense of self gives him or
her a sense of well-being and a positive feeling of self, as well as
the inner strength to express those buried emotions. We know that
unexpressed, buried emotions can sabotage the healing process.

I would like to present a way of looking at the task of strengthening the self that I have found to be successful in my work with children of all ages. This model is not necessarily linear—activities and experiences are presented as determined through observation and my interaction with the child. In another chapter I have discussed my working model based on the normal development of the child. To repeat briefly, the healthy infant comes into this world as a sensuous being: she must be held to thrive and suck to receive nourishment. As she grows she looks at everything, listens to everything, touches and tastes everything. Her senses are in full play. She becomes aware of what her body can do and uses it zestfully. Her emotions are expressed without inhibition. She uses her intellect to its full capacity to absorb and learn about the world.

She makes use of all the aspects of her organism in an integrated, vigorous fashion. But as she matures, various developmental aspects begin to mould and shape her existence and those modalities that make up the organism are often restricted and inhibited. The child who experiences trauma in her life is severely prone to a loss of her natural capacity to use the various modalities of her organism to meet the world. She may restrict her senses, inhibit the use of her body, block her emotions, close down her intellect. It is well known, for example, that children who have been molested will anaesthetize themselves as a form of protection. Once this happens, it is difficult to undo and becomes the child's way of dealing with all stress, if not all life. The child's self is inhibited and often lost.

Giving the child experiences with those lost aspects of the self is essential to helping her build her sense of self.

Most of the children I have seen have had two large, general problems regardless of what has brought them into therapy. One, they do not feel good about themselves (even if they won't admit it) and two, they have difficulty making good contact—relating well to either parents, teachers, peers, books. To make good contact one must have good use of the aspects of the organism: the senses, the body, awareness of and expression of emotion and the use of the intellect. All of these, functioning together in an integrated fashion, provide the means for each of us to make good contact with our world. Those aspects (senses, body, intellect, emotions) are the very same ones that actually make up the organism—the self. So it makes sense that if any one of these is impaired in some way, it will affect both the self and the ability to make good contact—to be fully present in every situation.

What exactly is the self? When we talk about self-problems, we generally refer to words like "low self-esteem" or "self-concept". In this chapter I will use the expression "sense of self" since I believe that this is a more integrating definition. Having low self-esteem, for example, implies judgment of one's self, as, in fact, does having high self-esteem. Having a poor self-concept refers to how we see and experience ourselves. Both of these terms seem fragmenting to me, a splitting of the person. It is not so much, I believe, to have a great opinion of ourselves, as it is to be fully aware of ourselves and what we have available to us—what our organisms consist of— to interact with the world.

It is interesting to note that *Webster's Dictionary* defines the self as:

1. the identity, character, or essential qualities of any person;
2. the identity, personality, individuality of a given person; one's own person as distinct from all others;
3. a person in his best conditions; and
4. the union of elements (as body, emotions, thoughts and sensations) that constitute the individuality and identity of a person.

It is this last definition that I particularly agree with. I believe the child is born with the potential for a good, strong sense of self. Though he or she may get that sense of self in the beginning from mother's voice, face and touch, the child, from the onset, struggles to find her own self. With appropriate nurturing, the child revels in her self and as she grows and develops, she discovers more and more of her self. Sadly, this phenomenon becomes thwarted.

I have delineated a variety of elements that I feel are essential aspects of the child's self. To achieve a strong, integrated sense of self, each of these elements must be strengthened. They are:

1. *the senses*: looking, listening, touching, tasting, smelling;
2. *the body*: becoming aware of all that the body can do, as well as the breath and the voice;
3. *the intellect*: making choices; defining the self; owning projections;
4. mastery;

5. power and control;
6. the use of boundaries and limits;
7. playfulness, imagination, humour;
8. looking at negative introjects to achieve integration;
9. the use of one's aggressive energy;
10. the sixth sense: using intuition and trusting the self.

I may begin by giving the child experiences that stimulate and intensify the use of the senses, an important step toward empowering the self. Experiences with seeing, hearing, touching, tasting and smelling—modalities that are actually the functions of contact—focus new awareness on one's senses. Activities, of course, are designed to meet the developmental level of the child. From this base we move on to other self-strengthening exercises.

In the following pages I will discuss each of these elements, giving examples of activities I have used. You may know of others, and often the children give good suggestions. Each is presented as a game or an experiment that may take up the whole session or five minutes of the session.

Stimulating and enhancing the senses

Looking

Where's Waldo? books.
Looking at pictures with much detail.
Drawing, painting, or sketching flowers, fruit, trees.
Experimenting with the feel of something, as clay, with eyes closed and then with eyes open.
Looking at things through glass, water, cellophane, magnifiers, kaleidoscope.

Listening

Meditating on whatever sounds come into awareness.
Painting while listening to music (finger painting is especially good).

Making loud and soft sounds, higher and lower, with percussion instruments.

Matching sounds.

Having a conversation with sounds.

Sound recognition game.

Comparing sounds with feelings.

Touching

Putting objects in a bag and guessing what they are just by feeling them.

Describing the feel of various textures with fingers or bare feet.

Finger painting, using wet clay, running one's hands through sand.

Listing words that describe some touching sensation (as bumpy, fluffy, slippery, hard, soft, smooth, sticky, gooey, warm, cold, hot, freezing, rough, holey, prickly, tingly, feathery, rubbery, thin, spongy, mushy, silky, hairy).

Assigning colours to these words.

Drawing pictures to represent these words.

Acting out these words in some way, for the therapist or children in a group to guess.

Tasting

Doing the orange exercise described in Chapter 3.

Discussing favourite and not-so-favourite tastes.

Bringing in samples of things to taste and comparing taste and textures.

Pantomime eating various foods.

Smelling

Talking about favourite and not so favourite smells.

Pantomime smells of various things for the other person to guess the smell. (A favourite with children is my pantomime of walking merrily along and then smelling something awful and realizing what it is on my shoe.)

Providing experiences with various kinds of smells as flowers, fruit, grass—place distinctive aromas in opaque containers—perfume, mustard, banana, apple and onion, for example, and ask the client to guess the smell.

Talking about memories evoked by specific smells (or drawing pictures of them.)

A case example

Joey was extremely hyperactive when I first met him. He literally did nothing but run around the room the first few sessions, with me attempting to join him by running with him or behind him. Joey had a severe "contact disorder"—that is, he was unable to stay still long enough to make contact with anyone. Medication had not made a difference. One day in session he noticed an object on the window-sill that somehow drew his attention. It was a kaleidoscope. I suggested he look through it and to my amazement he did. We spent the whole session taking turns looking through it all around the room and through the windows, sharing what we saw with each other. "Violet, look at this!" he said as he handed me the kaleidoscope and I, in turn, would say, "Joey, you have got to see this!" Joey was definitely in contact with me during this session and our sessions thereafter.

Another case example

Eli made me think of a wooden puppet whenever he walked. He was cooperative and intelligent and unable to express any feelings. In fact, he seemed unaware of what feelings were. I decided to do an experiment with him—to help loosen him up. I had had great results with a group of very disturbed 11–14-year-old boys with finger painting and decided to introduce this activity. Eli commented that he couldn't do such a "baby" thing, but I put out two old cafeteria-style trays, put some paint on them and I started painting. He watched for a while and then joined in, using only his index fingers. I placed some paper over my tray, pressed down and voila! Out came a beautiful block print. Eli watched and said, "I can do that!" He immediately threw his whole body into the task, and soon had a wonderful block print (actually four) of his own. There appeared to be a decided shift in Eli after this experience and he was eager to try other interesting sensory and body exercises. He painted to angry music, for example, and was soon receptive to dictating a list of things that made him angry, sad, afraid and even happy.

The body, breath and voice

Experiment with different ways to breathe and how the breath affects the body.
Blow up balloons and keep them in the air with breath.
Blow cotton balls across a table in a race.
Play the harmonica.
Experiment with voice sounds together with percussion instruments.
Sing.
Role-play various voices (as pleading, angry, fearful, etc.).
Have a screaming contest.
Fall in creative ways onto pillows.
Pantomime various games and sports.
Have an Encounter Bat fight as various characters such as king and queen, two very old people, two babies, etc.
Throw soft balls in various ways.
Use a very large ball (the kind you can sit or lie on).
Exaggerate various movements.
Show all the movements you can make with various parts of the body.
Play Twister.
Dance to music tapes.
Show how you can exercise sitting down.
Pantomime situations, starting with fingers and then using different parts of the body.

An example

I remember a session when I played a game called Hawaiian Punch with a client, 14-year-old Jenny. This is a board game (no longer commercially available) where you move a play-dough pineapple made from a plastic mould according to the number thrown on a die. Each person playing has a different colour play-dough pineapple, and the board has corresponding boxes of these colours. If I were to land on my client's colour, she could say to me, "How would you like an Hawaiian Punch?" but no matter what my reply was, she could smash my pineapple till it looked like a pancake. I then had to move this pancake until I might land on a "remould" box. Anyway, to make the game more interesting I suggested trying different voices to try to get the other person not to smash the pineapple. These were voices such as crying, whining, pleading, screaming, begging, arguing, authoritarian command and so forth. In one turn, Jenny landed on my colour and I said the prescribed, "How would you like an HP?" and there was silence (certainly another response), and as I started smashing it (we used a rubber mallet on a separate wooden board), Jenny decided to scream. At first her screams were tentative and rather weak, but then they got fuller and louder until they were blood curdling. I became alarmed and stopped my smashing and looked at Jenny and said, "That was amazing screaming. Have you ever screamed like that before?" Jenny replied, "No, this is the first time. But I wish I had screamed like that when my father used to come into my room at night and touch me." I knew that Jenny had been sexually molested; but this was the first time she openly and willingly talked about the abuse. It was a beginning to her healing.

Mastery

Children who live in dysfunctional families, have suffered trauma, have had alcoholic parents, often miss out on experiencing mastery. Mastery is an essential part of the child's development as he grows. An essential component of mastery is struggle, not to be confused with frustration. A baby learns from struggle, and with each mastery experience develops the strength to deal with frustration. A baby struggles to insert the block into the larger one. He uses all of his energy and concentration. When he is finally successful, mastery occurs. If he tries to put a block into a smaller one, he soon becomes frustrated and cries. Parents need to tell the difference between struggle and frustration, and allow the child to pursue his goal without intervening; when frustration sets in, the parent must quickly find the larger block to help the child achieve that wonderful feeling that comes with mastery.

Many children come into therapy clearly deficient in mastery experiences. Sometimes these children are labelled as having a "narcissistic disorder" since they never seem to be satisfied with anything, always want new things, give up easily, can't stay long with one task. It is as if these children have not had much opportunity to struggle. This may come about for many reasons: the parents did too much for the child right from the beginning, not allowing her to experience the struggle so necessary for mastery; the child experienced a great deal of frustration lacking proper support from parents who thought frustration was the way to teach; the child did not receive enough nurturing as an infant—perhaps her mother was ill when the child was in the earlier years and no one took over the task of providing necessary mastery experiences; and so forth. Whatever the reason, the child now, at this time of her life, needs as many mastery experiences as possible. Since the child cannot sustain contact by herself for very long with a given task, the therapist must find ways to provide mastery experiences together with the child.

From my case notes

An 11-year-old boy attempted to make a bird fly in a sand scene he was creating. He asked me for a stick and some string. I knew that the string wouldn't work, but wisely kept my mouth shut. He soon discovered, after many tries, that he couldn't tie the bird onto the top of the stick with string. His energy began to fade, his contact with the task was broken and any minute I knew he would decide to stop working on his sand scene. Sensing the onset of frustration, I gently said, "I have an idea that might work. Would you like to hear my idea?" The boy nodded and I said, "Maybe wire would work, or even something like masking tape. I don't know—what do you think?" The boy opted for some picture wire—it worked—and his energy and smile and big sigh indicated to me his mastery experience. (I did not say, "Don't forget, that was my idea".)

Making choices

I give children choices whenever possible. I put out three sizes of drawing paper and crayons, oil and chalk pastels, coloured markers, coloured pencils (crayons are the last to be chosen). I will ask, "Do you want to use clay or do a drawing today?" I might say, "Shall we play *Connect–4* or *Uno* for our last ten minutes?" Whenever children are given choices, the self is strengthened. Some children have such fragile selves that choices make them anxious. "What if I make the wrong choice?" I have seen a child stare at a pile of coloured construction paper for a long time, unable to commit to the three colours. I have asked her to choose. When I notice her energy fading, I say, "What about red, blue and yellow?" She is relieved not to have to make her own choice. Or sometimes she may say, "No, I think I want green instead of blue."

I tell parents to give their children choices when it's appropriate and feasible. Don't ask a child what he wants for dinner. Give him specific choices, but don't include chicken if there is no chicken available.

Power and control

Children don't have much control over their lives and certainly don't have much power in this world. Most children aren't concerned about their lack of power in the world at large. They are not aware that they are actually second-class citizens, particularly since they don't vote. (Politicians have a very narrow view and tend to forget that children are future voters.) Children are happy to give their parents the power and control in their lives as long as they feel heard, encouraged to voice their opinions, know that the rules are fair. They can then feel some power and control in their own skins. When the child has a good sense of self, she is not threatened by the power of her parents and in fact welcomes it for her own safety and security. She feels that she does have some control over her life when her parents give her choices, listen to her, honour and respect her. Children who are rebellious or engage in power struggles feel very little power or control. In fact things are often out of control in their families. Or parents are too authoritarian or too vague. In my office I attempt to give such a child as much power as I can within appropriate limits and boundaries. This experience is generally in play: the child knows this, but it is the experience of control and power that counts. Sometimes the child will suddenly take control over the sessions in a wonderful way. This represents to me a fine evidence of therapeutic movement.

Case examples

Eric, the very hyperactive child I had mentioned previously, suddenly took over the session one day. He became the playwright and the director of our interaction. He noticed on the shelf a badge, a set of handcuffs and an old wallet. He said, with much enthusiasm, as he pinned the badge on himself, "Let's play where you are a robber and you steal this wallet and I am a policeman and I catch you and put these handcuffs on you." So with great drama we acted out the scenario. Along the way he would often tell me what I was supposed to do and say. At the end of the session he commented, "I wish I had a rope so I could tie you up."

Not only was Eric experiencing a feeling of power, but in this play he opened up the possibility of re-enacting his trauma. Eric and his brother had been found in an abandoned car when they were 4 and 5 years old. They were tied up tightly with rope so that they couldn't move. Previously Eric had refused to talk about this experience, claiming he just didn't remember anything. At the next session I brought in some rope and in the course of the play, he tied me up. When it was too tight I came out of my role and told him I did not want the rope to be so tight. Eric complied. In the role, I cried and screamed and complained with clear direction from Eric. We enacted this scenario several times before he felt finished with it and let it go. Although he wouldn't own his own experience at this time, some kind of closure seemed to have occurred. His subsequent play involved "principal's office". He set up a makeshift desk, toy telephone, my stapler and a few other such supplies and busied himself pretending to write and talking on the phone. He directed me to be in another "office" as the therapist who called him for advice with various children. When I called him to ask what to do about a boy who was very destructive, he said, "Tell him to draw his angry feelings!"

Alicia was from Korea and was adopted by a Caucasian family when she was 5 years old. Her mother died when she was two and her father kept her locked up in a box with a small breathing hole while he was at work. When she got to be too big for the box, he took her to the countryside and asked his mother to keep her. He said he just did not want her. The grandmother became ill and called the authorities who took her to an orphanage until she was adopted. Alicia suffered from separation anxiety and nightmares that prompted the adoptive parents to bring her into therapy when she was 6 years old. She spoke English quite well by this time and refused to mention anything related to her Korean life. We established a relationship quickly and after a few sessions she began to take over the sessions, directing me in various play scenarios. We played school (she was the teacher) and restaurant. (Restaurants fascinated her.) Then one day she told me we were going to play mother and baby. She gave me a doll and took one for herself saying, "These are our babies. Your home is in that corner and mine is over here. I'll tell you what to do." After we were settled, she called over, "Now you are feeding your baby." Then after a while, "Now you are putting her to sleep." And then I heard Alicia singing a beautiful Korean song as she rocked her baby. When the play was over, I mentioned the song and she told me that her grandmother used to sing it to her. This was the beginning of a new phase in our work together.

I often suggest to parents that they set aside some time each day (or whatever they can manage) to be "Jimmy's time". This could be a 15- to 30-minute time span. A kitchen timer is used to keep track of the time. During this time, the child is the boss and the parent does whatever the child wants within appropriate boundaries. During this time the child feels some sense of power and control albeit in play. The experience is what strengthens the child's sense of self.

Boundaries and limits

A child has difficulty feeling a sense of self without boundaries and limits. He will become anxious if they are not present, and often act out to find them. In my office it is clear that we are in the safe container of that place, that certain items are off limits (as my telephone), that we begin and end on time and so forth. All children are expected to help me clean up, except for the sand tray scenes. At first some children may resist, but I leave time for clean up and begin to do it myself in spite of the child's resistance. Soon most children gladly participate. I often help parents set limits for their children, and emphasize that although they may protest, it is beneficial for the child's development. Of course these limits must be fair and age appropriate, and the boundaries stretched as the child ages.

Self-statements, defining the self

It is essential for children to have awareness of themselves—a definition of the self—for healthy growth. Picture a circle with nothing inside of it. In order for the edges of the circle to expand meaningfully, there must be some substance inside of the circle. Whenever a child makes a statement, expresses a like or dislike, gives voice to a thought or curiosity or opinion, the child is filling up the circle and allowing his boundary to stretch. When the self is fragile, there is no self-support and it is difficult for the child to grow and develop in a healthy way. Further, without a strong sense of self, the child cannot express his emotions meaningfully. So we make it possible for the child to make many statements. In this way he is defining himself, becomes stronger and matures. These statements come about in many ways. We sometimes make lists of things we like and don't like. Games such as the *Ungame* or the *Talking, Feeling, Doing Game* will elicit statements. Books such as *The Children's Question Book* ask interesting questions for the child and for the therapist. It is not a common experience for adults to listen to the child's statements and they sometimes are surprised at the therapist's interest.

A colleague of mine told me this story: She was working with a 6-year-old girl, who had been sexually molested at a pre-school. She presented herself as a model child, smiling, doing what she was told, never expressing angry feelings. She suffered from frequent stomach-aches and the mother was advised by her physician to seek therapy for her. The child was cooperative and friendly but never in any way expressed much feeling either at home or with the therapist. One day the therapist suggested a game in a session with her mother (a single parent). Each person would go around and say the name of a fruit they liked and a fruit they did not like too much. In the next round they mentioned vegetables. The girl said, "I don't like peas," and then turned to her mother and said vehemently, "And I don't like it when you leave me someplace and then go away!" It was almost as if the experience of saying what she didn't like, in an acceptable way, gave her the strength to express a heretofore forbidden feeling. The therapist told me that this was the beginning of some good healing sessions.

I have found that children have amazing ideas and insights.

An 11-year-old boy said to me when I encouraged him to talk to me as the super-hero he loved to draw, "I know why you are asking me to do this. You want me to feel some power inside of me."

Owning projections

Statements are closely connected to owning projections. The goal of the projective work we do is to help the child say something about herself that was expressed as a metaphor in the story but actually is an expression of something about herself. Whatever we do, whether drawing pictures from guided fantasies, doing clay exercises, sand tray scenes and so forth, we create powerful metaphors of our own lives.

Making statements about the self and owning projections allow for awareness of the self and one's place in the world. It is through this awareness that not only is the self strengthened, but change takes place. Arnold Beiser, M.D., writes about this phenomenon. "... *change occurs when one becomes what he is, not when he tries to become what he is not.*" ("The Paradoxical Theory of Change" in *Gestalt Therapy Now*, 1970, p. 77.)

Examples

In my book, *Windows To Our Children*, I give examples of children making such statements from a clay exercise. A girl aged 12 made, with her eyes closed, a sun. As the sun she smiled (a rare occurrence for this child), and talked about how she warmed everyone and was bright and shiny. When she finished talking she resumed her usual scowling facial expression. When I asked her if she ever felt like the sun in her real life, she said, "No! I can't let myself be like the sun. If I do, everyone will think things are good in my life and nothing will change." This was an important statement of her being. Prior to this she never had anything to say about her perpetual bad mood.

A 13-year-old who drew a snake living in the desert all by itself (after a guided fantasy where she found her own place), talked, as the snake, about her loneliness and isolation. She was able to own her own loneliness and proceeded to draw a figure of a girl standing in the desert. She said, "This is me. It's really me on the desert, isn't it."

An 8-year-old boy drew a volcano just because he wanted to. When asked to be the volcano he described his hot lava. I said, "What would a boy have that was like the volcano's hot lava?" After a pause, he shouted, "Anger!" We then spent some time listing all the things that made him angry.

These are just a few examples of "owning the projection". In each case, the window to the child's inner self is opened wider.

Aggressive energy

Contacting one's aggressive energy is an important prelude to expressing anger. It provides inner strength and self-support. Many therapists shrink at the term "aggressive energy" visualizing aggression when they hear it. This energy is akin to the kind one uses to bite an apple. It requires outward action. It is obvious that children who are timid and withdrawn have lost this kind of energy. What is important to know is that children who are acting out, aggressive and outwardly expressing anger are also lacking in this energy. This energy comes from an inside place—it has the feeling of calm power. The acting out children are not functioning from their core, but are totally outside their boundaries with no inner support. Children need this experience in order to find the strength to express emotions locked inside of them.

There are some essential elements and guidelines that must be followed when providing this experience in order that it will be effective.

1. *There must be contact with the therapist.* Though children may engage in aggressive energy type activities on their own, the therapeutic value comes from contact. The therapist is fully involved.
2. *The child must feel safe.* The therapist's office is a safe container for the child. He or she has already had the experience of knowing this.
3. *There are clear limits—the therapist is always in control.* This is what

makes the child feel safe. He knows that the therapist will always keep things from getting out of hand.

4. *There is a spirit of playfulness and fun.* Even when children are dealing with serious issues, playfulness in this situation is essential. The child does not have the strength to deal with heavy material without this.

5. *The activity is exaggerated.* Because children have lost the ability to engage in this important experience, only exaggeration helps.

6. *Content is not necessary. It is the experience that counts.* Sometimes content is involved, but my focus is helping the child feel permission to engage in the activity with her senses and her body.

Aggressive energy activities can be provided using games, Bataca fights (encounter bats), pounding clay, making music, pounding a drum, through puppets, creative dramatics, body movement and playing with toys. These activities can be played out in the sand tray, in drawings, through lists and statements, storytelling and books and dialoguing with clay figures, drawings and the empty chair. One needs to take into consideration, of course, the child's age level (though many do regress—a positive phenomenon) as well as the specific characteristics of the child.

Example

A girl, aged 11, had been molested by her stepfather for many years. She refused to talk about it, and preferred to engage in safe activities. One day I asked her to pick a puppet—any puppet. To my surprise she chose an alligator with a big mouth. I chose a crocodile who also had a big mouth. Our dialogue went something like this:

Crocodile:	Hi! Wow, you have a big mouth and lots of teeth. I hope you won't bite me.
Alligator (child):	Oh no. I will be you friend.
Crocodile:	Oh yeah? Well I think you'll bite me! (*the crocodile moved closer to the alligator*) I'm sure you will!

Though the alligator moved backwards away from the crocodile, the crocodile found itself in the alligator's mouth. The alligator made a slight, almost imperceptible, movement with its mouth. The crocodile shouted, "Oh! Oh! You bit me," and fell to the floor.

The child exclaimed, "Do that again! Do that again!"

We repeated this scenario with every "bad" puppet I had, to this child's delight. By the third puppet, she, as the alligator, grabbed it with its mouth, and bit hard.

We struggled before my puppet inevitably yelled, "You bit me! You bit me!" and fell to the floor. When there were no more "bad" puppets, she said, "I'll wave my magic wand and make them all alive again," and we proceeded to struggle with all of them again. When our session was finished, this child was glowing, standing straight and tall, and offered a firm goodbye. This was in great contrast to her previous posture and demeanour.

It was after this session that we were able to begin to address the issue of her molestation.

An adolescent, who denied any angry feelings, was able to begin to talk about his anger at his father after smashing a lump of clay when I asked him to show me how hard he could hit the clay.

I have seen examples like this over and over. The aggressive energy play appears to strengthen the self, allowing the child to delve into difficult issues.

The sixth sense

The sixth sense actually involves learning how to trust the self. Some people think of this as intuition or something spiritual and elusive. I believe that as we become stronger within ourselves, we know what is right for us. The inability to do this implies, to me, a fragmentation of the self as well as some kind of inner block to the truth. I came upon this idea when I was working with a couple who were divorcing and arguing about how to split their belongings. After listening to their bickering for a while, I asked them to stop and try an exercise. They had been arguing over such things as vases, dishes and so forth. I said to the wife, "Visualize the vase you are speaking of and say out loud 'I want this vase.' Then ask you body, 'true or false?'" To her surprise she knew immediately that she did not want it at all. We went through some of the other things they couldn't agree on and, except for two or three items, they had no difficulty coming to decisions. This exercise had the effect of not only tuning into each one's inner wisdom, but of seeing the other much clearer. They smiled at each other and left amicably.

Children do very well with this exercise. We try it with choices: Do you want the red paper or the blue paper? Do you want to do a sand tray or work with clay? We talk about the signals the body gives us. At first we try it with very obvious kinds of things: Is my name Mary or John? Or, do I want a cookie or a sprig of broccoli? It is very difficult to describe the actual body sensation that gives us the answer we look for, but some children say when it's true they feel it in their stomach, and when it's false they feel it higher up, perhaps in the chest area. Of course it doesn't always work! When a child cannot sense the signal for something he wants, we may dialogue with the choices. For example, I may ask the child to have the red and blue paper talk to each other. Or, talk as the red paper and then the blue paper: "If Jimmy takes me (red paper) I will be very bright and noticeable". "If Jimmy takes me (blue) I will be mellow and I know he'll get tired of that red colour, but not with me". Soon Jimmy knows which one he wants to use, depending on his current need. These exercises lead to more significant choices in the child's life. He learns to trust himself and to recognize the dialogue within himself.

This is akin to the top dog/underdog exercise I use with children, particularly adolescents. One 16-year-old girl, Alise, was offered a part in a movie. She had auditioned for this part since her goal in life was to be an actress. She actually was quite talented and had appeared in many school productions as well as community plays. However, she found out that she would need to leave her school to do this movie. She came to see me for help with her dilemma. Her parents and friends had plenty of advice, but Alise was torn. We had her "top dog" talk to Alise, and since the top dog has introjected much of her parents' admonitions and desires, she soundly argued for staying in school. (Alise, the actress, loved this exercise.) Alise's parents, by the way, had agreed to support whatever she chose to do. When the underdog spoke to Alise, the message was whiney and passive. She was clearly paralysed about this. I asked her to step away and look inside herself to find out what she, Alise, wanted. She had difficulty doing this since her fragmented parts fought to take over. So I asked Alise to sit in one chair and be the part of herself that wanted to be in the movie and to exaggerate what this part represented. Then I asked her to sit in another chair and be the part that didn't want to leave her friends and her school. After some rounds of this exercise it was clear that Alise's energy was high when she talked about school. I then asked her to make the statement, "I want to stay in school." "That is totally true!" she shouted. I then suggested she make the other statement, "I want to leave school and be in this movie." "Ughh," she said. "I feel awful when I say that one. I think I felt that I might never have that chance again. But really, I'm not ready."

Often the body knows things before the intellect. I once asked a young man to tell me some things that made him angry. "I'm never angry. I know how to work things out," was his reply. (It was clear from his behaviour that he was a very angry boy.) So I suggested that we do an exercise with clay. He wanted to experiment with the various tools I usually put out, and when he picked up the rubber mallet I asked him to show me how hard he could hit the clay. He began to hit it harder and harder and finally I asked him what he was thinking about at that moment. "*I am so mad at my father!*" he shouted. Another child continued to stroke her hair as we talked, seemingly unaware of what she was doing. I asked her to focus on her stroking and to give words to her hand. ("I want to stroke you to make you feel good, etc.") She began to weep, telling me that she missed her grandmother who had recently passed away.

The integration achieved through connecting the body to the heart and mind is strengthening and satisfying.

I might add a note here about experience. In many of the activities described beginning with enhancing the senses and so on, the experience given to the child is invaluable. To experience a part of oneself that has been hidden or dulled gives the child a new sense of self. As the self is strengthened, the child can then deal with painful emotions.

CHAPTER FIVE

The many faces of anger

A nger is the most misunderstood of all emotions. Why do I say that? Well, first of all, what looks like anger may not be anger at all, and, conversely, what doesn't seem to be anger, often is! Secondly, anger has a bad press; that is, we're all brought up to believe that it's bad, wrong to be angry and we attempt to avoid that feeling at often great cost to ourselves. Children learn at a very early age that anger is dangerous, and so do not learn healthy, appropriate ways to express this normal, human emotion. Anger is at the root of most of the problems that bring children and families into therapy.

In this chapter I will focus on this emotion and how it relates to the self, how children manifest anger and the difficulties these manifestations generate, the steps of the therapeutic process in working with anger and techniques for helping children express anger in healthy ways. I will also give examples throughout of specific anger work with young children, adolescents and families.

Anger and the sense of self go hand in hand. Anger is an expression of the self, and the self is diminished when one inhibits anger. A young child may appear angry, but is in actuality attempting to get her needs met, to take care of herself. The 2-year-old yells, "NO!" to the carrots her mother places in front of her. She may even push them on to the floor. She is mobilizing all the strength and power she has to make her statement. She does not have the cognitive ability to say mildly, "No thank you, I don't feel like having carrots today." She is perceived as angry, and the parent will often express disapproval and anger toward the child. The child responds to this disapproval by feeling that she is a bad girl, and is confused and frightened by her parent's reaction.

The growing child acquires belief systems about himself and about how to be in the world that will affect him for the rest of his life. How parents meet the child's needs and wants, and react to his expressions of them, how they react to the undaunted development of his senses, body, emotional expression and intellect, profoundly affect his belief system about himself. During these early years many negative messages, sometimes called introjects, are taken in because he has not yet leaned the art of spitting out or rejecting that which is toxic for himself. Developmentally he cannot as yet discriminate between that which is true about himself and that which is not true. The child, who is normally egocentric at these early stages of growth, blames himself for everything that happens, every traumatic event that occurs in his life. At the least, he becomes confused, lost and bewildered.

The suppression of emotions, particularly that of anger, is basically connected to her adoption of negative introjects. A child's emotions form her core, her being. When her feelings are not validated, neither is she. When her feelings are scorned, explained away, ridiculed, responded to harshly, she feels deeply rejected. Though she may find some way to express some feelings in an oblique quest for health, the child nevertheless harbours the constant notion that she is bad, that something is wrong with her. She does not consciously choose feelings—they just well up. In dismay she feels unentitled to have them; and when she does have them she feels unentitled to be, to exist, particularly since these feelings as well as she herself cause her parents so much concern, disapproval and anger toward her. The more the child absorbs negative self messages, the more she tends to feel an actual loss of self. She begins to interrupt and constrict her own process of growth. She shuts down her senses, contracts her muscles, withholds and blocks expression, closes off her mind. Her sense of self becomes diffuse, and she engages in a variety of defensive behaviours to maintain some semblance of feeling alive.

In opposition to all of this is the fact that children have a powerful thrust for life and growth and will do anything they can to get through the task of growing up. This life force is a positive one that runs counter to the negative belief system regarding the self. However, it gets children into trouble with parents, teachers, society in general. The organism in its healthful surge for growth seems to make its own determinations about how to function in the world. Let me explain.

The child thrives upon acceptance, approval, love. At an early age when he is still fairly congruent, he may express an angry feeling toward his mother, for which he may meet disapproval, rejection and what feels to be a loss of love. He begins to learn that the expression of angry feelings is full of danger to himself, and he must do whatever he can to avoid further injury. Since anger is unavoidable, he must make some determination about what to do when he feels it. He usually decides to push the feeling down, to keep it inside of himself. "I go to my room until it goes away," one boy told me when I asked him what he did when he got angry. But the unexpressed emotion lies within the child like a rock, interfering with healthful growth.

Further, since the expression of anger is an expression of the self, that self becomes diminished.

The organism relentlessly seeks to achieve homeostasis or balance. If an emotion lies below the surface, it must be expressed in some way for some sense of closure and subsequent equilibrium to be achieved, so that the organism can deal with its next need, and so on in its everlasting cycle of growth. So the organism appears to choose some kind of expression of the emotion with or without the cooperation of the child's awareness in its attempt to expel the energy of the emotion and achieve some balance. The child, as well as the organism itself, is trying to get rid of the angry feeling. But the attempt is usually inappropriate for healthful growth and doesn't do the job. Here is an example of one child's experience with angry feelings.

As an infant Sally cries to get her needs met. Her parents think she's wet and check her diaper. She cries louder since she really wants to be held. Finally, her mother picks her up and she stops crying. It's hit or miss with crying as her only tool for communication. In a few months her cries begin to take on meanings, giving her parents better clues for meeting her needs. Also her facial and bodily expressions begin to show that she has more awareness of her own needs. As she grows older she realizes that sounds and words are an important tool to use to get needs met, but she doesn't have a good repertoire of words to express what she wants to say. "I want milk" is easy; emotional expression is abstract and difficult. She says, "I hate you!" to her mother because she doesn't know how to tell her mother that it bothers her when her mother talks on the phone. Sally's mother reacts in shock, disapproval, or perhaps sadness that her own child hates her. She may yell, "Don't you ever talk that way to me!" Sally is confused at the many reactions she hears, sees, senses. Even the most enlightened mother may flinch at her child's hateful remark. Although Sally did the best she could to express her inner feelings and make her statement, she feels disapproved of, rejected and invalidated. Later, Sally says to her brother who just pinched her, "Don't!" and when he continues, "I'll kill you!" She uses gross terminology since she doesn't as yet have the vocabulary that may seem less violent. Her father rushes in and says, "Don't you *ever* talk that way again!" in a very loud, angry voice. After a few more of such interactions, Sally decides that, for her own survival, she'd better find some other way to deal with her feelings. So she keeps her feelings to herself, not knowing what else to do, but is plagued with stomach-aches.

The process gets more complicated from this point on. Sally continues to have angry feelings sometimes, and, though at the beginning they're pretty mild, she feels guilt, anxiety and fear for having them. As she gets older, her guilt harbours intense feelings of resentment, or her anxiety causes her to feel so bad, shameful and invalidated that her sense of self shrinks like a wilted flower. She tries harder and harder to suppress and hide her angry feelings; she actually loses awareness of even being angry. Meanwhile the organism wants to get rid of this angry energy, and causes Sally to unexpectedly explode at odd moments. Her diminished self fights for survival as well, and she secretly steals candy to make herself feel better. It gets pretty intricate. Because the individual life force of the child is so strong, she continually looks for ways to survive the dilemma. She does not, however, have the developmental, cognitive capacity to evaluate what she, and her organism, are doing with her angry feelings.

Children express angry feelings in all sorts of inappropriate ways—ways that are harmful to them, get them into trouble and certainly do not bring a sense of peacefulness and satisfaction. One child, like Sally, retroflects his anger. Retroflection can be defined as doing to yourself what you might like to do to someone else, turning the energy in, rather than out. So she might give herself headaches or stomach-aches, gouge herself, pull her hair out, become withdrawn, stop talking and so forth. Another child may deflect the anger. He feels he cannot express the authentic feeling, and after a time even forgets what that feeling was. Nevertheless, the energy remains and must be expressed. He punches out, hits, kicks. He feels good when he does this, but only for a moment. So he hits again to get that good feeling back. He complains, screams, blames others. Still another child's body expresses the feelings through bedwetting, or through one of her only means of power and control: withholding her bowel movement, until the body, in its need to rid itself of toxicity, expels the faeces at unfitting times. Some children project their wrath onto others, imagining that everyone else is angry with them. Some have nightmares of horrible monsters—projections of their anger. To deflect or dispel anger energy and feel a sense of self and power, some set fires. Others, to actually avoid feeling anything, become hyperactive or daydream and appear spacey. Some are so fearful of the power of their internal anger that they pull in to try to hold themselves together, and appear withdrawn, silent, sullen, cold, or paradoxically, overly pleasing and good—following every rule tenaciously.

Anger seems to have the most insidious effects in our society, perhaps because it is the least tolerated emotion. Most of the symptoms and behaviours that children evidence that may eventually bring them into therapy, directly relate to the suppression of anger.

The behaviours that bring children into therapy are the very ones that they have been using to gain some feeling of self, to achieve some sense of power in a world where they feel so powerless, to express who they are and what they feel. They use these behaviours, inappropriate as they may be, to survive, to contact the environment, to attempt to meet their needs. These behaviours are actually evidence of the organism's crusade for equilibrium. They often become the child's way of being in the world—her pattern, her process. Without therapeutic intervention, this way of being may haunt her throughout her adult life. A 40-year-old woman that I worked with remembers clearly that at the age of four she stopped talking since it appeared to her that her questions made her mother angry. Since she did not have enough self-support to express her own displeasure at her mother's lack of response to her, she chose to stop talking, thinking that this would keep her mother from being angry at her. And now, at the age of 40, she still had difficulty speaking in a natural, easy way.

When a child is brought into therapy, I know that I must assist his quest for strength and self-support. I must find a way to help him remember, regain, renew and strengthen, that which he once had as a tiny baby but which now seems lost. As his senses awaken, as he begins to know his body again, as he recognizes, accepts and expresses his buried feelings, as he learns to use his intellect to make choices, to verbalize his wants and needs and thoughts and ideas, and to find healthy, satisfying ways to get his needs met, as he learns who he is and accepts his uniqueness, he will once again find his rightful path of growth. I must help him learn that some of his survival behaviours are non-productive and that new behaviour choices can yield more satisfying results for himself. I must help him understand the faulty messages about himself that he has come to own, and how he might manage and cope with these messages.

Working with anger

Phase one

I recognize three phases in working with children's anger. The first phase is the talking *about* phase. Many children are so out of touch with their feelings that we need to do a great deal of just talking about feelings. They are particularly not acquainted with all the subtleties and nuances of feelings, and the more experiences they have with these various forms and descriptions of feelings, the better they are able to communicate them. Anger, for example, can range from mild irritation and annoyance, to downright rage, wrath and fury. Besides just talking, children draw or paint pictures of all kinds of angry feelings, using scribbles, colours, lines and shapes. We use the beat of a drum and other percussion instruments to express various forms of anger. We use music to illustrate various degrees of angry feelings. We use creative dramatics to show anger in many forms, a good way to involve the body. We tell stories with puppets and read books with angry themes. We play games with cards that say things like "Say something that bugs you", or "What makes you feel sad?" A very successful technique is list making. I might make a list, as they dictate, of all the things they don't like about school, or a list of foods they like and foods they don't like.

I would like to emphasize the importance of working with polarities. The young person is frightened of the splits within her, as well as those she sees in the adults in her life. She is confused when she finds herself feeling angry and hateful toward someone she loves. She is bewildered when someone she sees as strong and protective acts weak and helpless. It is important to help children understand that it is all right to have mixed feelings about things. She can be happy that school is over for the year, she can be sad that she won't see her school friends and she can be angry that she got a lower grade on a subject than she expected. In many of the exercises we do to help children understand feelings, we use the concept of polarities. I might ask the child to draw something that makes her angry and something that makes her feel calm. Or I might ask her to make some kind of abstract shape with clay to show how her body feels when she is strong and how it feels when she feels weak. You can see that we actually have fun with anger.

In this talking about phase, we not only talk about anger in a general way, but also personalize it by examining the kinds of things that might make us angry, do make us angry, what anger feels like in the body and what it does to the body and how we express our anger—our anger process.

In order to find more appropriate ways of expressing our angry feelings, we first need to have some awareness of how we presently express these feelings. Children do not connect retroflective, projective or deflective behaviour with the expression of anger, but they can begin to gain some insight about themselves. For example, I asked a group of boys, 11- and 12-year-olds, to tell me all the words they use or think about when they are angry. I wrote them on a chalkboard as they yelled them out (regardless of the shock value of some of them.) We looked at the list and found that some were attacking, striking-out words, while others were inside feeling words. We talked about this for a while and then discussed our own individual ways of handling anger—inside or outside. I then asked them to close their eyes while I led them in a relaxation exercise. I then asked, "What kinds of things make you angry? Pick one thing that makes you angry or has made you angry now or in the past. What do you do? Do you go inside or outside?" They drew pictures of what it felt like inside their bodies to be angry or what they do when they are angry, using colours, lines, shapes, scribbles or symbols. Each child's anger process was clearly depicted. One boy drew a maze with stick figures of his friends in one corner and a figure of himself in the opposite corner. He said that when he and his friends got mad at each other, he felt lonely and separate, and didn't know how to get back to being friends again. He labelled his picture "loneliness". Another boy drew dark scribbles all over the page around faces of his parents. He said that when he was mad at his parents he felt crazy, and was afraid of what he would do! In an individual session a 16-year-old drew a thick black square around a circle of bright yellow and orange. She said that when she felt angry the good feelings were squeezed in by her anger, and she didn't know how to get her good feelings out. Her body felt squeezed in the same way, she said.

Phase two

The second phase of the anger work involves giving children new or satisfying ways to express their anger. Children need many suggestions for getting rid of angry feelings that will not be harmful and destructive. Adults do not want, nor usually accept, the anger of children, so they do not learn how to express this emotion that must be expressed.

Before a child can even begin to engage in healthful expression, we must go through several essential steps. First, I need to help the child to become aware of the anger, to recognize the anger. This is the first step in the child's feeling strong and whole, instead of fearfully running from, and avoiding angry feelings, or discharging them in indirect ways that might harm themselves or alienate others.

Second, I need to help the child learn that anger is a normal, natural feeling that we all feel sometimes; that anger is merely anger—an emotion that is neither good nor bad, and that it's OK—he's OK—if he's angry. I want to encourage the child to accept his own feelings of anger. Third, I can then hopefully help him to make a conscious choice about how the express the anger: whether to express the anger directly, or to express it privately in some other way, since the emotion must be expressed. Finally, I need to give the child many techniques for expressing his anger—that is, how to express anger directly or how to express it privately.

Here is a summary of these essential steps:

1. To be *aware* of the anger. "I'm angry".
2. To *accept* the anger. "It's OK to be angry".
3. To *choose how to express* the anger.

Expressing anger directly is no easy matter for children. They learn at a very early age that to express anger directly, making their statement forcefully and clearly, brings disapproval, punishment and other harsh consequences. One boy said to me, "If I told the school principal what I really want to say about the school, he'd probably throw me out." It is particularly in relation to the expression of anger that children hold the status of second class citizens! When children discover that to be direct and straightforward with angry feelings causes problems for them, they turn to other ways to express themselves, ways that usually cause even *more* problems for them. So it is an extremely important task for the therapist to help children through this dilemma. Adding to the problem is the fact that children often regress when attempting to express their feelings. They lose intellectual abilities and become much like the very young person mentioned above, using gross, global, often indecent expressions along with loud voices.

Working with the whole family as well as educating parents about anger is an important part of this work. I always ask parents in family sessions how the family deals with angry feelings, and it is interesting and enlightening to hear the different views. Each person has their own point of view about everything, including each child, and each of these views is valid for that person. Lively discussions sometimes ensue as a result of my question. An exercise I often do in family sessions is to have each person in turn say, to every person in the family, something they appreciate or like and something they resent, that bugs them or they don't like. Sometimes one of the family members has trouble thinking of something they don't like (or at least has trouble verbalizing it). Sometimes it is the first time a sister, for example, will hear something that her brother likes about her. After a few rounds we discuss what has happened. I present my feedback and each person gives his or her reaction or rebuttal to what has been said. Practising being direct with angry feelings is important for the whole family and often the dynamics of the particular family goes through a radical change when I provide this experience. All kinds of material to be worked through can emerge.

Ellen, a 15-year-old girl who suffered from bulimia, an eating disorder involving binging and forced vomiting, expressed intense, direct, angry feelings to her parents in an exercise as described above. Her parents were astonished. They were a family that were loving and nice to each other and avoided conflict. It was as if a lovely house was built on a rotten foundation that was hidden from view. As we began to unearth the rot so that we could see it, deal with it, work through it, Ellen no longer choked on her own anger. Before this particular family session, several things had to happen. One, the parents needed to be educated about anger—to understand the detrimental effects of suppressing one's anger and to understand particularly the difficulty that children have in expressing direct anger. Secondly, the child needed to gain some self-support before she could express her feelings directly to her parents in the session. And even before any of the points just mentioned, I needed to establish a good relationship with the child as well as her parents. If there is not good will between us, if the parents feel criticized and attacked and become defensive, the pathology will be exacerbated rather than healed. It is my responsibility, I believe, to build that relationship.

Ellen and I spent a number of sessions together before that pivotal session with her parents. We went through many of the steps regarding anger work that I mentioned earlier. At first Ellen had very little awareness of her anger. She categorically denied being angry at anything or anyone. Two sessions stand out in my mind. In one, Ellen made a great big mouth with lots of teeth out of clay following instructions to make something, anything, with her eyes closed. I asked her to describe herself as the mouth. She said, "I'm a big mouth with lots of teeth." I asked her what she could do. "Well, I can eat a lot of food at once. I can bite a lot. People better watch out for me, or I might bite them!" I asked if there was anyone she'd like to bite. Ellen laughed and said she couldn't think of anyone. Then, to ease the tension further, I think, she playfully suggested that she was Mick Jagger's mouth! I then asked if anything she had said as the mouth reminded her of anything about herself or her life. She thought for a moment and said, "No, nothing I can think of." I replied, "What you said reminds me of something." She looked at me with interest. "It makes me think of why you are coming here— eating and then throwing up." She was absolutely astonished. "I can't believe I did that! I can't believe I made that mouth!" she repeated several times.

At a subsequent session she made a sand tray scene with several large animals and snakes attacking some smaller animals. In describing her scene to me she said, "And this animal will gobble the smaller one up, and that snake will gobble the other one." She added that the animals were fighting because they were really mad at each other and wanted their own space back. After some further work with the scene, I again asked her if anything in her story reminded her of her life and again she said no. When I pointed out how she had used the word "gobbled" she again reacted in surprise. "I just can't believe I did that again!" she said. Gradually, Ellen began to own some of her angry feelings, particularly at her parents. She was terrified to directly tell them what bothered her, but as she gained strength from our sessions together, she was willing to participate in the family session described above. That particular session was a turning point for Ellen.

Even a very young child can learn to be direct with anger. A 4-year-old boy, Todd, was brought in by his parents because he had a severe stutter. The parents were divorced and had joint custody. Todd lived half the week with one parent and half the week with the other. Todd spent several sessions playing with the dolls' house, creating stories about happy, intact families, stuttering all the while. He included me in his storytelling, directing me to be one character or another. Every now and then I would softly interject a remark as "I bet you wish your family lived together like this one." "Yeah!" he would say. Then one day he played in the sand tray with Superman and Batman figures. I took a large lion with sharp teeth off the shelf and said, "I'm going to get that Superman." He yelled, stuttering severely, "Put that away! Put that away!" I did, mumbling that I was sorry. After a moment Todd said, "Get the lion." So I did and said, "I hope Superman doesn't hit me before I can get him," and as I came closer Todd lightly tapped my lion with Superman. I yelled, "Oh! Oh! He got me!" and dropped the lion to the floor. Todd said, with not a trace of stuttering, "Do that again!" We enacted this scene over and over with varied instructions from Todd, with no stuttering. At another session while Todd played with clay, I made figures of Todd and his parents out of clay. I told him who the figures were and asked him to have the clay boy tell each parent something he liked and didn't like. He said to his mother, "I like it when you read stories to me. I don't like it when you yell at me." To his father he said, "I like it when you take me places. I don't like it when you go away." Again there was no stuttering. At another session, Todd described a dream he had the night before. "I was in my house sleeping. My Mommy and Daddy were there too. It was raining hard. They woke me up and threw me out of the house in the rain. A big bird came at me and then flew away. I didn't like that dream—it scared me." We created the whole dream scene out of clay and Todd enacted each part. He said he didn't like that his parents threw him out in the rain and that it made him mad. I had him tell the clay parents that. I asked him if he wanted to change the ending of the dream. He said he would kill the bird and proceeded to smash it with his fist as he spoke. He then told me that he feels like they throw him out in the rain, even when it's not raining, when he has to go back and forth and back and forth. In a family session Todd was able to tell all of this to his parents. I instructed his parents to allow him to express his feelings, even if they did not want to change anything. (The idea of joint custody is a good one, but the child needs a safe container for expressing his feelings about it.) I suggested that they provide a Mad Session for Todd where each night he could say what made him mad, without any explanations or lectures from them. Todd's stuttering markedly decreased and his parents noticed that when he began to stutter they needed to stop and say something like, "I bet you are mad at Daddy for going on one of his business trips,"—paying attention to what was happening and helping him articulate what might be bothering him.

There are situations when children are angry and know that they cannot be direct with their feelings. I want to give them techniques for expressing those feelings in ways that will not be harmful to them. As indicated above, the child must first *recognize*—know that he is angry. He must *acknowledge* the anger to himself. He must *accept* his anger. "I'm mad and it's OK for me to be mad." Then he can *choose* how to express the anger. If he cannot express it directly, there are many other safe ways he can rid himself of this angry energy. He can tell a friend he's angry. He can write about his anger. He can list all the angry words he can think of. He can draw, paint or scribble his anger. He can squeeze or smash lumps of clay, plasticine or play-dough. He can tear newspaper to shreds, wad up paper, squash or kick a can with his foot, jump up and down, punch a pillow, hit his bed with a tennis racquet, run around the block, scream into a pillow, yell in the shower, or wring a towel as hard as he can. We make lists of things he can do and practise some of them in my office. I will often give children assignments to experiment with at home and report the results to me.

I asked one 16-year-old girl who had terrible yelling fights with her mother to write down each argument so I could know how often these fights occurred She told me that after a fight she ran into her room and angrily wrote about the argument in the notebook I had given her, and found that her rage dissipated and she wasn't mad any more. Prior to this her angry feelings simmered within her for many hours, if not days.

Kevin, aged 6, retroflected his anger by literally tearing at himself and destroying things he owned. He would not ever admit to being angry. Kevin lived in a foster home and beneath his retroflective behaviour he harboured numerous emotions ranging from grief to rage at his abandonment. As Kevin gained more self-support through our work together, we began to sort out some of these emotions. He had already developed a very harmful anger process by turning his anger in to himself with every instance in his life that might cause him to be angry. So I not only needed to help Kevin uncover his deeper buried feelings, but to learn how to deal appropriately with angry feelings that might come up in his everyday life. We begin with the current surface feelings, before going deeper.

One day as we played with clay I asked him to tell me about the other children at school. His body tightened, as did his voice, when he mentioned the name of one boy. I very gently asked if the boy sometimes made him mad. Kevin, as usual, denied any angry feelings. I then asked if the boy had ever done anything to Kevin that he didn't like. I have discovered that using the expression "don't like" is much less threatening to children like Kevin than words such as angry and mad. Kevin nodded and told me how the boy sometimes teased him about being in a foster home. I asked what he did when it happened and he didn't like it. He hung his head and said, "I don't know." I made a big lump of clay and said, "Let's pretend that boy is sitting on this clay. What could you say to him?" "I don't know," he said. "Well, I know what *I'd* like to say to him," I said. "*I don't like it when you tease my friend Kevin! That makes me mad!*" Kevin giggled at this. I asked him if he could tell the boy he was mad. Kevin shook his head. I started to punch the clay and said, "I'd like to punch you for teasing Kevin!"

Kevin laughed out loud. (Kevin rarely smiled, much less laughed.) I asked him to try it himself and he tentatively punched the clay. I reassured him that we would never really do this, that this was just clay and that the boy couldn't even know we were doing this. I suggested that we do it together and we both began to punch with Kevin laughing and giggling all the while. Soon we were both talking to our imaginary adversary. I told Kevin he could punch a pillow or his bed whenever he felt mad at someone. His foster mother reported that he did this every day after school for a long while, and that he had stopped gouging himself and breaking things.

Kevin had experienced a hard life in his 6 years. Abandonment as well as physical abuse had left him deeply disturbed. In many ways he showed signs of not wanting to live, of feeling unentitled to exist. The survival part of him felt a deep rage, a rage that terrified him. I felt that in our work I could provide him with some needed tools for dealing with feelings that frightened him, as the smallest anger did. As we directed his aggression outward in safe ways, he began to develop a stronger sense of himself. At each session he worked on his process of dealing with anger in his everyday life. He expressed little bits of anger in many ways: through puppets, through clay, through storytelling, through sand tray scenes. At the same time that he was projecting and then owning his angry feelings, he was feeling validated by me. His FEELINGS were validated. He began to feel a stronger sense of self with every statement about himself that he made. Soon he was able, at my suggestion, to act out his physical abuse with doll figures, as well as scenes depicting his abandonment. Many other feelings related to these episodes emerged, in small segments, feelings of grief, loneliness and particularly worthlessness. Children who are abused and abandoned generally feel that it is their fault, that they are bad and worthless. Kevin was soon strong enough to deal effectively with his own bad feelings of self, and was able to learn how to become more accepting and nurturing of himself.

Expressing in small doses is the essence of child therapy. A child comes to therapy with resistance as his only ally, his only means of protecting himself. As the child begins to trust me, and as he begins to feel more of his own support, he may choose to allow himself to open, to risk, to be a little vulnerable. We meet resistance over and over during therapy. The child opens a bit, then closes. Each occurrence of the child's closing is actually a sign of progress, for it's the child's way of saying, "This is enough for me right now. The rest will come later." And the rest *does* come later, a little bit at a time.

Billy, aged nine, had been deflecting his anger. He was referred to me by his school because of rebellious behaviour: hitting, kicking, fighting on the playground, disruption in the classroom. Because of his father's Navy career, Billy's family had moved many times and, in fact, Billy had never finished a school year in one school. From the first session with the parents it was clear that the whole family was in trouble. Billy's mother was visibly depressed. His father denied the existence of any problem. A younger sister, not present at this session, was later disclosed to be suffering from eczema, asthma and chronic bedwetting. Because Billy aroused the most attention, he was the one brought in for help. The parents refused any parent or family therapy and just wanted me to "fix" Billy.

I am not averse to working with a child, even though it is clear that the whole family needs therapy. Billy had already formed a belief system about himself and a process of living that was self-debilitating. If his parents were willing to bring him in for therapy, I was willing to help him gain as much strength as possible.

At our first session Billy huddled in the corner of the couch as his parents rattled off a list of complaints about him. It is important for me to have the child present during this first session to hear everything the parents tell me. I want him to know everything I know. It is my time to begin to make some contact with the child, and to let him know that although I am listening to the parents, I am just as aware and respectful of HIS point of view. It is also an opportunity for me to begin to change his stance of being brought into, perhaps dragged into, therapy, to one of choice and responsibility for coming. As the parents talked I often made eye contact with Billy, asking him if he agreed with what they were saying. He shrugged and said, "I don't know." I smiled at him as we, the parents and I, continued. I spent five minutes alone with Billy at the end of the session, telling him a little bit about how I work with children and showing him my office, and he agreed that he would be willing to come back for a few times.

At our next session the rebellious child came in quietly, no words to say, body constricted, face pinched. I saw him glance at the paints which happened to be out on the table, so I asked him if he would like to paint a picture, anything he wanted to paint. His face lit up and he proceeded to paint with great absorption. When he finished he told me that his class at school was studying volcanoes, so that's what he painted. I asked him to tell me about his volcano. He said, "This is not an active volcano—it's a dormant volcano. It has hot lava that hasn't erupted yet—but it might. This is the smoke coming off the volcano because it has to let off some steam." These were his exact words indicating to me that he must have been in class when volcanoes were studied. (The counsellor had indicated that he was never able to remain in the classroom due to his behaviour.) I asked Billy to stand up and imagine that he was the volcano and to tell me about himself. To his puzzled look I said, "Pretend the volcano is like a puppet and you have to be its voice. Start by saying, 'I am a volcano.'" So Billy said, "I am a volcano." To my questions he added, "I have hot lava inside of me. I haven't erupted yet, but I will. I have grey smoke coming out of me so I can let off steam." I said to Billy "If you really were a volcano, if your body were the volcano, where would the hot lava be?" Very thoughtfully Billy placed his hand on his abdomen and said, "Right here." "Billy," I said softly, "What would that hot lava be for you, a boy?" After some moments of thought Billy looked up at me with very wide eyes. "Anger!" he whispered. I then asked Billy to paint a picture of what he thought his anger looked like, just using colours, lines and shapes. He painted a large, thick red circle with various colours inside the circle. When he finished I wrote the description of his anger circle that he dictated to me, as well as the things that made him angry. "This is Billy's anger inside his stomach. It's yellow, red, grey, black and orange. I get mad when my sister messes up my room and when I get in fights and when I fall off my bike." At this point Billy couldn't think of anything else to say. He had opened as much as he was willing for this session, and he then enveloped himself in his protective wall.

At this session Billy was not ready to give much expression to his anger except through painting. Furthermore, he would only admit to very surface angers. At each subsequent session he was willing to own more and more of his angry feelings through clay, the sand tray, drawings and puppet figures. As he expressed angry feelings, other feelings began to emerge: grief over the loss of friends each time he moved, fear of making new friends because he knew he would have to move again, feelings of despair and loneliness, feelings of helplessness and self-blame regarding his depressed mother, anger at his father for leaving so often.

In one session Billy made a circle of animals in the sand tray. A lion came onto the scene and attacked the surprised animals. I said, "Say you had to be one of those animals. Which one are you?" "I'm the lion," he said. "What about the lion reminds you of you?" "I don't know." "Do you ever feel like attacking someone like the lion did?" Billy answered, "Yeah!" "Who would you attack?" "Well, there are kids who bother me at school." "Billy, what do you do when you get angry at your Dad?" Billy pulled back in fear. "I don't get mad at him! He'd whip me!" "How about your Mom?" I asked. "Sometimes she yells at me and I yell back. But she tells my Dad." One could see Billy's dilemma clearly. At our next session I introduced the idea that anger needed to be expressed and we experimented with some ways he might do this. He enjoyed tearing up old newspapers and magazines and I have to admit I had a lot of fun doing this myself. After I had seen Billy for about four months, I called the school to see what was happening with Billy there. His teacher reported that she hadn't had any problem with him for the last two months, and she supposed that he had just been going through some kind of stage!

Sometimes I have the opportunity to work closely with a child's teacher, but not often. Many teachers do not have the time, or the willingness. When I can involve all the people who are part of the child's world, my job becomes easier.

Phase three

The third phase in working with children's anger has to do with helping children uncover and express locked-up angry feelings due to past, or perhaps current, trauma in the safety of the therapeutic setting. This kind of anger may be so buried that the child has absolutely no awareness of it; yet because of the child's symptomatic behaviour we can be sure that it has a detrimental effect on the child's healthy functioning. These angry feelings will be released usually in small increments; children rarely experience a catharsis as an adult might. The power of the feelings, as they emerge, is frightening to the child.

Sometimes I am aware of the trauma, due to information given to me by the parents. Other times, the child's drawings and other projective work indicate to me that something is happening or has happened that has created terror for this child. I realize that I may be interpreting the projections incorrectly; however, the material presented indicates that the child needs help in uncovering *something*. If a child is plagued by nightmares or night terrors, if she is severely phobic, if she is torturing animals, if, in my office, she viciously attacks clay with a knife, as one child did, over and over, if her drawings and sand tray scenes and stories are replete with horrifying symbols, I need to pay attention. It is quite likely that the child has endured trauma that has been buried so deeply that she cannot remember it. Children will often split off, fragment as a way of handling traumatic events. They truly do not remember that anything happened. The organism, however, in its thrust for integration, attempts to get rid of the feelings that are buried within the child. It pushes relentlessly. If the child is given the opportunity to draw and enact and use clay in a therapeutic session, the kind of projections mentioned will come through.

When I work with such children I want to help them express the angry feelings that are projected into monsters and frightening symbols. I want to help them OWN these feelings in order to feel their own energy and power. Sometimes it is too difficult to expect a child to remember the traumatic event, particularly if it happened at a pre-verbal stage. However, the anger is simmering and I must help the child own and release it, even if we cannot identify it.

An example of this phenomenon is the child I saw several years ago who was exhibiting behavioural manifestations indicative of severe trauma. However, in looking at her history, there was nothing to indicate that anything had ever happened to her. She had never been in the hospital, had never moved, no one in or close to the family had died, her parents were loving and concerned, etc. The family system was quite healthy as I observed it. Yet she was severely phobic and had terrible debilitating nightmares. It was only later, 5 years later, that I discovered that she had attended a local pre-school where children had allegedly been molested over a period of time. She denied, even 5 years later at the age of 12, that she had ever been molested. In our sessions together, when she was 7 years old, she drew pictures of devils and monsters, stabbed clay repeatedly and intensely with a butter knife and could not get enough of very wet sand and water as she poured water with a fierce energy. After three months of these activities in once-a-week sessions, all of her symptoms disappeared and she has been a very happy, well-adjusted young lady ever since. She never discussed her possible molestation, nor articulated any deep angry feelings. I could only assume from this experience that she underwent some kind of catharsis through her activities, and that whatever had been at the root of her intense activity was so deeply buried that she could not bring it to consciousness. Perhaps more would emerge at a later developmental stage.

Another example is a young boy who was severely physically abused by his father, yet had no memory of the abuse. He has exhibited numerous symptoms to indicate interruption of healthy organismic development. In our sessions he too intensely used very wet sand, never seeming to be able to get his fill of it. He poured water into the sand tray until I needed to ask him to stop before the water spilled onto the floor. His stories, drawings and sand scenes were replete with symbols of conflict and anger in the most intense way. His nightmares and other symptoms stopped after about 3 or 4 months though we continued to work together since his work continued to be rich with expression. He was able at this time to express anger directly and appropriately, and was doing well in school, with friends, and at home. He was relaxed and full of happy energy. Yet the intense symbolic feelings continued to pour out. He was unable to articulate anything about his trauma. Fortunately, his parents continued to bring him for his sessions knowing that he was still doing significant work. At the point where our sessions took on the aura of "hanging out" together, I knew it was time to stop. Perhaps at some future developmental level he will be ready to explore a deeper level.

Sometimes the child does own and articulate blocked feelings of anger, and healthy integration occurs rapidly. Susan, an 11-year-old girl, was severely beaten by a burglar who entered the unlocked door of her house. He stumbled into her room and she awakened and screamed. He beat her to silence. In therapy Susan was unable to feel any anger. She could express, through many forms of expressive techniques, her fear and terror, yet anger eluded her. I knew that until she could express some anger, she would continue to remain a frightened victim of her assault. Before the incident Susan, according to her mother, had always been able to express angry feelings openly and directly. One day, after three months of once a week work together, we sat working with clay. I picked up the rubber mallet and asked Susan to hit the clay. I said, "Imagine you're mad at the clay and give it a hit." She made a face at me but complied. I said, "IF you were mad at someone, who would it be?" She answered, "I guess that guy." "Then imagine it's that guy you're hitting." Susan listlessly allowed the mallet to fall on the clay. "What would you say to him if you could talk to him?" "Well, I guess I'd say, that was a terrible thing you did. You are a bad person, or something like that." I encouraged Susan to repeat these words, and she began to hit the clay with much more energy. Suddenly she dropped the mallet and looked at me in horror. "What is it, Susan?" I asked very softly. She whispered, "It's not him I'm mad at, it's my mother for leaving the door open that night and for not hearing me scream when I did." Although her mother had asked Susan over and over again if she was angry with her, Susan had always denied it, probably needing to protect her sorrowful mother. I insisted that she share her angry feelings with her mother, explaining that if she didn't there would always be a wall between them. It was only after Susan did express her anger toward her mother that she was finally able to fully, wholeheartedly, direct her anger toward her assaulter thus regaining her own sense of self and power.

Clay is an excellent medium for helping children contact, express, and work through hidden angry feelings. Since these feelings have been lying dormant within the child like heavy rocks, the child usually needs assistance. I cannot emphasize enough that these hidden feelings rarely burst forth in one cathartic experience, but emerge in small bits. Children do not have the self-support to handle too much of these feelings at one time. The feelings are terrifying in themselves. Because they are so scary, I will often need to give the child a little push, as I did with Susan, at the same time focusing on the issue in a light, non-threatening way.

Another example is of an 11-year-old girl who had been physically and sexually abused by her stepfather. She too had much difficulty expressing her anger—at him or at anything. One day I asked her to make a figure of him out of clay. She worked a long time making only his head. Finally I asked her to finish her work and to talk to the clay head. She seemed agitated and upset in spite of my reassurance that it was only clay and he would never know. I asked her if I could talk to the head. I said, "I don't like what you did to my friend. You make me so mad!" She laughed at me, but was still unable to say anything to him. I picked up the mallet and asked her to hit the clay, reminding her again that it was only clay and her stepfather would never know. She asked me to do it for her, but I refused, saying that this was something she, herself, had to do. She was terrified, yet took the mallet and gave him a couple of punches. "You'll get more later," she said to him. In subsequent sessions, gradually, she was able to more and more directly, openly and with energy, express her anger toward him. As she did this, her whole demeanour and posture changed from a timid, restricted child into a strong, happy, forthright, assertive, young lady.

A boy that I saw, aged 8, deflected his angry feelings by destroying flowers in the garden, torturing the cat and other destructive behaviours. In a clay session one day he made many tiny clay figures he labelled Mr. Perfects, placed them in a clay spaceship, and proceeded to slam the ship down as hard as he could. He did this over and over for many sessions, never owning his feelings. His father, who, according to his mother, expected the boy to be perfect at all times, would not come to see me. I asked Tommy if anyone he knew wanted him to be perfect. He couldn't think of anyone. I asked him if his father ever wanted him to be perfect. He shrugged. I said, "If my father wanted me to be perfect, it would make me mad." "Yeah! I know!" he said. After that he was able to identify all his Mr. Perfects as his father, as he smashed them inside his spaceship. Since his father refused to come in, I insisted on speaking to him on the phone, and gave him the assignment of withdrawing any criticism of his son for a whole week. The father defensively denied that he criticized, yet after I gently explained the kinds of things that a child might take as criticism, the father burst into tears. He, himself, had been severely criticized as a child. Needless to say, much progress was made after that phone call.

Sometimes, as children's angry feelings are unleashed, parents express the fear that I am teaching their children how to be angry, even violent, through encouraging hitting pillows, smashing clay and so forth. It is vital to educate parents about the role of anger, the harm it does when not expressed, the need to help children move through angry feelings. Soon after my first book, *Windows To Our Children*, was published, I was interviewed for a news programme in Los Angeles regarding my work. They came to my office and filmed me in an actual working session with a child (with the child's and parents' permission, of course). John, aged 11, told me that he was very unhappy because he had no one to play with at school or at home. His general stance in life was as a retroflector. He walked around with hunched shoulders, restricted body and was sad and whiney a great deal of the time. I asked John to draw how it felt to have no one to play with. He drew two pictures, just using grey and blue lines across the paper. He said, "This is how it feels at school— bad. And this is how it feels at home—bad." I said, "What's it like for you to feel bad at school, bad at home, bad all the time?" John answered, head down, shoulders crunched, "Bad." At my request, he drew another picture with flat lines and dull colours. We spread the pictures out and looked at them. "John, when you look at these pictures and see how you feel all the time, what do you thing of? What's it like feeling bad at school, bad at home, bad, bad, bad? Do you like it?" John answered, "No! I don't like it." "Well," I said, "Draw a picture of how you don't like it." John proceeded to draw somewhat lethargically, and then got more and more engrossed and involved in his drawing. He drew dark black and red swirls, a gun with bullets shooting out of it, a knife with blood dripping from it, some boxing gloves. The television camera caught it all. When he was finished I asked him to tell me about his drawing. John stood up and shouted, "I feel so mad I'd like to stab someone! I feel so mad I'd like to shoot someone! I feel so mad I'd like to punch someone hard!!" As he yelled, he made thick black marks all over his paper. I watched this public display of violent anger in panic, wondering what to do next. Then I looked at John, and noticed that he sat down, was taking a deep breath, his face was glowing, he was smiling, his head was up, his shoulders straight and he looked happy and relaxed. I said, "How do you feel now, John?" He said, "Good! I liked doing that!" I asked him to draw how he felt at the moment and he drew a lovely picture pf pinks and yellows and a rainbow and a bright, smiling sun. He said to me, "I feel really nice now, not like I felt before. Why did just drawing these pictures make me feel good?" It's not unusual for children to ask such questions when I direct their awareness to their feelings. John had been angry at his plight, but had retroflected his anger, his process for most of his life, and as a result felt bad and hurt. He was lethargic, flat, devoid of energy. When some of his angry feelings had an opportunity to be released, he felt good instead of bad. He felt energetic, calm and peaceful. We could then begin to deal with the issue of making friends. By the way, the newscaster's comment at the end of the session was, "If I hadn't seen that with my own eyes, I would never have believed it!"

Throughout this chapter I have alluded to anger work with various age levels as well as families. There actually isn't much difference in helping children of any age work through angry feelings. Very young children may do more of their work on a symbolic level than older children who have more cognitive development and language skills. At the same time young children are quite pragmatic and are able to understand and respond more than most people realize. Though they may play out their angry feelings using monsters and angry looking animals, they will express their own feelings in concrete, uncomplicated ways. It is important to help parents of young children to understand the developmental level of each child and the art of communication with young children.

Since most children, and particularly younger children, feel small and powerless, many of them, in frustration, engage in power struggles. A temper tantrum is not necessarily an expression of anger, but an indication of powerlessness. As children begin to feel some control and power in their lives with the limits and boundaries of safety, they become calmer and easier to get along with. Sometimes in our sessions young children will spend the whole time directing and controlling me in the session, deriving great satisfaction. I will often direct parents to provide such a scheduled time at home.

Adolescents are not unlike young children in their quest for separation and power. The adolescent, as the very young child, is struggling to establish the self. When the young person can be assertive and direct regarding her likes and dislikes, her wants and needs, and when her anger is accepted and respected, her task of individuation becomes easier. The parents of the adolescent need guidance and reassurance regarding their child's struggle to establish the self. I find that most adolescents have great wisdom. They very much appreciate my explanation of the therapy process and are willing to participate and are responsive to our work together. They too enjoy using many of the projective techniques described here to unearth hidden feelings. You can read more about adolescent work in the next chapter.

Often I will use projective techniques in family sessions to view the family dynamics and to help them share feelings with each other. I will explain all of the phases of anger work in family sessions: talking about anger, providing experiences to express anger directly and symbolically and finding ways to help the family become aware of and express hidden angers. An added aspect to family work is the effect of each individual's experience and process on the whole family. This experience includes the parents' own childhood experiences with anger. I may ask the family to draw something that made them mad—directing the adults to draw from their own childhoods. The children, regardless of age, are fascinated to hear about their parents' childhood angers.

Anger work is something like a spiral. As the child feels some self-support, inner strength, through activities to enhance and strengthen the senses, body and self, she can express an angry feeling. The resistance then comes up since she no longer can tolerate opening to further expression. We continue the work, giving her opportunities to achieve further inner strength, and further expression emerges. This process continues until the child has achieved enough integration and strength to maintain and sustain greater levels of expression. The spiral continues upward until the child's organism takes on its own natural flowing and evolving task of healthy self-regulation.

CHAPTER SIX

Working with adolescents

T he adolescent is not some mysterious breed of human as many seem to think. She is going through a developmental process that is normal and necessary. We have all been in that very same place. I have worked with hundreds of teens and find that they are quite responsive to the kind of experiences I offer. I find them to be wise, insightful, funny, and eager to know themselves. Of course each is an individual with unique needs.

I have often named workshops regarding adolescents as "Working with the resistant adolescent." This title draws the attention of therapists since the word "resistant" resonates with their image of this age group. In fact, most adolescents are by nature resistant. Some are more honest about their resistance than others. If they are compliant and appear to be totally cooperative in the beginning, they are probably presenting a false self. Actually, resistance is a good thing. It implies to me an honouring of the self. "Why should I trust this lady when I don't know anything about her?" "Why should I open myself and show her my deepest feelings?" "Who is she, anyway?"

In this chapter, I will present some techniques, along with case examples, that I have found to be helpful in my work with this age group. Let me first say a few words about the adolescent, words you probably know but which bear review.

The major developmental task of the adolescent is to individuate and find an identity of her own. This is not really a new task since it begins with infancy—that early struggle to establish a separate self. But at adolescence it becomes all-important. At each stage of the child's development she is seeking a self and discovering her boundaries. By adolescence the task is crucial. It is at this time that she must separate from her family and face a menacing future.

Mark McConville, a renowned Gestalt therapist, in his important book on adolescence (1995), writes extensively regarding this new, emerging self. He postulates that the adolescent, particularly the young adolescent, does not question who he is. It is not a cognitive process. This adolescent self emerges through his emotions and his senses—it is a visceral experience.

Yes, the adolescent brings a lot of baggage with her to this important task, making it very difficult. At an early age the child has developed a way of being, a process of living and coping and surviving, which stays with her as she grows, and this process becomes even more rigid in adolescence. The younger child learns to get her needs met in any way she can and develops this process in a misguided attempt to get those needs met. For example, at an early age, say about four, the child learns that it is not OK to express her angry feelings. She faces the wrath, or disapproval, or maybe sadness of her parents at the expression of such feelings and she has little guidance, experience or maturity in expressing them gracefully and diplomatically. Fearful that approval will not be met and that abandonment may be just around the corner, she keeps her anger in. But the organism, in its everlasting quest for health and regulation, must discharge the energy in some way. And so the child may deflect or retroflect her feelings. She may become withdrawn and quiet and develop headaches or stomach-aches. She may project her anger onto others. She is rebellious, has tantrums. She is hyperactive or spaced out or both. She wets the bed, becomes encropetic, has nightmares. These are just a few of the behaviours or symptoms that may occur, and they become her way of being in the world—her way of handling any stress that comes her way. Along with this comes a decreased sense of self since anger is actually an expression of the self, and when it is inhibited, the self is diminished.

In adolescence these behaviours may become transformed into more sophisticated ways of anaesthetizing herself to avoid feelings, since she has learned that feelings are fraught with danger. The use of drugs, increased sexual activity, eating disorders, anti-social activity, suicidal tendencies—these are the behaviours that plague the adolescent population.

The young child, precursor to the adolescent, has introjected many faulty messages that affect his feelings about himself and these messages continue on through adolescence and adulthood. Feelings, memories and fantasies from the past interrupt the natural flow of the organism. He has a depth of feelings that he finds difficult to share with his family. He just can't put those feelings into words. He cannot risk being vulnerable because if he is, he will lose the fragile self he has. He needs assistance in expressing his feelings of anxiety and loneliness and frustration and self-disparagement and sexual confusion and fear. He needs to see how he interrupts his own healthy growth. This is the job we face.

An article I read back in 1985 captures the plight of the adolescent so well, I would like to quote it here. Even after all these years, it is still pertinent:

> The transition from child to adult is perhaps the most traumatic of life's many processes, but it is the chaos of adolescence that is the normal process of identity formation. Part of this formation is what we refer to as acting-out behaviour. This behaviour is a manifestation of the child's experimenting with his or her own identity. The child may not listen, may rebel, become obstinate or verbally abusing. You may feel that the child is acting-out, but he is actually experimenting with issues of autonomy and dependence. The greatest thing—the most difficult thing—to recognize is that this rebellion, in moderation, is important to the child during the formation of identity. The bottom line is not what the child is doing, but to what degree—what is truly destructive and what is not.
> [From a newsletter put out by Vista del Mar Hospital in Torrance, CA, "Is there such a thing as 'Normal' Adolescence?" by Kevin Cox, MD]

So we know what is happening and have some idea of what we need to do. How can we do it? How do we help the child overcome his resistance to find himself and his boundaries of self, so that he can live a healthy, productive, good life in this very stressful, faulty society?

My teen years

I haven't even talked about the era in which the adolescent lives today, and what he faces in the world. I was a teenager during World War II. The focus for everyone was to win the war—everyone rallied around this objective. This was a war that we considered a just war and one that brought the whole country together. Seventeen-year-olds joined the service, as my future husband did. Eighteen-year-olds were already training or fighting. Younger boys waited impatiently till they could join. Meanwhile, they and the girls joined organizations like the Civil Air Patrol Cadets to do their part, just like I did. As a 16-year-old I spent many hours dancing with young soldiers and sailors at USO canteens. We were able to get jobs like no other time since older young men and women were involved in the war effort. I had jobs that would astonish today's teens. Our identities were handed to us in a new and different way. We grew up fast. We learned quickly who we were or thought we were. (Actually we didn't think about such things.) We planned for the future—anything was possible.

We teens, here in the US, were on the "home front." Our young men went across the oceans to fight, but we were never in danger, as teens in Europe and Asia were. We did without some things, but I never felt this to be a problem. My two older brothers were overseas, one in Europe and one in the South Pacific, and I was proud that my family displayed two stars in our window. But then the war came home to me when, just a few months before the war's end, one of my brothers was killed in action in Germany. And we began to learn about the terrible slaughter of the Jews that had taken place. I remember thinking that if my parents hadn't emigrated to the United States when they did, we would have been among those that perished. This was a sobering thought to me, and hastened my maturity. I wonder sometimes how my own rebellion manifested itself. Perhaps the war kept me and other adolescents from typical ways of achieving identity formation. We had other ways to define ourselves. I grieved deeply for my wonderful brother, and tried hard not to show my grief since my parents were so devastated. Instead, I became even more responsible. I did leave home at an early age to make my way in the world—perhaps this was my way of rebelling.

Today's youth face a totally different kind of life and, as I write this, our country is at war with Iraq. The future is not easy to plan for. Professions become obsolete quickly. Companies are down-sizing or out-sourcing.. The economy is in terrible shape. Lack of funds affects educational opportunities. Nothing is simple and easy for today's adolescent.

Meanwhile we therapists have a job to do. Let's move on to the task of how we work therapeutically with troubled youngsters.

Psychotherapy

An important implication for the therapy we do involves the polar-ities that exist for the adolescent. It's as if she has two separate selves. One self feels the pull of past experience. The old self of childhood doesn't magically disappear. This is the *introjected* self that clings to the goals and standards of her parents. This self gets its esteem from parental approval and accepts the adult world at face value without much conflict. The other self is the emerging ado-lescent self. This self is very much tied to sensory experience that is intensified by the body's changes. She feels a heightened sense of herself, and begins to identify with her experience and separate it out from the interpersonal and family milieu. She becomes acutely conscious of the divergence of her experience from the familiar framework provided by the other self (McConville, 1995).

She becomes uncomfortable as her thoughts, feelings, urges, per-ceptions and choices conform less and less to what they should be. When the adolescent can recognize this struggle, she is for the most part healthier and more mature than if she is totally aware of what's going on. She needs to let go of the old self but this is not easy. It's akin to Fritz Perl's idea of the "fertile void" or "death place"—that place between old ways and new ones, without the usual support systems (Rubenfeld, 1992). Many kids bury any awareness and disown this kind of struggle. They project everything onto the adult world. They have no problems; it's the adults who cause the problems. They are the victims. (And to some extent this is true.) But without taking some responsibility and seeing things as they are more clearly, they will only sink further and further into this victim place.

The most common defense mechanisms I see with adolescents are projection, denial and fantasy. The defense mechanisms, often seen as resistance, are the adolescent's way of taking care of herself, coping and surviving. The more she is enmeshed with her family, the greater the hold they have on her, the more confluence there is, the stronger the defense mechanisms become.

Family work is a different kind of work—a time when we can assess communications skills, degree of confluence, roles taken and assigned, articulating wants and needs, road blocks, helping to express feelings and know the messages behind what is actually said and so forth. Certainly this is important work, a kind of work that might be adjunct to the individual work I may do. The troubled adolescent can benefit greatly by the work we do individually in terms of bringing out into the open the polarities that exist for him. He has one foot in the family and one foot out in the world. Both places are filled with stuff that creates anxieties and fears. His self-esteem suffers based on his family experiences and those negative introjects. I believe he needs to do this work himself to assist in the task of separating and finding his own boundaries, defining the self and begin to have some awareness of what his feelings are and learn how to articulate them.

When I work with an adolescent I follow my policy of seeing the parents with her at the first session, if at all possible. There are many exceptions: when the young person comes in on her own and refuses to have her parents present, when she is in a foster home and bonding has not taken place, or she is living in an institution or group home, for example. If at all possible I want to see the adults that this child lives with. I can get a sense of the child's life, the various points of view, clarify the reason for the referral, assess the dynamics. I need to know the divergent life views—what the parents say and what the kids say, and maybe uncover what they all really mean to say. At this session I will ask the child if she would be willing to come for a few sessions alone so I can get to know her in her own right, away from her family. After that we can decide which path to take. She may not agree on her own, but this approach does dilute the idea that she is the sick one. So I begin with what is presented to me.

There are times, though, when a teen will adamantly refuse to come by herself. A single mother, who was having, in her words, great difficulty controlling her 16-year-old son, managed to bring him in for a session. I felt that we had a pretty good first session, but he refused to come in again and his mother felt helpless in the face of his strength. I suggested that the mother come in by herself. In the course of our work together, Mom realized how much she clung to this boy and needed him for her own self-esteem. As she worked on letting go of him and building her own sense of self, she reported that he began to hang around her in ways she had previously hoped for. He often asked her what she talked about in her therapy, though he was still unwilling to attend any sessions.

Relationship

Building a relationship with the child is of course a pre-requisite to any other work. My non-judgmental, non-manipulative, authentic stance generally quickly builds this important I/Thou relationship. I need to accept the child without judgment.

A 14-year-old-girl was referred to me through the courts. She was involved in a programme that diverted adolescents to counselling when they broke the law in some way. I saw her about three times before I realized that I needed to refer her to someone else. She never responded to me, never looked at me and generally sat stiff and silent. I decided to give it one more try. I went out to the waiting room and noticed that she was reading a magazine. She may have been doing this at the other sessions, but in my haste to usher her into my office I never paid attention to what she was doing. This time, I sat down next to her and asked, "What are you reading?" She quickly moved the magazine toward me and then went back to reading. This was the first response I ever got from her. I said, "I didn't see it." So she held it toward me a bit more slowly. I saw that it was a heavy metal music magazine. I asked her if we could look at this magazine together since I was pretty ignorant about this kind of music and yet had clients such as her that liked it. So we went into the office and spent the whole session looking at the magazine. She talked about the different groups and the ones that were her favourites. We tried to find some of the music on my radio, but couldn't. I asked if she could bring in some tapes and she happily agreed. Needless to say, we established a great relationship and the words to some of the songs provided fertile material for our work together!

I learned how important it was to pay attention, to notice, to be fully in contact myself. In another, somewhat different situation, I was confronted with a highly resistant 13-year-old boy. He had been in seven foster homes by the time I saw him, and was now eligible to be sent to a state hospital where there was a unit specifically for "incorrigible adolescents." At the time I was providing outside therapy to various children who were severely emotionally disturbed and living in the foster care system. It was decided that this child would receive some therapy with me before this drastic move. The social worker told me about the child's background on the telephone and then brought him in and dropped him off. He walked in "tough" and stood in the middle of the room. I stood in front of him and said, "I know you probably don't want to be here, but since you are, let me tell you what I know about you so you can tell me if it's right." I proceeded to tell him what the social worker had told me. He dropped his tough stance somewhat and made a few corrections. Then I said, rather firmly, "Jason, just sit down." He sat down on the couch. I told him that I planned to take him on a fantasy journey and that when he was done I wanted him to draw something from that journey. I generally provide two or three sizes of paper and crayons, pastels, markers and coloured pencils and I pointed those out to him. (Children rarely choose the crayons.) I asked Jason to make himself comfortable and close his eyes as I took him on the journey. (I generally close my eyes when I do this since most children keep their eyes open—I know this since I peek to see what they are doing.) Jason kept his eyes open at first and then leaned back and closed his eyes as I spoke. I did a brief relaxation exercise, ending with the tone of a Chinese gong, before I began the fantasy. I took him on a rather long journey through a meadow, up a mountain, through caves to a door that would open to a place of his own (see *Windows To Our Children*, p. 3).

When I was done, Jason, to my surprise (I actually thought he was asleep) opened his eyes and began to draw using the markers. We had an amazing session that I will describe later. I saw Jason weekly for four months, and he never did go to the hospital, though he did move to another foster home by his own request.

I learned from this experience the importance of meeting the child where he is—he was "tough" and I was firm. Sharing what I knew about him was key here. At our ending session I asked Jason what impressed him most in our work. He said, "I remember that first session. You didn't lecture me about shaping up, like everyone else did. We did that fantasy and drawing and you never once said anything to me about what I was doing to get into trouble." It's true that I don't focus on behaviour. I see behaviour as a symptom and rarely can the young person consciously change this behaviour.

At the first session I often ask the client to draw a picture of a house, a tree and a person on one sheet of paper, adding anything he would like to add. The child will come in and feels awkward and anxious, wondering, I'm sure, what will happen. There is not generally enough of a relationship for him to pour his heart out. The House–Tree–Person (Jolles, 1986) drawing is not difficult since most children draw houses and trees at a very early age. I will say, "There's something I would like you to do. I want you to draw a picture that contains a house and a tree and a person and anything else you want to put in the picture. Don't worry about making a wonderful picture—in fact I would rather you didn't try to do your best since we just don't have enough time. When you're done, I'll tell you what this drawing tells me about you and you can correct me."

I have set out crayons, pastels and markers but it seems typical for 12- to 16-year-old boys to ask for a pencil, or use a black marker. Some even ask for a ruler. I now put all of those items out as well. I do not use this drawing as an interpretive test. When the child is finished I will tell him what I think it means and ask him what is right or wrong. I sometimes give my own thoughts or sometimes read directly from the *Manual* (Jolles, 1986).

Watching the child's progress can be revealing. A 12-year-old boy was brought in to see me because he had set fire to his house. Lee was an only child who lived with his father. His mother had died when he was six. At our first session with his father he remained totally silent. His father was mystified at his son's fire setting. He said, "He is usually pretty good—spends a lot of time with himself.

I work long hours but I generally don't have to worry about him. The only problem we have is that he never does his homework or chores I assign. I guess he's pretty lazy." In our time alone I asked Lee to draw a house, a tree and a person. He drew a large house and proceeded to make bricks along the side of the house. He picked up a brown marker and began laboriously to colour in each brick. I realized that he would never finish the drawing if he did this so I said, "Lee, I'll know that all the bricks are brown coloured, so just do the rest of the picture." When he finished I said, "This picture tells me something about you, but I'm not always right so I need to check it out with you. First, I noticed how hard you worked to colour the bricks, but I stopped you because I knew that you would never finish. I wonder if this happens in your life? Do you want to do a very good job on things—set high standards for yourself—but can't finish since it's just too much? And then people think you are lazy!"

Lee burst into tears. "Everyone thinks I'm lazy! My father, my teachers. And I try so hard!" Lee cried for a while. Lee left with a smile on his face. I knew that we had to find the root of his problem: his mother's death, his aloneness, his father's long work hours.

His fire setting was, for sure, a desperate cry for attention.

This is one of the most successful exercises I have ever used for beginning a relationship, getting to know a child and for the child to feel heard. Kids desperately need someone to listen, validate and support them in a non-threatening safe place. When I do this at a beginning session I never go deeper than what is presented. I have used this exercise with children as young as six, but find that adolescents respond with great enthusiasm. A fairly resistant 16-year-old girl totally changed her attitude about coming in for sessions and asked if her mother and sister could do this exercise at the next session!

Contact

I have discussed contact in a previous chapter. The child (and the therapist) must be in contact—fully present—for a successful session. Contact is different than relationship. I can have a relationship with a child who has difficulty sustaining any contact, or goes in and out of contact in the session. If a child shows an inability to be in contact, this, then, becomes the focus of the therapy. Here is one example:

A mother calls me up to say that her 14-year-old son chased her with a knife the previous night and she is very frightened of him. I agree to see them and don't know what to expect. I go out to the waiting room and the mother and boy stand up. The boy has a very large, live snake wrapped around him. I am startled and before I say anything the mother introduces herself and her son and she and I shake hands. The boy smiles broadly and holds the snake out toward me and offers to have me hold it. I decline saying I don't know how to hold a snake. (I'm assuming that it is not a poisonous one.) The boy tells me that it is easy to do it and plunks the snake into my arms. He assures me that the snake is friendly and likes to be stroked on the head, which I do very tentatively. He is very pleased and compliments me on my snake holding style. (I am quaking inside and trying not to show it.) I am very impressed with John's ability to make contact with me. What I find out in the course of our time together is that he can only maintain contact when it involves his snakes. (He brings in many snakes in subsequent sessions.)

He will not make any conversation about anything, except his snakes. "How are you?" is met with total silence. He is not interested in drawing or clay or games or anything in the office. And so we spend a lot of time with his snakes. At one session, as we lay on the floor having races with the snakes, I began to speak to John's snake. I said something like, "Hey snake, do you like racing my snake?" John responded for his snake. In this projective way, John was able to express many thoughts, ideas and especially feelings. After several months he was actually able to put his snakes (which he always carried with him) into a bucket of sand and engage in other expressive techniques. He never once chased his mother with a knife during our year and a half together.

Here are more examples of establishing contact:

A family came in with a very resistant 16-year-old girl. She made hostile comments throughout the session and refused to make contact with me or with anyone, for that matter. She looked down at the floor most of the time. Her father told me she had warned them that she wouldn't talk at all, though she did talk in spite of herself, albeit in her hostile way. Her hostile remarks were actually quite perceptive and I told her that the family really didn't need me; they needed to listen to what she had to say since she was so good at assessing correctly the dynamics of this family system. The parents appeared shocked into silence, and contact between me and the girl was immediately established. My comments were totally sincere, by the way.

A mother brought in her daughter in desperation. The girl had joined a Jehovah's Witness sect and was obsessed with bringing her mother into the fold. The child was angry and felt that she had come to see me totally against her will. I asked the mother to leave, and I asked the girl to tell me about her beliefs. I told her that I was Jewish and had no intention of joining, but I knew nothing about this organization and wanted to learn more. She complied and began to tell me the whole story of how she was drawn in and what she had learned. I asked many questions about the group which she readily answered, though she realized there were many things she did not know. She spoke about her need to join this group and the good things it was giving her. Mostly she was worried about her mother's after life future but said her mother wouldn't listen. Contact between us was excellent, reinforcing my belief that to achieve contact the therapist must be honest, congruent, respectful of the client's position and above all, begin with where the client's interests are. What happened next? The mother learned to listen with acceptance, and after several months the girl left the group of her own accord.

The child learned about herself in our sessions and became more of her own person.

A final example of establishing contact:

A 15-year-old boy was referred to me by the courts as part of that programme that diverted young people into counselling if their act was a first offense. Jack had called in a bomb threat to his school and watched as the whole school was evacuated. Unable to contain himself, he began to tell other children that he was the cause of the evacuation. Word got to the principal and the police were called. Jack was very frightened when he came to see me and was eager to please me as much as possible. I realized that I was very uncomfortable with our sessions though at first I ignored my discomfort. However, the discomfort persisted and I finally sat down to figure out what was happening. It suddenly occurred to me that Jack was not really in contact with me at our sessions, though he appeared to be. So at the next session he and I sat facing each other and played out our little ritual, "Hi Jack. How are you?" "Fine." "Is there anything you would like to do today or talk about?" "No. Whatever you say." And then instead of my usual, "Well let's do . . .", I sat in silence thinking about what I should do next. Jack said, "Well, what do you want me to do today?" I replied, "I don't know, Jack. Something is missing and I don't know what it is." Jack became very agitated and anxious. "I'm doing everything you ask me to!" he almost shouted. "I know, Jack. You have been very cooperative. But something is just missing." Suddenly I knew what it was. "Your heart just hasn't been in it." Jack was astounded and began to cry. "I don't know how to do that." I said, "Let's go ahead and do something and maybe it will happen now. Or you could talk to me about what it's like for you to be here and what your feelings are. I know you must be scared and worried even though you always act as if everything is great. What would you like to do?" "I don't want to talk. Can we use clay?" And so we did. Our contact was strong and, through the clay, many of Jack's feelings were expressed. This experience taught me to trust my own feelings and body sensations. The discomfort in my own body was an important clue that I attempted to discount. It persisted, though, until I paid attention to it.

Enhancing the self and emotional expression

The major developmental task of the adolescent is to separate and individuate. As we discussed earlier, this is a major struggle and is the cause of much contention in the family. When I see an adolescent I know that a big part of my job is to assist him. Many teens will readily talk about their family's dysfunction, their siblings, their friend, or school. They are rarely introspective or self-aware. They do need to spend time talking about these things that interest them, and they need help to be taken to a deeper level. Becoming more aware is key to building self-support and defining the self. When the adolescent has more inner strength, separation becomes more natural. Self-work often promotes emotional expression as well. There are many projective techniques that enhance this work. Here are a few examples:

The rose bush drawing and other projective tests

I ask the young person to close his eyes and imagine that he is a rose bush, or any flower bush that we will call a rose bush. I do quite a bit of prompting, such as, "Are you tall or short? Are you full or scrawny? Do you have thorns? Flowers? If so, what colour are they? Do you have roots? Where are you? You can be anywhere: in the middle of the ocean, on the moon, in a yard—anywhere. Are there other bushes, trees near you, animals, birds, a fence? Who takes care of you?" I then ask him to draw his rose bush and whatever else is in the picture. When the drawing is complete, I ask him to tell me about his rose bush and write down the answers. I may ask questions to elicit responses. I will then go back and read each response. "Does this fit for you in any way? Or remind you of something in your life?"

I have done hundreds of rose bushes with children and find that adolescents are particularly responsive. A 17-year-old boy admitted that he wanted to die like the rose that had fallen to the ground. (He had had no idea, he said, that that rose represented his death wish when he drew it.)

Adolescents love projective tests. I never use them to diagnose or interpret, but will always ask the child if she agrees with what they may mean, as indicated in the testing manuals. I will read each sentence and stop and ask, "Does this feel right for you?" I have used the Thematic Apperception Test (Murray, 1943) that involves a variety of very old-fashioned black and white pictures to elicit stories. I write the short story down as we go through the cards. A picture of a child looking at a violin will have varied responses: "He is supposed to practice but he hates doing it and wishes he didn't have to." "Does this remind you of anything about yourself?" "Well, there are a lot of things I have to do and I hate doing them, but I have to." I can stay with this response for a while to delve deeper, or I can move on to the next card.

Other tests I have used are The Hand Test (Wagner, 1969), The Problem Experiences Checklist, Adolescent Version (Silverton, 1991) and the Luscher Colour Test (Luscher, 1971).

Using an astrology-type book, such as *Linda Goodman's Sun Signs* (Goodman, 1971), is very popular. I may read one sentence at a time for their particular birth date and determine with the child its relevance to them.

Clay

Pottery clay is very popular. I find that adolescents like to be given a specific exercise:

> Make something with your eyes closed (see *Windows to Our Children* for examples).
> Make yourself weak and make yourself strong is popular.
> Make an image of yourself.

A young woman who had been raped and wouldn't speak of it made herself from the waist up without being consciously aware of doing this. She was so surprised that she began to talk about her rape.

The toy exercise

I may ask a child to select a toy from the shelf or some object in the room and then speak as that toy. A 13-year-old girl invented variations suggesting that I pick one as well, and then that we pick one for each other. It truly is amazing to see how much of ourselves comes out through this projective exercise.

I was asked to visit a group of boys who were in the "incorrigible" adolescent unit of a state hospital. I brought a bag of various toys, the kind used in sand tray work. The group of ten boys were very restless, shouting at each other and their therapist, moving around, ignoring the therapist's pleas for quiet. When I emptied the toys in the middle of the room they immediately came around to look at them. I asked them to form a circle, look at the toys and then pick one to use for an exercise we would do. They noisily and readily did this. I then demonstrated with a toy that I picked: "I am a dump truck. I go around picking up people's garbage, and then dumping it, etc. Wow! A lot of that fits for me, I guess. People tell me their problems and somehow we get rid of them that way." The boys were respectful and quiet as I spoke. I then asked for a volunteer to go first. The boy had chosen a large snake and he said, "I am a snake. People are afraid of me. I won't hurt them but they think I will and they scream and run to get away from me." When I asked if anything he said fit for him, he said no. The other boys began shouting, "Yes, it does! You scare people because you're so big and black!" "But I would never really hurt anyone!" he said. The other boys agreed that this was true. Each boy took their turn in a friendly, happy atmosphere. The therapist told me that he had not done any exercises with this group because he thought they would never work. He was astounded and promised the boys he would do more activities like this one.

This reminds me of an experience I had at another hospital for mentally ill children but this did not involve the use of toys. I was asked to meet with a group of adolescent boys and girls, to give their therapist some ideas. It was a very large group—perhaps 20 children. I passed out paper and crayons and asked them to draw an image of themselves as weak and then as strong using colours, lines and shapes. About half the group refused to participate and walked away. The rest of the group worked diligently, and when done I asked for a volunteer to talk about their picture with me. Jill, a 16-year-old, sat next to me and described the parts in her drawing, elaborating when she felt weak and when she felt strong. We processed this a bit and I then asked the group to divide up into pairs to share their drawings with each other. As they were doing this, the young people who had left the group filtered back and eavesdropped on the conversations. As I was leaving, several asked if I would come again since they hadn't done the drawing and now wished they had.

Puppets

Adolescents love puppets. They are not just for younger children. The problem is that the adolescent is embarrassed to show his interest so puppets need to be introduced surreptitiously, though there are exceptions to this rule. A 15-year-old boy came in for his session and noticed a turtle puppet on the coffee table. He grabbed it and held it as we talked about his life. I suddenly took another puppet from a large basket of puppets and began to talk to the turtle.

Hey turtle, what's that thing on your back?
That's my house.
Why do you carry it on your back?
When I'm tired, I go in there. Also when I'm scared so no one can see me. (*Pause*) And I can also use it to punch someone when I need to (*gently punching me with his hand in the turtle*).

We went on in this fashion for quite some time. Each time the boy came in to the office he searched for this puppet. "Where's my turtle?!" he would say, and proceed to put his hand in it for the rest of the session. He definitely was more verbal and forthcoming as his turtle.

The adolescent enjoys putting on puppet shows, particularly in groups. The group is divided into pairs and they choose a card from a stack on which I have written themes. Examples of some of the themes are related to the issues that plague adolescents, as body image, peer pressure, loneliness, feeling rejected and left out, feeling different and so forth. I encourage the children to exaggerate the characters which inevitably brings forth a great deal of laughter.

Video

I brought in a video camera one day thinking I might videotape some sessions. But the children immediately decided to use it and so it became a very successful therapeutic tool. Adolescents particularly love inventing scenarios.

Charlie's father brought him in because he had been caught stealing from a neighbour's house. This 15-year-old had a traumatic childhood: he sat in a shelter for six months while his birth mother decided if she wanted to keep him (the father was unknown); he was adopted by a couple in hopes that a child would save their marriage (it didn't); his adoptive father moved to another state and remarried; as he grew his mother had more and more difficulty controlling him; he was shipped to his father's house and his step-mother was not happy to have this child living with them. Charlie was very withdrawn and silent during our session with his parents. When I saw him alone he showed somewhat more energy and was willing to draw a House-Tree-Person but was not willing to say much. Everything changed when I brought in the video camera. Charlie came alive. The first scenario he wrote and directed involved a therapy session with me as the patient and Charlie as the therapist. The camera sat on a tripod. As the patient I was sullen and angry. As the therapist he lectured me. We watched our scene on the monitor and both of us laughed uproariously. I asked Charlie if he wanted me to lecture him in our sessions. He admitted that he did bad things but did not know what to do. I explained that he was reacting as a young child, the young child he was, out of desperation to be loved and have attention and basically get his needs met. I explained to him the kind of work that I would do to help him feel better about himself and happier in his life. He couldn't wait to get started. Working with Charlie was one of the most gratifying experiences I have had in my career. (Among the projective techniques that I introduced to him, the video camera remained a favourite.)

Another child, a girl aged 13, responded to the camera more than any other tool. I drew up a list of questions on a card and told her that we were going to have a "talk show"—I would be the host and she would be the guest. I introduced her to the "audience" as she giggled, and then began looking at the cards and asking her questions. She was extremely responsive and thoughtful about her answers. The questions started out simple, as "How old are you? What grade are you in?" and then, as I flipped the cards, moved to deeper places. "Could you say a few words about how your parents' divorce affects you?" We watched the "show" on the monitor and again laughed so much we could hardly hear what we were saying.

The sand tray

I received a call one day from a young man who had been my client when he was 15 years old. He was having difficulties with his girl-friend and thought that I might be able to help them. When he came into the office he immediately went over to the sand trays and explained to his girlfriend how they worked and actually described to her some of the trays he had made. I was flabbergasted! My memory of this boy, now 21 years old, was that he was extremely "resistant" and nothing much had happened and that he never said much. He turned to me and said, "I loved doing those trays. You helped me so much!"

I find that adolescents, both young and older, do love the sand trays. They are fascinated by miniatures. When asked to make a scene, any scene, the girls will often make an idyllic, peaceful place. The boys will use cars and motorcycles or monsters. After a while I will give specific directions: make a safe place in one tray, and an unsafe place in the other; make a scene that represents the divorce in the family; make a scene about how you might feel in different situations, and so forth.

When asked to make a scene about the divorce in his family, Eric, aged 15, quickly got to work. He put two figures, a man and a woman, at either end of the tray. Then he placed some very large marbles, followed by smaller marbles, making a sort of path. On the side he put miniatures to represent a hospital with a figure in bed, another figure on crutches. An ambulance stood by. He said, "These figures are my mother and father. The big marbles are the big problems we had, but now it's getting easier so I put smaller marbles. I'm the patient on the bed since the whole thing made me sick, but now I'm on crutches because it's getting better, but I'm not completely well yet. The ambulance took me to the hospital and is ready to take anyone else who needs it."

The beauty of this work is that it is so enjoyable and gives great support to express painful material. Eric was able to express his feelings in a way he could not do just with words.

Exploring polarities

The adolescent is plagued by polarities. She feels one way inside and presents herself another way outside. She wants to be independent yet is fearful of losing the support she needs from her parents. She has mixed feelings about many things and can't make up her mind.

The empty chair technique is often thought of as "Gestalt Therapy". Of course we know that it is merely a technique and ludicrous to think it involves all of the theory, philosophy and practice of Gestalt Therapy!

The chair experience is a very helpful technique and allows the therapist to help the client put things into perspective. One of my clients, aged 16, told me she had an opportunity to be in a movie. She had been in a number of short commercials but to be in this movie she would have to leave school and be tutored. Her dream was to be an actress in a movie and here was her opportunity. At the same time, she enjoyed school and had many friends and hated to miss her senior year. She felt paralysed by this dilemma. I asked her to sit in one chair and talk to me about accepting the movie. "This is the part of you that wants this more than anything."

After she had fully expressed her desire to be in the film, I asked her to sit in a facing chair and only talk about staying in school. Soon the two parts were actually talking to each other as she moved back and forth. Finally she was silent. I waited. "You know, I would love to be in the movie but I'll have other chances to do that. I will only have one chance to do my senior year and graduate, so that's what I'll do." She was very relieved and left with a much lighter step.

I had explained to her that it's never easy to make choices when both choices have advantages. "If you hated school, the choice would have been simple," I told her.

The top dog/underdog exercise is similar and in fact two chairs can be used. Another client had an important paper to finish and hand in the next day. But his grandmother had arrived for a visit and the whole family was going out for a celebratory dinner. "I want to go and be with everybody! But I know I should just stay home and write the paper. I wish I hadn't put it off to the last minute!" he moaned. The word "should" is a red flag for me since it implies that there is a message he has introjected which probably would foster resentment and maybe paralysis and would certainly interfere with writing a good paper. I explained that the top dog is the part of us that always tells us what to do. It is generally harsh and critical and is never satisfied. In opposition is the underdog. This part responds to the top dog by being rebellious or tired or whiney. No matter how strong the top dog is, the underdog generally wins since it keeps us from doing anything at all.

I asked my client to sit in one chair as the top dog and talk to himself in the other chair.

"You are bad for not getting your paper done before this! You'd better get to work on it or you'll get a terrible grade on the course. You shouldn't think about doing anything else." Sitting on the other chair as the underdog, he said, "I can't do it! I hate it! I don't care if I fail. I'm not going to do it. I want to be with my Grandma and the rest of the family. They'll all be having fun and eating great stuff and I'll be alone eating nothing. Anyway, I'm just too mixed up and tired to think about it." We did several rounds of this and finally I asked him to sit on a third chair and tell me what he, himself, wanted to do. After a period of silence he said, (in a calm voice), "You know, my grandmother doesn't come very often and I really love her. It's special to have a family dinner like this. I'm going to the dinner and when I get home, I'll write the paper even if I'm up half the night." And he did.

Story books

I have read pre-school books to my teen-aged clients. I'll usually say, "I have this great book that I got a kick out of and I want to read it to you to see what you think" (or something like that). I have read *There's a Nightmare In My Closet* (Mayer, 1968), *Where the Wild Things Are* (Sendak, 1963) and *Alexander and the Terrible, Horrible, No Good, Very Bad Day* (Viorst, 1972). The books elicit great responses about their own dreams and anger and bad days. There are many wonderful books like this. I use myself as a test; that is, if I enjoy it, I'm pretty sure my clients will. Sometimes I just say, "I need your opinion about this book."

Sherry was a 14-year-old who had spent many years in foster care, and was now adopted into a family. She would never talk about her years in foster homes. Someone in one of my training programmes sent me a book he wrote about foster care, *I Can't Live With Mum and Dad Anymore* (Smith, Rothenbury, & Campbell, 1996). The book was written from the viewpoint of a young child and was illustrated with stick figures. It addressed many issues such as abandonment, loneliness, confusion in a lively, interesting manner. I casually asked Sherry if I could show her this book and if she would give me an opinion about it. I began reading to her and she suggested we take turns reading. At the end of the fairly short book, with tears in her eyes, she said, "Wow. This guy" (the author) "must have been in a foster home. He sure knows what it's like!" Over the next few sessions Sherry told me about her own experiences, often requesting that we look at this book once more.

Medicine cards, Oh cards

There are many interesting cards on the market that offer wonderful projective opportunities. *The Medicine Cards* (Sams & Carson, 1988) are pictures of North American animals with a Native American focus. I have asked children to pick a card that reminds them of how they used to be, how they see themselves now and how they would like to be. I remember using these cards with the family of a 15-year-old. The father remarked to his son, "I never knew you felt that way."

There are numerous picture decks such as the *Oh* cards (Eos Interactive Cards, Victoria, BC, Canada). All of them have wonderful pictures of places, people and the like and include instructions and suggestions for their use. They are so intriguing that adolescents are quickly drawn in. We sometimes do a continuation story using the cards, or pick one at random, tell a story about it and then talk about how it might apply to ourselves. Of course one can make cards from magazine pictures; however these cards are so appealing that it can be worth the expense of purchasing them.

The use of checklists

When an adolescent is withdrawn and unresponsive, I have found that checklists seem to draw the child out. I will put the list, as the *Problem Experiences Checklist*, adolescent version (Silverton, 1991), on a clipboard and tell the teen that I will make some statements and he only needs to say "true" or "false" or "yes" or "no." There's something about the paper on a clipboard that appears to put distance between me and the child and this creates enough security that he usually will answer the questions quite thoughtfully. Some questions are "My teacher dislikes me," "My parents say things that hurt my feelings," "My friends do things I'm not ready for" and so forth. The statements are divided into groups representing school, opposite-sex concerns, peers, family goals, crises, education, recreation and many others. The therapist may choose to limit the statements at her discretion. The one grouping that does not appear on this checklist are physical concerns which used to appear on the old *Mooney Problem Checklist* (Mooney, 1951). An answer of "sometimes" is perfectly acceptable. I generally do not delve further at any statement until a subsequent session. I might say, "You said yes to 'I frequently get angry'—could you tell me more about that—what kinds of things make you angry?"

Other techniques

I have mentioned some techniques and materials that I have used with adolescents. This is by no means a complete list. Here is a brief list of some other techniques that have been very successful with adolescents of all ages:

> In a family session ask each person to rate their family on a scale of 1 to 100%, then ask what is missing to make the score 100%.
> Ask: If you could change one thing in your life, what would that be?

See *List Your Self: Listmaking as the Way to Self-Discovery* (Segalove and Velick, 1996) for some great ideas for list making. Sometimes I have the client dictate the list to me and sometimes I ask him or her to make the list at home.

Mark McConville in his book *Adolescence: Psychotherapy and the Emerging Self* describes the use of the dart board. Some successful therapeutic games for adolescents are: *Your Life Story*, *Likes and Gripes*, *The Ungame*. Be on the lookout for attractive games.

I have taught numerous teens how to do self-hypnosis, as well as the ideomotor finger response.

Collage making is very popular.

The Scribble technique is described in detail in *Windows to Our Children*. Adolescents particularly like this exercise since the drawing comes out cartoon-like. One 16-year-old found a person on a motorcycle in his drawing. He told a brief story about the man on the motorcycle and his freedom. He owned having such a wish and was totally enamoured of his drawing.

I use many fantasy exercises followed by drawings with adolescents. Two intriguing ones are the *Pawn Shop* and the *Boat in a Storm*.

The Pawn Shop (short relaxation exercise followed by the sound of the gong): "Imagine you are in a time machine that will take you back to the middle ages. You land safely and when you emerge you see a cobblestone street with many shops of all kinds and people walking up and down. You notice an interesting shop with unusual items in the window and you enter what turns out to be a pawn shop. The proprietor greets you warmly and invites you to look around. He sees you are someone from another time and offers to give you a gift of anything you choose. There are beautiful stones and unusual boxes, and instruments, and jewellery and figurines—many wonderful-looking things. Finally you choose something. Soon you must leave and you get back into the time machine and here you are. I want you to draw the item you chose, and anything else you feel like including in your drawing."

The Boat in a Storm (after relaxation exercise): "You are a boat, or maybe a ship. You can be any kind of vessel—a canoe, a sailboat, an ocean liner, a submarine—anything. You are in a body of water—an ocean or a lake or a river—any kind of water. You are happily moving along when suddenly there is a terrible storm. The rain comes down in torrents, the wind is howling, there is lightening and thunder—it is a massive, angry storm. What happens to you? I would like you to draw yourself before the storm, during the storm and after the storm. You can choose to draw just a before and after picture if you like."

This is a wonderful process-oriented picture; that is, it considers how one handles conflict and chaos. A 14-year-old boy drew a canoe with himself and several friends. After the storm the boys were in the water and hanging on to the canoe. He said, "We are hanging on for dear life. If we let go we will drown." And before I could say anything, he added, "And that's how I feel in my life. I don't know how I'll get through my parents' divorce."

I would like to describe one last technique which I call "self nurturing work." I have described this in detail in a previous chapter and would like to emphasize its use. Most of us have many parts of ourselves we don't like and wish we could change or get rid of. Teens particularly feel this way, though they may deny having such feelings. Here is an example of this work:

I asked Jill to close her eyes and think of a part of herself she didn't like. "There may be several," I said, "but pick one. Now I would like you draw that part—you can make it funny and weird as much as you want to." When she was finished I asked her to write the name of this part on the paper. She wrote "The Deceiving Part."

Step 1   Tell me about your part. "This is the part of me that tells lies and steals money from my mother's purse."

Step 2   Be the part. "I'm this part and I steal and tell lies. I know it's wrong but I just can't help it. I get so mad sometimes and it makes me feel better when I do these things."

Step 3   Talk to the part. Jill, what do you think about this part? "I hate it!! It just makes things worse and I get into so much trouble. I'd like to kill it!" Tell that to the part, Jill. Jill, looking at picture, "I hate you! You get me in trouble!"

Note: This is the most common response and also a healthy one. The child is now expressing energy outward rather than holding it in.

Step 4   In this case I asked Jill to tell me how long this part has been with her. "Since I was about 5." (Jill was adopted by her present family at age 5.) Tell me about being 5, I say. "Well," Jill answers, "I came to live with this family when I was 5."

We talk for a while about what that was like for her. She was frightened and missed the foster mother that she lived with when removed from her birth mother whom she scarcely remembered.

I tell Jill that at that time, when she was adopted and felt frightened and needy, she stole things to feel better. It's as if the 5-year-old is still alive in her. She needs to let the little girl know that she loves her even when she takes things, and understands why she does it.

I ask Jill to make a quick drawing of her 5-year-old self and tell her these things. "All this week," I say, "whenever you steal something, tell the little girl that you love her even when she does that, and that you will find ways to make her feel better that won't get her into trouble." Jill said she thought this was a bit weird but that she would try it. Actually she never stole or told lies that whole week. When she came in we spent the session making a list of what she could do to make herself feel better when she felt rejected. Some of her ideas were: take a bubble bath, call a friend, listen to music she liked, write me a letter, draw a picture with rainbows and others. We had a great time coming up with ideas that would appeal to her. I asked Jill to do one of those things every day, even if she felt fine, and to tell me the following week about it. It is important for children to know that they can do nice things for themselves without having to wait for someone else to do them. Doing them with awareness is key.

Regression

One thing I have noticed is that children will often regress when in my office. I see this as a positive event. I have seen pre-teen and younger children do this, as act like a baby, or engage in play activities much younger than their present age level. These children have not had the opportunity to engage in these activities freely when they were younger and seem to feel safe at some point to meet their needs in our session. Jill was no exception. One day she announced to me that she wanted to play store. She eagerly placed various items and toys around the room on the round table we used for clay and drawings. She put little stickers on everything giving their prices. I had a pre-school type cash register that she filled with play money. She gave me some of the money and told me that I would be her first customer. And so I acted out, in an exaggerated way, a customer, picking up and examining things, oohing and aahing and finally buying something. Jill giggled in pleasure all the while. We cleaned up when the time was up and she whispered, as she left, "I loved doing that. But don't tell anybody, OK?"

CHAPTER SEVEN

Loss and grief

G estalt Therapy is an ideal discipline for work with grieving children since it is directive and focusing. If the child who has suffered a loss is fairly well-adjusted, the course of the therapy can be quite brief. In longer-term situations, the sessions become a sort of dance: sometimes the child leads and sometimes the therapist does. In short term work, the therapist becomes, for the most part, the leader. She must assess what will best serve the child's therapeutic needs to provide the best experience in the sessions available, while being heedful of the child's developmental level, capability, responsiveness and resistance level. She must not be forceful or intrude upon the child's boundary—she must tread lightly without expectation.

Preliminary to doing work with grieving children, the therapist must have an understanding of the issues involving loss and grief.

Stages of grief

Elizabeth Kubler-Ross (1973) postulated five stages related to the reaction to the death of a loved one: denial and isolation, anger, bargaining, depression and finally, acceptance. Most therapists have generalized these stages to fit many kinds of loss situations. Lenore Terr, in her excellent book *Too Scared to Cry* (1990), discusses the process of mourning as presented by John Bowlby in his three-volume work, *Attachment, Separation, and Loss* (1973–1983) as four phases particularly relating to children: denial, protest, despair and resolution. Children, she argues, can become stuck in any one phase for long periods of time. The therapist cannot push the client through any of these stages. However, as specific issues are dealt with, movement begins to take place.

Issues

There are numerous possible issues involved when a child suffers a loss, and the therapist must be aware of these. Some of these issues include: confusion, abandonment, loss of self, blaming the self, guilt, fear, loss of control, feelings of betrayal, feeling the need to take care of parents, unexpressed feelings of sadness, anger, shame and misconceptions. The therapist must make an assessment regarding the issues besetting the child so that she can provide a focus to the therapy. Certain issues are particularly prevalent at various development levels. For example, the 4-year-old who loses a parent will feel responsible for that loss, since he is basically an egocentric individual. Generally, it can be assumed that every child is troubled by most of the issues mentioned.

Kinds of loss

Children suffer many different kinds of loss throughout their development. These losses affect the child deeply: the loss of a favourite toy, a friend, a neighbourhood, a loved teacher, a pet, a parent through divorce and the loss that comes about through some kind of physical impairment, all impact the child. The death of a parent, sibling, friend, or grandparent is certainly a traumatic loss. As children grow, the accumulation of these losses, without appropriate expression of grief, causes havoc to healthy development. It is not unusual for the child to develop worrisome symptoms and behaviours months, or even years, after a particular loss. The child certainly has the capacity to go through the grieving process naturally. However, he generally has interjected many messages regarding the expressions necessary for this work: It is not OK to cry. It is certainly not OK to be angry about the loss. The child feels responsible for the well-being of the adults in his life. He may be holding a secret fear that he is responsible for the loss. In short, the child needs much support for and guidance through the grieving process. When the process is encouraged, and any issues that impede his grief are addressed, the child often responds rapidly.

Short-term work

Often combined with the task of helping children through the grieving process is the therapist's mandate to do it quickly, often a seemingly impossible task when working with children. The therapist may feel pressured to achieve results quickly. This pressure can be a detriment to the work and the therapist must find a way to shed this burden and trust the process, even if not successful. When the child who has suffered the loss has functioned well prior to the loss and appears to have a fairly strong sense of self with good support in his environment, only a few sessions can help the child move through his grief. Further, if the therapist can feel a thread of a relationship, and the child can sustain contact when working with the therapist, good results can be achieved. Contact must be assessed periodically, since the child will cut herself off, break contact, if the work becomes too intense for her—if she lacks the self-support to deal with the task at hand. The therapist must be sensitive to this phenomenon and when it happens, she must honour this resistance and perhaps suggest that the remaining time be filled with some non-threatening activity, such as a game of the child's choosing.

When the relationship and contact are prevalent, the therapist must then make some determinations that will best fit the model of short-term work. In spite of the goals the therapist may have, she must be vigilant in avoiding expectations. She will set the framework for each session, present the activity, but to anticipate results is a breeding ground for failure. Every child is highly sensitive to expectations that may be present; this attitude can severely affect and cloud the session. Expectations present a dynamic that becomes a living part of the encounter. The therapist must take an existential stance: whatever will happen will happen.

Several points involving short term work need to be considered and can be helpful:

1. See the situation as "crisis intervention". Tell the child you only have a few sessions to make things better.
2. Look at the number of sessions there are and plan what you will do (without expectation that what is planned will happen.) For example, the first session would be used for establishing the relationship by getting to know the child, engaging in non-threatening activities and providing safety for the child. When the therapist is respectful, genuine, congruent, accepts the child however he or she presents the self, and is, herself, contactful, relationship and safety will be established.
3. Do not become enmeshed with the child. Often, when dealing with a child's loss, the therapist can feel she must take care of the child, make things better, feel emotional, feel so sorry for the child, that she allows him to do whatever he wants, even going beyond limits. If the therapist cannot maintain her own boundaries, and have the child adhere to the limits by which she operates, the child becomes confused and anxious.
4. List the issues you determine are involved with this particular child and set priorities. Cut right to the core of the issues and feelings. (Examples are given in the next section.) Depending on the age of the child, the therapist can share some of these items with the child, giving the child the choice to decide what she want to work on.
5. Include parents in some of the sessions if possible. Explain to them the process of your work. Assess the communication level regarding the loss. For example, a child whose father lost his job

felt he needed to cheer up his parents, reassure himself and look at the "bright side" of things, totally cutting off his fears. Other symptoms, such as falling grades and inability to concentrate, cropped up. In family sessions he admitted he was terrified about what was going to happen to the family. The parents admitted that they never showed their own fear, much less discussed it with the child, thinking that this would be detrimental to the child. As they began to talk to each other about what they were feeling, the child's symptoms faded away.

6. Therapy is intermittent with children. Termination is generally temporary. At each developmental level, new issues arise. The child can only work at his particular developmental level. Parents need to understand this.

7. Be honest and clear with the child about the reason she is having sessions with you. Even a very young child can understand if the therapist uses appropriate developmental language.

Case examples

The following are condensed accounts of work with grieving children on a short-term basis.

Case one

Twelve-year-old Jack lost his mother to cancer when he was a 7-year-old. His parents had been divorced for some time and his father had remarried. Jack had a good relationship with both his parents who had joint custody, did well in school, had friends and appeared to be fairly well-adjusted to life in general. When his mother died he moved in with his father and stepmother whom he liked very much. His father reported that there had been no problems with Jack since his mother's death. When I asked how Jack had handled his grief, his father realized that actually Jack had shown very little effect outside of some brief crying when he was first told of her death.

At his present age of 12, certainly a crucial developmental age, various symptoms appeared. His grades began to fall, he preferred to stay at home rather than play with his friends, was upset when his father was not at home and began to have trouble sleeping. His parents did not associate his symptoms with the death of his mother 5 years earlier. However, I saw this traumatic event as a red flag, particularly since the parents reported that he handled her death "so well."

Session one

At the first session, Jack came in with his parents. It is during this session that I learned the child's "story," and the concerns of the parents. It is important that the child be present at this session to know what his parents tell me. Jack agreed that he would like to work on sleeping better since he saw himself as something of an athlete and admitted feeling too tired to do anything, presumably due to lack of sleep.

Session two

At the second session I evaluated Jack's ability to make a relationship and observed his contact skills. Jack was a bright, friendly child who quickly related to me and appeared to be quite contactful. He, from all appearances, was a good candidate for short-term work.

The first session with Jack alone was primarily a time to help him feel comfortable and to promote the relationship. After some conversation, I asked Jack to draw a safe place—a place where he felt safe. Jack drew a camping scene and talked about how much he enjoyed camping outings with his Dad and step-mother. He offered that he liked being with them and doing things together and that the stresses from the regular world did not get in the way. I made a list of some of these stresses as Jack dictated them. The session concluded with a game of Uno, Jack's choice from several easy, fun games.

Session three

At the next session, I asked Jack to close his eyes and think about his mother and see what memory might come to the fore. He was invited to draw the memory, or just share it. He reported that he had very few memories of his mother, but proceeded to draw a beach scene. When finished, he talked about how he remembered going to the beach with her when he was little. I asked Jack to give the little boy in the scene a voice and immediately began a dialogue with the boy, "What are you doing?" and Jack, in spite of his initial resistance to such a silly request, answered, "I'm building a sand castle." I encouraged Jack to dialogue with his mother in the picture as the little boy. At the conclusion of this little exercise, Jack stated with a smile, "That was fun." Again the session was concluded with Uno.

Session four

Pottery clay had been set out on two boards on the table along with a rubber mallet and some other tools. As Jack and I played with the clay, I casually asked him to tell me more about his mother and some things he remembered about her. Clay has a powerful quality of providing a nurturing, sensorial experience along with promoting expression. Jack was surprised that he actually had numerous memories. I shared with him that I believed his sleeping problems and difficulty separating from his Dad were related to the loss of his mother at age seven. Jack was astonished and startled at this information. I asked Jack to make a figure of a 7-year-old boy out of clay and to imagine what it was like for this little boy to lose his mother. I engaged the "7-year-old" in a dialogue, again inviting Jack to be the voice of the little boy. I encouraged Jack to "make up" what he imagined a little boy would say.

Therapist: Were you scared when your mother got sick?
Jack: When she went to the hospital I was very scared.
Therapist: Yes! That's a very scary thing for a little kid.

Jack offered much information to my casually stated questions, much to his own surprise. I told him that children at that age had difficulty grieving and that they needed help to know how to go through the grief stages. Jack was fascinated by the various stages and more memories of that time began to flood back for him. "I remember that I was mad when my Dad said she died! I was sure he was lying and I ran from the room and wouldn't talk to him. That's like denial I guess. My Dad seemed mad at me for that. I guess he didn't know about the stages." And Jack talked about his anger that seemed to get him into a lot of trouble, so he suppressed it assuming that he was very bad to feel such an emotion. I placed a large lump of clay in front of Jack and invited him to pound it with the rubber mallet. Jack did this with much gusto. When I asked him to put words to his pounding, Jack stood up and hit the clay with tremendous force. He began to cry as he shouted, "Why did you leave me?!" obviously now talking to his mother. I articulated encouraging words, as "Yes. Tell her!" I knew that if I remained silent, Jack would suddenly realize what he was doing and stop himself from his noisy outburst. Jack continued for a while and finally sat down. Quickly I praised him for being able to allow his anger to come out. I fashioned a little figure that I labelled 7-year-old Jack.

Therapist: Jack, this is your 7-year-old self. Imagine you could go back in a time machine and talk to him. What would you say?
Jack: I don't know.
Therapist: Try saying, I'm sorry you lost your mother.
Jack: Yeah. I'm sorry you lost your mother. You're just a little kid and you need her. It's not right.

Jack continued in this vein with encouragement and suggestions from me.

Therapist: Jack, that little boy lives inside of you. He's been quiet for a while, but now that you are twelve and can do a lot of things, I think he has been trying to get your attention. I think he's been stuck at that age because he never expressed or even knew his feelings. He needs you now. When you are scared when your father goes away, it's really him thinking something will happen to his Dad. It's really him keeping you from sleeping. But now he has you and of course you will never leave him since he's part of you. He needs you now. So every night this week when you go to bed, I want you to talk to him and tell him you will never leave him and that he's a very good kid. And maybe you can tell him a story while you're lying in bed.
Jack: My mother used to tell me stories.
Therapist: Now you can do it. You're good at this kind of thing so try it. This is your homework for the week!

Jack declined to practise this exercise in my office and agreed he would do it at home.

Session five

At the fifth session Jack reported that he was sleeping better but not great yet. I asked Jack to close his eyes and imagine he was in bed at night and to report the feelings he experienced. Jack said there was still some fear but he wasn't sure what it was about. I asked Jack to draw the fear, using colours, lines, curves, shapes.

Jack:	This is how I feel. Lots of weird lines and circles, mostly black. I think I'm afraid my father will die like you said last week.
Therapist:	We don't know what will happen in the future about anyone, but when a boy loses someone close, especially a mom, he naturally begins to think that it will happen to someone else close, especially his Dad. You need to let the little boy in you know that it's OK to be afraid—that you understand it. Here he is (drawing a quick stick figure)— tell him.
Jack:	Yes, it's OK to be afraid.
Therapist:	Do you believe that?
Jack:	Well, it's OK for him to be afraid. I don't think I should.
Therapist:	That's why I'm asking you to talk to him. I think if you give him permission to be afraid, you won't be so afraid.
Jack:	OK. You can be afraid. It's natural.
Therapist	Remind him that you are with him and will never leave him and that you know how to do a lot of things he couldn't do.

Jack practised this for a while.

Session six

At the sixth session Jack reported that he fell asleep before he finished talking to his 7-year-old self and that he forgot to worry about his Dad. He was too busy.

I reminded Jack that every now and then he would feel lonely for his Mom and to remember that he needed to let himself do that, and maybe do something nice for his 7-year-old self.

Session seven

At this last session Jack and his parents participated. We talked a bit about what Jack had learned. Jack was anxious to enlighten them, particularly about stages.

A follow-up session was held one month later—all was well.

This work was accomplished in a total of seven sessions, including the last one.

The first session involved the family while the next two were relationship building as well as providing a base for focusing on the death of Jack's mother. I made the assumption that this was the cause of his present symptoms, particularly because of his attachment disorder. The issues that emerged spontaneously were fear of abandonment, anger and sadness. Learning to nurture the self and gaining skills to take care of the self are important and effective.

Case two

Ten-year-old Susan lost her father to suicide. Her parents had been divorced since Susan, the youngest of three children, was a baby. Susan's dad was very involved in Susan's life and she was very close to him. There was an agreement that she would live with him for a year, and just prior to her move, he killed himself. Susan's mother brought her into therapy six months later when Susan's behaviour appeared to deteriorate into angry, aggressive outbursts and the teacher had complained that she was not doing her work and had become quite belligerent. It is common for parents to bring a child into therapy after a traumatic loss such as this, after a few months have gone by and symptoms emerge and accelerate.

Session one

The first session took place with mother and daughter. The mother stated that ever since the father died, Susan has been having difficulties at school, and their relationship has deteriorated. "Things are getting worse," she said, "and not better as I thought they would with time." At this session Susan was quite withdrawn and would not participate. I asked the mother to go into the waiting room, and then asked Susan to draw a house and tree and person on a single sheet of paper. Susan appeared to be relieved that she didn't have to talk and worked diligently.

Therapist: Susan, this is really a test but I'm not using it that way— I'm using it to get to know you better. It tells me some things about you and I need to check them out with you to see if it's right.

Susan: What does it tell you?

Therapist: Well, for one thing, it tells me you keep a lot of things to yourself.

Susan: It's true. How do you know that?

Therapist: Your house has very small windows and dark shades and sometimes when someone draws windows like that, it could mean that.

Susan: (*showing interest*) What else does it tell you?

Therapist: It also might show that you keep in a lot of anger because maybe you don't know how to get it out. Does that fit for you? The person looks kind of angry.

Susan: Yes!

Therapist: See how the house is tilting? Maybe you don't feel very sure about anything right now. And the girl is at this corner far away from the house so maybe you don't know where you belong.

Susan: (*very low voice*) That's right.

I noticed tears in Susan's eyes and gently told her that we would try to work these things out together in the sessions. I wrote each finding on the back of Susan's paper and read them back to her. Susan listened intently. I then suggested that we spend the final few minutes of the session playing a game. Susan selected *Connect–4*; the relationship appeared to be taking hold.

Session two

At the second session I asked Susan to make her family out of clay. Susan fashioned her two sisters and her mother. When asked to include her father, she refused. "He's not here anymore." I quickly fashioned a rough figure. "This is your father," I said. "He'll be over here." I placed the figure at the far corner of the clay board.

Therapist: I would like you to say something to each person.

Susan: (*to oldest sister*) You don't care anything about me. You're always off with your friends.
(*to middle sister*) I wish you wouldn't tease me so much.
(*to mother*) I wish you didn't have to work so much and could be home more.

Therapist: Now say something to your father.

Susan: I don't want to.

Therapist: OK. You don't have to. Susan, sometimes when a parent commits suicide, kids blame themselves, and are ashamed to tell anyone. I wonder if that's true for you.

Susan: Other kids feel those things too?

Therapist: Yes, they are very common feelings!

Susan: I don't know what I did, but I was supposed to move in with him and then he went and killed himself. I thought he was glad I was coming. And I don't want anyone to know. They'll know it was because of me.

Therapist: It's hard for you to feel those things. I'm sorry.

Susan nodded and closed down. This was obvious by her lack of contact, her body posture and decreased energy. I suggested we stop talking now and play *Connect–4* again. Susan visibly brightened and took down the game with renewed energy. I told Susan that her mother would be joining us at the next session.

Session three

At the third session with the mother, I asked each one to make something that made them angry. Susan watched her mother draw and then finally began to work on her own picture. The mother drew an incident that happened at work and talked a little about it.

Susan: I didn't do what you asked me to. I just drew my family.

Therapist: OK. I notice that you didn't draw your father. Just make a little circle up here in the corner for him. Susan, tell each person in your family something that makes you angry or you don't like that they do.

Susan complied, but again refused to talk to the father figure.

Therapist: (*to mother*) I wonder if you would be willing to say something to your ex-husband over here. It is hard for Susan to do it. Anything you would like to tell him.

Susan's mother immediately began to express intense anger at him for killing himself, causing so much hurt and pain to his children, especially to Susan and leaving her to be responsible for the three children.

Susan began to cry and said she was angry too and that she was sure it was all her fault. I directed Susan to tell this to the father figure. Susan's mother voiced astonishment and emphatically assured Susan that this was not the case, that her Dad had financial problems and she thinks that's probably why he did it, and that he loved Susan very much. But it just got too much for him.

Susan continued to cry as her mother embraced her.

Session four

At the fourth session I suggested that Susan draw a picture of something she had enjoyed doing with her father. She drew a picture of a swimming pool and talked about how much fun they used to have swimming together. She then asked if she could do a sand tray and proceeded to make a graveyard scene, announcing that one of the graves belonged to her father.

Therapist: Susan, I would like you to talk to your father's grave.
Susan: Dad, I hope you are happy where you are. I miss you a lot. I'm sorry things were rough for you.
Therapist: Could you tell him you love him?
Susan: Yes! Dad, I love you. (*long pause*) Goodbye.
. (*to therapist*) Do we have time to play a game?

Session five

Susan and I had one more session together. Her mother was unable to attend and sent a note saying that Susan's inappropriate behaviours were no longer present. I asked Susan what she would like to do at this goodbye session and Susan opted for clay. She made a birthday cake with toothpicks for candles stating, with much gaiety, that her Dad's birthday was coming up and she wanted to have a cake ready for him.

This work took five sessions. Here again, as with Jack, the relationship was established quickly and Susan was quite responsive in spite of her initial resistance. The issue of responsibility for her father's death appeared to be dispensed with quickly. Anger and sadness were expressed. I called Susan's mother to tell her that Susan worked on the loss of her father at her particular developmental level but deeper feelings may emerge at later developmental levels involving issues that she did not have the self-support to deal with now.

Case three

Six-year-old Jimmy was brought in by his Dad. Jimmy's sister, 2 years younger, was killed in an automobile accident and the parents and

Jimmy had sustained minor injuries. Jimmy's father said that Jimmy seemed to be functioning well but he felt that he needed help to deal with his sister's death since he never spoke of her. Jimmy's mother, extremely grieved and barely functioning, was under a psychiatrist's care. Jimmy remained stoic. I assumed that Jimmy was afraid to show his grief for fear of abandonment—he needed to be strong for his mother. Further, Jimmy's Dad told me that the children got along quite well, played together all the time, but that Jimmy loved to tease his sister, sometimes hit her and seemed to enjoy making her cry. Jimmy, still at an egocentric developmental level, probably blamed himself for her death, particularly in light of his behaviour toward her. I felt that this latter issue, plus his fear of losing his mother's love and attention, seemed to be priorities for our work together.

Session one

At the first session, as the father talked to me, Jimmy refused to talk and sat at the sand tray, running his hands through the sand. I could see, through his body posture, that he was listening intently.

I asked the father to wait in the waiting room after asking Jimmy if that was OK with him. Jimmy nodded, his back still to me. I drew Jimmy's attention to the shelves of miniatures, inviting him to set them in the sand to make a scene. Jimmy proceeded to put all the trees he could find in the sand, and under one of them he placed a very small rabbit. "I'm done," he said.

Therapist:	Jimmy, could you tell me about your scene?
Jimmy:	It's a forest with lots of trees.
Therapist:	What about that little rabbit?
Jimmy:	He's hiding under that tree.
Therapist:	I'd like to talk to him. Would you be his voice, you know, as if he were a puppet?
Jimmy:	OK.
Therapist:	Rabbit, what are you doing?
Jimmy:	I'm hiding.
Therapist:	What are you hiding from?
Jimmy:	Sometimes big animals eat rabbits. I'm hiding from them.
Therapist:	You have a good hiding place; I can hardly see you! Do you feel safe?
Jimmy:	No, I'm still scared.
Therapist:	Is there anyone around to help you?
Jimmy:	(*very low voice—body scrunched*) No.

Therapist: Oh, that must be hard for you.
Jimmy: Yeah.

At that point I told Jimmy that we could play a game for the five minutes until the session ended. I asked him if it was OK if I took a picture of his scene and postponed putting the objects away so I could look at it. He readily agreed.

Session two

Jimmy came in asking if he could make another sand scene and proceeded to make the exact scene he had made the previous week, except for another rabbit that he placed near the first one. "Now the rabbit has someone to help him," he said. It was my guess that Jimmy was acknowledging the help he might receive from me.

Therapist: Jimmy, I am so sorry that you lost your sister. I would like it very much if you would draw a picture of her so I could have an idea of what she looked like.

Jimmy drew her picture willingly, explaining as he drew about the colour of her hair, her eyes, the clothes she was wearing, as well as other details.

Therapist: Jimmy, I am going to make a list of some of the things you and your sister did together. Tell me one thing.
Jimmy: Well, we coloured pictures from a book she had. We played Captain Hook and Peter Pan—I was Captain Hook. We built stuff with blocks. She was only four and I had to show her how to do things.
Therapist: I know you were a good big brother. Big brothers sometimes tease their sisters too. Did you do that? I know my son used to tease his little sister and she would run crying to me. Now they are grown up and are good friends. I bet you and Julie would have been very good friends as you got older.
Jimmy: Your son teased his sister? Yeah! I teased Julie a lot! I could make her cry easy. She bugged me sometimes too and I would hit her. Then she would cry and run to my Mom who would get mad at me. I liked her really.
Therapist: I bet you miss her a lot.
Jimmy: (*Nodding with tears in his eyes.*)

I offered to do a puppet show for Jimmy. In the first scene, two animal puppets—a dog and a cat— are playing and the dog begins to call the cat silly names. The cat begins to cry. In the second scene, a larger animal, an eagle, tells the dog that there has been an accident and the cat has died. The dog begins to cry saying he didn't mean to tease her. The eagle assures him that the cat didn't die because of his teasing. In the third scene, the dog tells the eagle how sad he is to lose the cat. The eagle hugs him.

Jimmy watched this simple show intently and immediately asked if he could do it himself. His show was actually more involved, with the dog telling the eagle about hitting the cat and being mean some-times, with the eagle continuing to assure him that these actions did not cause her death.

Jimmy's last statement on leaving this session was, "I loved this puppet show!"

Session three

I asked Jimmy if he thought his mother was very mad at him since she was so upset. Jimmy began to cry. Because of his developmental level, it was logical that Jimmy would feel that his mother's intense grief was his fault.

Therapist: Jimmy, I think your Mom is just so sad about losing Julie that she is sick from it. I don't think she's mad at you at all. Is it OK if we ask Dad to come into the session so we can talk about this?

Jimmy nods.

I asked Jimmy to tell his Dad about thinking his Mom is mad at him. Jimmy looks at me, and I ask if I can tell him. He nods vigor-ously. Jimmy's father is horrified at this idea and with much emotion tells Jimmy how much he and his mother love him. Jimmy climbs on his Dad's lap and sobs.

Session four

Jimmy tells me that his mother seems a little better. She smiled and hugged him this morning, he reports. I guessed to myself that Jimmy's Dad spoke to his Mom about our last session. I direct Jimmy to make his sister out of clay and to talk to her. Jimmy tells the clay figure that he misses her very much, is sorry she died and that he will think about her a lot. He then spontaneously picks up the figure, kisses it and says goodbye. "I want to play that game (Blockhead) before I leave today."

This was actually the last session. Dad called to say that he felt that Jimmy did not need any more sessions. I advised Jimmy's Dad to watch for any new symptoms that might emerge since there were many issues that had not been addressed that may affect Jimmy. Developmentally, perhaps Jimmy had expressed as much as he could handle at this time, and that as he became stronger, some of the other issues may need to be dealt with.

Case four

Another situation involved a 9-year-old girl whose mother had been physically abused by the father; finally, she had managed to escape to a new city and there was no contact at all with Dad. The girl had become sullen, abusive and aggressive toward her younger sister and the mother. The mother advised me that they could only come in for five or six sessions. Based on previous experiences with similar situations, I felt that the child may have conflicted feelings involving the loss of her father and anger at the mother for taking her away from him as well as her friends, her school and her previous home.

Session one

At the first session, Sally appeared quite anxious as her mother spoke, sitting with hunched shoulders and pursed lips. I directed my "intake" questions to Sally, "Do you sleep OK? Do you have bad dreams sometimes? What's school like here?" and so forth. Sally actually responded readily, visibly relaxed and then asked what all the toys and stuff were for that were in the room. I explained that they were used, along with drawings and clay and the sand trays, to help kids express what was going on inside of them instead of just having to talk. The mother was very nervous at this session and seemed anxious to leave. I invited her to wait in the waiting room while Sally and I became acquainted with each other.

I encouraged Sally to go around the room and look at everything in the room. Sally was drawn to the doll house and began arranging and rearranging furniture. After some time I suggested that she choose a family that would live in the doll house. Sally selected a mother, a father, a small boy and a medium sized girl and placed them in various parts of the house. I remarked that the family appeared to be a pleasant, happy one. Sally agreed, and suddenly clearly lost her energy and enthusiasm with the doll house. I suggested that we play a game and Sally, with renewed contact, selected *Uno*.

When a child suddenly loses interest in a task, breaks contact when there had been good energy toward the task, it is generally a fairly reliable clue that something has occurred that has caused the child to close down. It seemed evident that the "happy family" in the doll house touched a painful spot in Sally.

This type of closing down is actually a positive event in the therapeutic process since it indicates that just behind this resistance feelings are emerging.

Since the mother had been clear about the number of sessions, I mapped out a programme for the therapy, always cognizant of the fact that expectations would be anathema. My plan for Sally consisted of the following.

At the next session I would present a non-threatening mode of expression such as the scribble technique that is fun and easy, and can lead to important projections. At the third session I thought that I might ask Sally to make figures of her family, including her father, out of clay and request that Sally dialogue with each of them. I might help her to focus on anger, self-blame and sadness at the loss of her father as well as her familiar home. At session four I thought that I might incorporate all of these feelings, including, perhaps, the child's confusion over her feelings in general, through drawing or painting. In this way the varied feelings become more explicit, making it easier to work through them. Further, if there was time, the percussion instruments could be used to "play" with feelings providing a nurturing, enjoyable atmosphere around these emotions. At session five I would suggest that Sally make a sand scene about her life, and finally, at the last session, I would meet with Sally and her mother and spend some time giving the mother suggestions for helping Sally express her feelings appropriately, as well as refining their communication skills.

The following is a summary of what actually took place.

Session two

I introduced the scribble technique—asking Sally to make a scribble and find a picture to colour within this scribble. Sally appeared to enjoy this task and found a picture of a large cat surrounded by trees. She told this story about the cat: "Once upon a time there was this cat who lost her way. She was walking home from a visit to a friend and somehow got lost. She had taken a short cut through the forest and now she was lost. She didn't know where she was or which way to go to get home. It got dark and she heard all kinds of noises and got very scared."

Therapist: Then what happened?
Sally: She got very tired and curled up under a tree and went to sleep.
Therapist: What happened when she woke up?
Sally: When it was morning the cat recognized where she was and ran home. The family was very happy to see her and pet her and fed her. The end.

Therapist: That was a good story! Sally, is there anything about your story that fits for you and your life?
Sally: I don't know (*long pause*). Well, maybe I don't know where the home I used to have is.
Therapist: Tell me about it.

Sally begins to describe the house she lived in, her neighbourhood, her school, her friends. She was very animated while doing this, watching me carefully (for my reaction?). I realized that it was not possible for Sally to talk about these things at home since any mention of her previous home was probably very upsetting to her mother. In the last ten minutes of the session, I decided to introduce instruments, and Sally and I played, with much gaiety, happy, sad, crazy, lonely and especially mad.

Session three

At the next session I put out the pottery clay, boards and tools. We sat at the table playing with the clay and I, after a while, asked Sally to make her family out of clay. Sally ignored this direction and proceeded to make various kinds of food. I dropped my plan and joined Sally in pretending to eat the food. Sally giggled at my dramatic enjoyment of the food. In between bites, I, myself, fashioned rough figures of Sally's family: mother, sister, as well as her father whom I placed some distance from the rest of the family.

Therapist: Sally, I want you to say something to each person here—maybe something you like about them, something you don't like or just anything you want to say.

Sally:	(*to sister*) I like to play with you sometimes. I don't like it when you take my stuff.
	(*to mother—long pause*) I like it when you play with me.
	(*to therapist*) She's always working and tired.
Therapist:	Maybe that could be the thing you could tell her you don't like.
Sally	Yeah. I don't like it that you are always working and tired and don't have time to play with me very much anymore.
Therapist:	Now say something to your father over here in the corner.
Sally:	I don't want to talk to him now.

With this statement Sally picked up the rubber mallet and began to hit a nearby mound of clay.

Therapist:	Sally, show me how hard you can hit the clay. Stand up if you have to.

Sally begins to pound the clay with all her might, holding the mallet with both hands.

Therapist:	What are you thinking about, Sally, when you do that?
Sally:	Nothing.
Therapist:	I bet there are a lot of things in your life that make you mad. Just hit the clay—you don't have to tell me what they are.

Sally continues to hit the clay as I cheer her on. The time is up and we clean up.

Session four

At the fourth session Sally's mother tells me that there can only be one more session since she has changed jobs and cannot bring her daughter in after this session. I urge her to accompany Sally for the last session and she reluctantly agrees.

Feeling desperate for lack of time, I decided to offer Sally a puppet show. The show consists of three scenes, hopefully addressing some of the issues relating to Sally's situation. In the first scene a mother puppet is singing to herself, "I'm cooking dinner, I'm cooking dinner." The father puppet comes in yelling, "What's for dinner? I'm hungry! I hope it's ready." The mother puppet replies, "It will be ready very soon, dear. It will just be a few more minutes." The father yells, "I want it now!!" and hits the mother squarely on the head. Sally murmurs from her audience place, "That's just like my life." I do not respond and changes scenes. Now two furry animal puppets, a monkey and a dog, are conferring. The monkey (the smaller of the two puppets) says, "Did you see Daddy hit Mommy again? I wish he didn't do that. It scares me." The dog replies, "Yeah. It scares me too. I'm mad that he does that. Why does he have to hurt Mommy like that!" The monkey: "You need to tell him to stop. After all you are the older one. You can tell him. Maybe he'll listen if he knows how we feel." The dog agrees he will try. At the next scene the dog calls Dad who says, "Yes, son, what is it?" With a great deal of difficulty and emotion the dog says, "Daddy, you have to stop hitting Mommy. It scares me very much and it scares my little brother. He thinks it's because he's bad sometimes. And Dad, it makes me mad that you do that!!!" The father puppet acts very upset, at first denying everything, but finally says, "I guess I do lose control. I'll try to stop. I don't want you and your brother to be scared of me. You are good kids and not at all bad." "Thanks Dad," the dog says, and they hug.

This was the end of the show and Sally immediately asked if she could do it herself. Sally repeated the show adding her own words. I offered to do another show in the remaining time of the session. This time the dog calls his mother and says, "Mommy, I have to tell you something. Don't get mad." She replies, "Honey, you can tell me anything." "OK," the dog says, "I miss Daddy." The mother puppet becomes very flustered. "You know we can't see him!!" The dog quickly says, "I know we can't see him. I just wanted to tell you I wish I could and that I miss him." The mother is quiet for a few seconds and then says, "I know you miss him. After all he was a good father to you. Maybe after a while you'll be able to see him." "Thanks, Mommy. I just wanted to tell you." And they embrace.

Sally was equally thrilled with this little show.

I was aware that Sally could never have told her father about her anger, but she wanted to at least bring out in the open the feelings that she might be having.

Session five

At the last session with Sally and her Mom, Sally wanted to put on both the shows for her Mom. I warned the mother that she might not like the content but that it was important to understand that Sally had hidden feelings that may be the cause of her behaviour, and that expressing them through fantasy at least was very relieving and healing for Sally. Sally did the shows with great gusto and her mother applauded generously as she dabbed at the tears in her eyes. We talked a little about the need for Sally to express her feelings while her mother listened without judgment.

I called Sally's mother a month later and she reported that Sally was much calmer and easier to live with, was no longer unusually belligerent and in general was doing quite well. The mother, who seemed calmer herself, thanked me profusely. I advised the mother to be alert for new symptoms as Sally reached new developmental stages.

I have often used puppet shows, such as used with Sally and with Jimmy, particularly in situations where the child has much difficulty expressing feelings. Children are fascinated by such shows, and are very forgiving if they are not "perfect". Significant issues can be presented in simple scenes in a dramatic way and the metaphorical messages are quite powerful. They seem to reach the child at a very deep level.

In this chapter, I have attempted to offer some effective methods for working with children around the issues of loss and grief on a short-term basis. These methods have at their base the theory, philosophy and practice of Gestalt Therapy. The projective techniques used (drawings, clay, fantasy, story-telling, sand tray scenes, music and puppetry) make it possible for children to express their deeper feelings in a non-threatening, often fun, way. The therapist must have an understanding of the myriad of issues involved in traumatic loss, and determine which ones are the most essential for focus. She must do this gradually, even when the time is short, to allow the child to feel safe and disclose the deeper parts of herself slowly. The therapist must take care not to intrude or push the child into doing or expressing anything the child resists. This resistance is usually an indication that the child does not have enough self-support to deal with the material presented; it must be honoured regardless of the short-term requirements. Though the therapist may have goals and plans, expectations can be toxic. The therapist must be infinitely sensitive to the child.

Prerequisite to any work is the establishing of some thread of a relationship. This relationship will build with each session. Contact, as described in this chapter, must be present each time, and the therapist must carefully observe the breaking of contact, generally evident when the child loses energy, the body deflates, the child's eyes become somewhat glazed, or the child does not respond to the therapist's question or request. It is futile for the therapist to attempt to ignore this evidence that the child is not fully present in the encounter. The child must be allowed time to withdraw from contact as needed. It is the therapist's responsibility to be fully contactful with the child, regardless of the child's inability to do so. The therapist meets the child with respect however he or she presents the self, with no anticipation for a particular response. She must be gentle, authentic and respectful without becoming enmeshed or confluent with the child.

In short-term work it can become evident that there are many other issues that emerge or become obvious to the therapist that cry out for attention. If the mandate is for brief therapy, priorities need to be followed. If good results are achieved, that is, if the child appears to make some closure regarding the loss incurred, the work must be deemed successful. What the child experiences in these few sessions will often carry over into other areas of her life.

Children do not know how to grieve and often are confused about the various feelings within them. The metaphors that emerge from the projective techniques offer a safe distance to children, allowing the therapist to gently help them own the feelings that are fitting. It is through this ownership that the child can move through the grief process. Therapists who work with children are privileged to have the opportunity to help children ease through difficult passages in their lives.

CHAPTER EIGHT

Helping children and adolescents become self-nurturing

S ome time ago, I discovered that no matter how much good work I did with my clients, something seemed to be missing. That something, I found, was helping the client nurture the self. In spite of increased strengthening of the self, completing unfinished business, expressing blocked feelings, particularly anger, there still remained a kind of void within the person. Becoming self-nurturing fills that void.

Children develop many faulty beliefs about themselves as they grow into adulthood in this stressful society. These negative messages become diffused through every part of the child's life. The child's very sense of self becomes impaired and fragmented, and deep down he or she feels worthless, shameful and lonely. Children who have been molested or abused, children who have chronic illness or have suffered some kind of trauma, children who have alcoholic parents, children who have been abandoned—these are only some of the situations where children are particularly susceptible to distorted perceptions of self and how to be in the world. To cope and survive, these children will restrict, inhibit, block and often totally shut down aspects of the self.

Regardless of the aetiology of these negative introjects, it has become clear to me that it is the child's work to change them. No matter what parents, or, for that matter, the larger society, do to alleviate the circumstances that may have caused these destructive belief patterns, they do not go away. They appear to persist in some way—sometimes going underground, only to emerge at a later time.

Learning to be self-nurturing is the final, essential step in helping a client work through those powerful negative messages that so often debilitate and sap our energy and life force.

Introjects are those negative messages about ourselves that we take in as children. Developmentally, young children are unable to appraise messages they receive from their parents, and later from the outer world. They believe everything they hear, or imagine they hear, overtly or covertly, about themselves. They are cognitively unable to evaluate these messages: "This fits for me. This definitely does not fit for me." These messages are carried by words, sounds, gestures, body language, behaviour, as well as misinterpretations based on the child's developmental level. It is at an early age that we begin to determine who we are and how we should be in the world to get our needs met. In other words, we form a belief system about ourselves and how to function in the world at a very early age, and we take this belief system with us right into adulthood!

I knew that if I could assist children to confront, manage and perhaps even change their negative self-messages, their healthful growth and development would be greatly enhanced. I experimented with ways of doing this with many of my adult clients with great success, and thus motivated, I attempted to introduce this process to my child and adolescent clients. To my dismay, I discovered that unless a child was ready for this step in the process of the therapy, she could not integrate the concept. I found that the child needs a certain amount of self support—inner strength—to engage in the process of self-nurturing. So when I would find, through a process of trial and error, that a child wasn't ready, I would focus on other aspects within the therapeutic journey: enhancing the contact functions, improving body awareness, intensifying consciousness of the self, assisting the child in expressing blocked, withheld feelings, providing experiences that promote a sense of mastery—all within the context of our own I/Thou, contactful relationship. And then, when I would feel that the child had reached a stronger level of support within herself, we would begin to focus on the issue of self-nurturing.

A prelude to becoming self-nurturing—accepting, caring, loving to the self—is dealing with those negative introjects I mentioned. As children begin to acknowledge, accept, respect and express their own feelings, they begin to feel a much stronger sense of themselves and of their entitlement. It is *then* that we can begin to look at some of their faulty beliefs of self.

Helping children express their feelings is crucial to the child's healthy development. All infants express feelings, regardless of the cultural milieu, through sound, facial expression, gesture and, as they grow, through language. The inhibition of feelings is a learned experience, and this inhibition leads to bad feelings of the self. Some children learn to inhibit feelings, most commonly anger, at such a young age that they have no memory of ever feeling them, no words with which to describe them, no skills with which to express them. These children have concluded very early that they are shameful beings. Every child who is emotionally disturbed has an impaired sense of self which in turn interferes with good contact with others. Deep down he feels that something is missing, he is different in some way, he is lonely, something is wrong. He blames himself— though he may outwardly and defensively blame others—and imagines that he is bad, has done something wrong, is not good enough, not smart enough. The young child does not have the cognitive ability to recognize those messages that are toxic and need to be rejected. If the child undergoes trauma, he will blame himself for that trauma. Developmentally the child has not completed the task of separation, and so he is unable to cognitively and emotionally understand that he is not, in any way, the cause of his injury, pain, loss or assault.

Even favourable messages can sometimes be harmful, for they too are not assimilated into the child's being as her very own. If the parent says, "you're so wonderful!" there is a disbelieving aspect of the child that says, "that's not really true. I'm not that good. I did something bad last week." And so fragmentation rather than integration occurs. A part of the child likes hearing that she's wonderful; but the disbelieving part makes its claim. The adolescent or adult who has never experienced the integration of those favourable messages often says, "I feel like a phoney" or "no one knows the real me." Parents need to learn to express their appreciation in very specific ways, such as, "I liked the way you cleaned the kitchen," or "the colours of your drawing give me a good feeling," or "I like that shirt you're wearing," and so forth. These clear statements strengthen the child's sense of self.

My task in working with a child becomes one of making it possible for her to remember, regain, renew and strengthen that which she had when she came into the world as a tiny baby. I need to provide many experiences to awaken the child's senses, to give her back the joyful, zestful use of her body, to connect her with her feelings and to feel and know her power. I need to help her use her intellect in conjunction with language to make declarations of who she is and who she is not, what she needs, what she wants, what she likes and dislikes, what she thinks about, what her ideas are. As the child begins to develop a stronger sense of self within our therapeutic relationship, we can then take on the task of confronting her negative introjects. It is very difficult for a child to admit openly, "I am bad," "I am a rotten person," "I don't like myself." Usually she is busily defending the small vestige of self she may feel. I have found that children have a very well developed critical self (usually well-hidden from their parents.) They often do a better job of criticizing themselves than their parents do. This judgmental stance is extremely detrimental to healthful growth. The child may say to herself, "I should do better," feeling and knowing that the enactment of this wish is beyond his power and comprehension. Thus, the will to "be better" or "do better" serves to enhance her despair. I cannot emphasize enough how each negative experience, each trauma, large or small, takes its toll in terns of not only unexpressed feelings, but the blaming of self as well.

Because of the child's intense life force and thrust for survival and growth, as well as the organism's continued crusade for equilibrium, the child will engage in many inappropriate behaviours and develop troublesome symptoms to overcome these suppressed feelings and loss of self. These behaviours and symptoms become *further* cause for the child's self-hatred and self-disparagement.

When the child or adolescent is able to recognize and admit to the existence of bad feelings about the self, we can then embark on her self-nurturing journey.

In my work I use many creative, expressive and projective techniques such as guided fantasy, graphic art forms, collage, clay, storytelling, puppetry, the sand tray, creative dramatics, sensory experiences, body movement, music, the camera and more. These techniques are important ways for helping children to express what is kept hidden and locked, and to experience and strengthen lost, interrupted, inhibited parts of the self. They are particularly useful for isolating and dealing with negative introjects and furthering the self-nurturing work.

As you read these examples of the self-nurturing work, you may feel disappointed because of their simplicity, and almost mechanistic form. I can only assure you that this kind of work is necessary and effective. The serious effect of trauma and negative introjects on children would appear to call for dramatic, intense work. But work with children is accomplished in very small segments. The child therapist must be reminded of several essential pre-requisites for the work:

1. The relationship is the essence of all therapeutic work.
2. Contact between the therapist and the child must be palpable at each session.
3. The clinician must meet the client where he is psychologically, emotionally, intellectually and developmentally. It is the task of the therapist to determine these levels and to be respectfully, with acceptance and no expectations, present with the child, following her level and rhythm.
4. The therapist must honour the child's resistance. When the energy fades, when the child withdraws from contact, the child is communicating in this way, "This is all I can do now, all I can take. I don't have enough support and inner strength for more." The therapist must respect this stance and be patient.

The following vignettes are presented in order to give you some idea of the nature of this self-nurturing work. The process of the work is almost impossible to present in a didactic, literal fashion although you will notice that there is some kind of sequence that does appear to present itself. This sequence is merely a guide; it is not to be seen as a mechanical list of directions to follow. Though I can present a theoretical rationale for what I do, my work is guided by my intuitive sense, my heart, my gut. The most powerful work with children is done that way. We enter a place together where we are in full communion—we are *with* each other. We understand each other; we feel understood by each other; we honour and respect each other. As I guide the work, I take my cue from the child at all times, always respecting her boundaries. I watch the child's energy flow. If it is present, I dance with it; if it is gone, I know enough to wait, or to stop. Please note that in all examples names have been changed and certain facts have been altered to protect confidentiality.

Example one

A 9-year-old girl, Jenny, tells me a story from her scribble picture that she calls, "A Girl With Messy Hair". I write the story down as she dictates, and then read it back to her. "Does that story fit for you in any way?" I ask. She answers, "Well, I don't like *my* hair." I ask her to draw a picture of how she perceives her hair. She draws a large face with very messy light brown hair. I ask, "Show me how you wish your hair looked." She draws a face with beautiful long blonde hair. "I wish I could have hair like this," Jenny says wistfully, with a big sigh. "Jenny, if you could talk to your messy hair, what would you say to it?" Jenny yells at the picture, "I hate you! Why can't you be like that?" (pointing to the blonde hair picture).

I ask Jenny if anyone in her life agrees with her about her messy hair. She answers, voice very low, "I don't know. Well, my father, I guess."

"How do you know?"

"Well, he always says, '*GO BRUSH YOUR HAIR!*' and things like that." (There's a lot of anger in her voice now.) "And he loves my sister's hair." Jenny begins to cry. I ignore the tears, knowing that if I focus on them, I may interrupt the work she is doing. I draw a round face with the words, "Go brush your hair", printed in a balloon coming out of its mouth.

"Here's your father. Tell him what you think about all this. Remember," I say in a conspiratorial whisper, "he's not really here." Jenny yells at the father picture, "I hate it when you tell me to brush my hair."

"Yeah! You tell him!" I encourage.

Jenny continues, "My hair is just as good as my sister's! You never tell her to go brush her hair." Jenny is yelling and giggling at the same time.

"Jenny, let's find a puppet that likes your hair. Imagine there's a puppet here that thinks your hair is terrific." Jenny, now high with energy, looks through the puppet basket and comes up grinning with a great furry bear puppet. She holds the puppet in her hand facing the messy hair picture and says, "I like your hair. It's not so bad. And besides, when you get older you can let it grow long and even make it blonde if you want to and your mother can't stop you!" She grins at me and says, "My Mom colours her hair but she says I'm too young to colour mine."

I smile at Jenny and say, "Jenny, can *you* say some of the bear's words to yourself?" I get a mirror. Jenny shyly repeats the words to her mirror self.

"How does it feel to say those things to yourself?"

"Nice," Jenny replies.

"Now, every morning this week," I say, "I want you to say those words, or words like them, to yourself in a mirror and then when you come in next week, tell me if it was OK to do it."

Jenny agrees, taking a deep breath.

Comment

It is obvious to me that a deeper feeling of rejection has been symbol-ized by discussing hair. It's as if the messy hair picture is a metaphor for her whole life. We actually have, in previous sessions, talked about Jenny's feelings of rejection from her father. Jenny's father lived in another part of the country and she saw him rarely. Even if her father had lived here and came into family sessions and worked hard at giving Jenny acceptance, Jenny would still be plagued by the feeling that she was not good enough. Negative introjects appear to go deeper into the self—they don't readily dissipate. It was time to call upon Jenny's own resources for acceptance. As we exaggerate and elaborate on her feelings, as we did in this session, she begins to feel validated and accepted. If I had said, "Oh, I think your hair is lovely" I would only have discounted her feelings. When she feels validated and accepted, when she gains some self-support by expressing her retroflected anger outward, she can then begin to experiment with self acceptance and nurturing. This was only the beginning.

A word here about polarities: Often, to achieve integration, one must examine polarities. The critical self surveys the child with a demanding eye. The parts of self the child hates are usually exaggerated and distorted. To help the child achieve a balance, we will call forth the polar opposite of the hated part—the idealized part. This part is usually far-fetched and unrealistic. The child views the aspects of herself she dislikes as larger than life and the opposite of that part becomes impossible to reach. As the child despises and turns away from those hated parts of self, she further broadens the gulf between her polar selves, causing increased fragmentation and self-alienation. We must encourage even further exaggeration and separation of both polar parts in order to achieve enough distance to examine them carefully. In this way an integration, reconciliation, or synthesis of one's opposing sides can be achieved leading to a realistic view of self and a dynamic and healthy life process. In work with children we do this through creative media, as puppets, drawings, clay, collage, creative dramatics and music.

Example two

I show 10-year-old Andrew a sort of colouring book about demons. It is about the parts of self the author doesn't like and includes very funny drawings representing each of his demons, as he calls them. Andrew and I talk about the parts of ourselves that get in our way, that we don't like. I ask him to close his eyes and think about one of those parts. Then Andrew draws a cartoon like figure with large legs and arms with bandages and blue and red splotches all over it. He says, "This is the part of me I hate. I'm always falling down, bumping into things, getting hurt. His name is Mr. Klutz." I ask Andrew to *be* Mr. Klutz while I talk to him—to be the voice of Mr. Klutz as if it were a puppet. I say to the picture, "Hello, Mr. Klutz. Tell me about yourself." Andrew answers, "Hello. I'm a klutz. I always bump into things. I'm always getting hurt. I have cuts and bruises and black and blue marks all over me. I never do anything right!" Mr. Klutz and I continue to talk to each other playfully and he tells me about each injury. I turn to Andrew. "Andrew, what would you like to say to Mr. Klutz?" He says, "*I hate you!* I wish you would go away. You get in my way. You make me feel bad." I encourage Andrew's outburst with remarks such as, "Yeah! Tell him!" Andrew makes faces and noises at Mr. Klutz. "Andrew," I say, "How do you wish you could be?" Andrew describes a lithe, athletic, beautiful fantasy person—a direct polar opposite of his Mr. Klutz. I ask Andrew to be this athletic person and describe himself to me and to move around the room as if he were this person. I am amazed at the power, energy and gracefulness Andrew displays as he portrays his ideal person. I say, "Andrew, imagine that you have a fairy god-mother. Let's get a fairy godmother puppet. You know how fairy godmothers are. They think you are wonderful no matter what." Andrew nods. "Imagine you have this fairy godmother and just as your Mr. Klutz part cuts you or bumps into something or falls off your bike, she suddenly appears on the scene. What do you think she might say to you?"

Andrew hesitates. "I don't know." I see that he is deep in thought so I wait. After a while I notice that his energy is fading—contact is breaking. Wanting to bring him back into contact, I repeat, "You know how fairy godmothers are. They like you no matter what you do or what happens." Andrew nods and is struggling for words. "She says, Uhhhhhh. Ummmm." I decide to help him out. "Try having her say, 'I like you.'" Andrew, obviously relieved to have something to say, repeats my words. "How did it feel to say that?" Andrew responds, "It felt good!" "What else could she say?" I ask. Andrew begins with, "Maybe she'd say, 'Don't feel bad'"—he stops, and then suddenly seems to have a burst of energy. "She'd say, 'You're O.K! I like you! I like that you do things. I like that you try things.'" (Andrew is on a roll, now.)

"Don't worry that you hurt yourself sometimes. That shows you do new things and I like you for that. You're not afraid to do things!!!" He stops and looks at me.

"Andrew, your fairy godmother suddenly disappears." (I grab the puppet and throw her behind me.) "And now you, Andrew, are here with Mr. Klutz. Can *you* say these things to Mr. Klutz?" Andrew repeats what his fairy godmother said. His voice is lower now but the intensity is still present. I ask, "How did that feel to say those things to the Mr. Klutz part of yourself?" Andrew responds softly, "Yeah! It felt good." I can see that Andrew has withdrawn into himself—he appears glassy eyed and distracted. I wait since I sense that Andrew is deep within himself. Suddenly he turns to me, fully present, fully in contact. He takes a big deep breath and his face breaks out in a huge delighted grin. He says, "I *do* try things!" Integration has taken place before my eyes.

Comment

In previous sessions we had dealt with Andrew's very athletic Dad's high expectations of him, so we already had a sense of where this feeling of klutziness came from. Andrew's Dad willingly participated in our monthly family sessions and owned these expectations of his son. In fact it was the only way he had known to relate to Andrew. In spite of his father's willingness to change, Andrew's bad feelings of self persisted.

The negative belief that the child develops about himself can never be totally changed by an outside agent. Self-acceptance of all of one's parts, even the most hateful, is a vital component of unimpaired sound development. Such self-acceptance comes about through the contact and growth of the child's own loving, nurturing part of himself, which must join with the "bad" self to accept, understand, comfort and love it. As the child experiences and accepts all aspects of himself without judgment, he grows and expands joyfully. As we dig out those darker aspects, illuminate them and bring them into contact with his nurturing inner self, the child experiences healthful integration.

Self-acceptance is an important prerequisite to this work. I asked Andrew to imagine that his fairy godmother appeared on his shoulder whenever he had a klutzy episode, and she said, "It's OK, I like you even when you fall down." Andrew agreed to try this experiment and reported the following week that he hardly had any klutzy experiences.

Example three

Twelve-year-old Ellen scratched herself till she had large ugly sores all over her arms. She was a lovely child who despised herself. She was born ill and for the first 7 years of her life cried almost continuously. After we had worked together for about a year, the following session took place. Both parents were present for this session as I felt that it was important for them to understand this work. They were both filled with guilt over Ellen's predicament and often this guilt would become unleashed in anger at Ellen, exacerbating the situation. I wanted Ellen's parents to know that it was now Ellen's work to heal *herself*.

I start: "Ellen, see this doll? Let's imagine it's you as a baby and she's sick and she's crying. How do you think she feels?" Ellen answers, "I guess terrible!" I turn to her mother and father. "Is there anything you would like to say to your baby?" Mother begins to cry. She says, "Don't cry, baby. I wish you wouldn't cry. I wish you wouldn't be sick. I'm so worried about you." Dad adds, "We're trying to find out what's wrong with you. We love you." I say to Ellen, "Imagine you are this little baby, and even though a baby like this can't talk, let's imagine that she can talk. What do you think you might say as the baby?" Ellen immediately responds, "Whaaa!!!!! Help me! Help me! I'm sick! I'm sick! Help me!"

I say, "What do you think the baby thinks about herself? You probably can't remember how you—the baby—really felt about herself." Ellen says, "I don't know. Yeah, I don't remember."

I explain to Ellen and her parents that when a child is sick and in pain, she, consistent with developmental theory, blames herself, feels that she is a bad girl. Also, when the baby cries so much, the parents are desperate, beside themselves with anxiety, feel terrible because they can't help the baby. The baby senses the parents' feelings, because babies are very sensitive, and blames herself for THEIR feelings too. These feelings appear to reinforce her bad feelings of self since the baby is totally egocentric and cannot understand separate experience. She can't comprehend that her parents have their own feelings separate from her. She feels she is the cause of their feelings, and in this case, she actually is. Ellen says, "I remember feeling like I was a bad girl when I was about four and I was sick. Like something was wrong with me as a person."

"Right! And you probably started feeling that way even as a tiny infant. Ellen, if you could go back in a time machine and talk to her, what would you say to her right now?"

Ellen asks if she can hold the doll. She cuddles her and says, "Baby, it's not your fault. You're a wonderful baby. You're really cute. You can't help it that you're sick." She rocks the doll, saying, "There, there. . . ." Her mother turns to me and says, "We kept telling her that." I say, "It was hard for her to believe you. Now she has to tell it to herself." Ellen is now very involved with the baby doll. She is rocking it and repeating over and over those loving words.

"Ellen," I say (she looks up at me), "Every time you feel bad inside, remember that it's the baby self feeling that way. She needs you to hold her and love her. And, Ellen, every time you scratch yourself, you are actually scratching the baby. I think you do that when you feel bad inside. So now, instead of scratching the baby, you can hold her and rock her and talk to her. Can you find something at home to be the baby—a doll, a stuffed animal, a pillow?" Ellen is sure she can find something and agrees to experiment with this new idea for comforting and loving the baby self inside of her. Ellen's parents are now crying outright and Ellen looks over at them, smiles and says, "It's OK. I'll take care of the baby."

Comment

This session was by no means a magic cure. It took a great deal of work and practice for Ellen to integrate this nurturing concept. An important part of the work was to help Ellen learn how to meet her own needs in her day-to-day life. We outlined her daily schedule on a large piece of paper and rated each event in terms of satisfaction and frustration. She talked about how she could improve the quality of her day-to-day existence on her own. This was not to imply that she could not ever ask for what she needed, but she did need to learn to take responsibility for asking for that help. This was an entirely new idea for her. In fact she felt, as many people do, that to do something nice for herself was selfish and to ask for help was a sign of weakness. This idea is the reason that children, and adults too, often try to get their needs met in indirect, regressive ways.

Ellen and I made a list of all the things she could do to make herself feel better and all the things she liked to do. I asked her to experiment with doing at least one nice thing for herself each day and to let me know at our next session what she did and how she felt doing it. Many adolescents tell me that they feel self-indulgent and think they already do a lot of nice things for themselves based on what their parents tell them. They find, however, that it is quite a different experience to do something nice for yourself with conscious awareness and wholehearted permission. Sometimes the belief that it is selfish to do nice things for oneself is so strongly ingrained in a person that we must spend time exploring and working through this detrimental idea.

Even when we have made great progress for achieving responsible, satisfying management of our lives, regression will occur. Some stressful or painful event or experience can cause fragmentation, that is, the younger part of ourselves that is vulnerable and easily injured, that baby or young child within us, splits off and is no longer an integrated part of the self. That younger part then seems to take control of our whole being and reacts to the hurtful event in old, infantile ways. It is at this time that we must remind ourselves that we are no longer the helpless young child. We must mobilize all the energy we can muster to soothe, comfort, nurture the injured child within us. The more we do this, the easier it gets. When we are new at this, we often do need someone to remind us, as a friend, a parent, a therapist. We must take care not to be judgmental of our regressive reactions. Remember that the child does whatever she knows to do in her attempts to take care of the self. And sometimes all she can do is cry.

Ellen had a bad experience at school one day that caused her to revert to her old self-destructive behaviour. Her mother called me on the phone in a panic. Ellen was scratching herself vigorously, crying hysterically, seemed unable to catch her breath and was completely inconsolable. I asked to speak to her. I spoke firmly and loudly above her wails. "What can you do right now to make the little girl who feels hurt inside of you feel better!" Through her tears I heard her mumble, "Music?" "OK" I yelled. "Do it!" Ellen reported later that she turned on the radio and fell asleep. By the next day she was able to consider the event in a more rational way, talk to her mother about it and accelerate her self-nurturing techniques until she felt her life was in balance again. The rejection and hurt she experienced that day at school opened old baby wounds. There was no way her mother or father could make amends for what happened to her when she was little. Nor could her future partner for that matter. Only Ellen, herself, could do it.

Example four

Angie, aged 7, and I were sitting on the floor with several puppets before us. I asked Angie to choose a puppet that most reminded her of how she felt right now. She chose a sad-looking green dog. I picked up another puppet and my puppet (me) begins to talk to the dog.

Me: Hi.
Angie: Hi.

Me: What's going on with you today?
Angie: Oh, nothing.
Me: I wonder what about you, dog, made Angie pick you.
Angie: Because I look sad.
Me: What are you sad about?
Angie: Oh, school.
Me: Are you having trouble at school?
Angie: Yeah, with reading.
Me: You feel bad about that?

Angie herself nods. My puppet speaks directly to Angie.

Me: What could you say to your dog puppet who has trouble reading?
Angie: (*to her dog*) You're so dumb!
Me: (*speaking to dog*) What do you have to say to that?
Angie: (*as dog*) Well, I try!

Angie again tells the dog how dumb she is. My puppet speaks to Angie.

Me: I guess you feel dumb like the dog when you have trouble with reading.
Angie: (*mumbles a yes*).
Me: (*to Angie*) Your dog says she tries. I guess you try and still can't get it and a part inside of you calls you dumb.
Angie: (*nods her head and makes a face*).
Me: What's that face about?
Angie: I *am* dumb.
Me: Angie, pick another puppet here that might be nice to your dog who tries and then feels dumb—maybe the fairy godmother puppet, or any other one that would be nice. (*Angie picks the fairy godmother puppet.*) What does she say to the dog?
Angie: (*as the fairy godmother says without hesitation*) You try hard. I know you do. And you're really not dumb because you can do other things. You're good in math. You couldn't be dumb and be good in math!
Me: (*to fairy godmother*) Can you tell the dog that you love her even when she's dumb?
Angie: (*as fairy godmother*) I love you even when you're dumb.
Me: How does it feel to say that?

Angie: Well, I don't think she's dumb. I think she'll get good in reading. She needs extra help.

Me: Angie, would you say that to your dog? (*She does and then hugs the dog.*)

Angie had been suffering from reading anxiety. At the next session she told me, "My tutor came yesterday and I didn't want to do anything. Then in my mind I was hugging the dog part who feels dumb, and I did good!"

Comment

Doing self-nurturing work with young children is very gratifying. Children are very responsive to this work. They don't seem to have the inhibitions and restraints to the idea of self-nurturing that some adolescents and most adults have. Children have an inner wisdom that they rarely show. I am deeply moved by the wisdom that I am often privileged to witness.

Example five

Doing this work with adolescents can be difficult, yet vitally necessary. Cathy, a 17-year-old young woman, had been sexually molested as a young child and suffered from many disturbing symptoms including obsessive behaviour and intense fears of every sort. Her self-esteem was non-existent. We worked together for 2 years before Cathy was able to accept the concept of nurturing herself. She made much progress in her therapy and finally I knew that we needed to tackle the subject of self-nurturing. I asked her to bring photographs of herself as an infant and young child. She was disgusted with each picture, feeling that she was ugly and unlovable. She could not muster any compassionate feelings for her child self until we looked at a picture of herself at about the age of one month. I noticed her face soften somewhat and quickly made her aware of this reaction. She began to cry and admitted to the innocence of that tiny baby. Each week we looked at her baby pictures and spoke to the images. She was completely amazed that I found her baby self to be charming and lovable and that I could say lovable words to the baby. Cathy could not even muster the energy to project loving statements onto a fairy godmother figure, nor fantasize loving feelings in any way. So, in this situation, *I* took the role of the fairy godmother. She was eventually able to admit to some fond feelings of acceptance of the baby and little girl up to the age of her molestation that occurred when she was 6 years old. Memories came flooding back. Up till now Cathy had had difficulty remembering childhood scenes. I told Cathy that the young child within her, so very much alive, had someone now that she had never had before, someone who was always with her. "Who?", she asked in amazement. "You," I said. "You are with her all the time—she lives inside of you." Cathy was finally able to grasp this idea and began to talk to the 6-year-old who had been so brutally injured and betrayed. At first I needed to feed her words—words such as, "It was *not* your fault! You are a wonderful girl. I love you. I will always be with you. I will protect you. I'll never leave you alone." After each statement we stopped to examine her reactions to saying these words. Slowly Cathy was able to own these words for herself, adding many of her own. Sometimes Cathy would literally hold her breath during these sessions and I would encourage her to take full deep breaths to feel her own life force. I watched Cathy blossom into a well-functioning happy young woman as a result, I am certain, of this work. She herself felt that she had a powerful tool of her own to use to help herself wherever she was.

Comment

Self-nurturing work is particularly essential in work with children who have been physically or sexually abused, as well as with adults who have been abused as children. Some debilitating effects of abuse include the blaming of the self, self-disparagement, fragmentation, anaesthetizing aspects of the self and feelings of powerlessness, shame and guilt. Helping the client contact and express outwardly the anger that is retroflected to the self is a first step. Only through self-acceptance and the nurturing of the self can complete healing take place.

Example six

Even a 2-year-old can respond to self-nurturing techniques. Such a child, Molly, who had been abused and abandoned was brought into a shelter. The therapist assigned to this child was in one of my supervision groups. One day, after discussing the self-nurturing idea, she went back to the shelter and approached the child who had cried non-stop since she been brought in. The therapist held a big doll and said to the child, "This is Molly—this is baby Molly." The therapist rocked the doll murmuring, "Poor Molly. I know you're sad. I love you. I'm here with you." She handed the doll to the child who immediately stopped crying, held the doll close and began to rock and croon to the doll.

Example seven

Here is an example of a session with a 16-year-old boy. John is very shy and particularly had had difficulty talking to girls. John's process—his way of being in the world—was to inhibit himself, restrict himself, talk as little as possible. We had been working for about six months when I decided to introduce the self-nurturing concept. I asked John to draw a picture of a part of himself he didn't like. He drew himself lying on his bed listening to music. He explained, "There's a world outside and all I do is stay in my room." I asked him to actually BE the boy on the bed and to describe what was happening. "I'm on my bed listening to music. That's all I ever do and I'm sick of it."

Me: (*focusing my remarks to the drawing of the boy*) What keeps you from going out into the world?

John: (*pausing, seemingly deep in thought and finally saying*) He's afraid no one will like him. He's afraid he won't have anything interesting to say.

Me: John, what do you think of this boy on the bed?

John: (*without hesitation*) I hate him!

Me: Tell him.

John: I hate you! Why don't you get up? Stop being afraid. What a wimp you are. You make me sick.

Me: John, can you remember a time in your childhood when you were afraid to talk?

John had many memories. He chose one when he was a 5-year-old in kindergarten. The teacher had yelled at him for talking when he wasn't supposed to and that had really scared him. I suggested that he draw a picture of that little boy.

Me: Imagine that you could go back in a time machine and be with him. What would you say to him?

John looked at the picture for a few moments. "It's not your fault. You didn't know you were not supposed to talk. The teacher was wrong."

At my suggestion he drew a quick picture of his teacher and proceeded to yell at *her*.

I explained to John that the small boy John was still alive inside of him and when he, John, was afraid to talk, it was a 5-year-old's fear he was feeling. But now he had 16-year-old John to be with him and understand him and help him. After all he knew a lot more now than he did then. He could even drive the younger John places. John laughed since he had just received his driving licence. I told John that for the next week, whenever he felt afraid to talk, he was to tell his child self that it was OK to be afraid and that he didn't have to talk. John was surprised at this assignment, but agreed. I explained to him that it was important for him to learn to be self-accepting before he could teach the young child ways to talk, that the more he judged himself, the more he would remain silent. Next I would ask him to allow himself to experience more fully the feelings he had when he couldn't talk—to *feel* the fear and the frustration, but without judgment. Finally, I would encourage John to hold his 5-year-old's hand so to speak, and to risk talking and to assure him that he was there to assist, teach him and support and love him no matter what happened. I can happily report that with the first step of self-acceptance, when John told himself it was OK not to talk, paradoxically he found himself talking more than ever before (especially to girls).

Comment

The hateful parts that we elicit can generally be connected to a time in early childhood. For John the school incident was probably one of many experiences that he had that reinforced the introject that he was a bad boy if he talked. The actual source is not always important—we use a memory as an example to work with. It is interesting to note that these negative introjects that we take in as young children and which cause us to engage in behaviours to avoid rejection and disapproval become our process throughout life and further our self-disparagement. John decided to stop talking to protect himself and through his growing-up years he continued this behaviour. Now in his teenage years he hates this part of himself. He feels he has no control over this behaviour—that it is an integral part of him. Since he has cut off this part of himself that he surely once had, he feels that he cannot contact it, that in fact he doesn't have it or has completely lost it.

Helping him to accept, reassure, love this younger child even as he doesn't talk is the amazing paradox toward finding his talking self.

Example eight

One more example of a self-nurturing procedure with a bed wetter. Julie, aged 10, had been a bed wetter all her life. Her parents had tried many different kinds of programmes and gadgets without success. Julie was very responsive to therapy and did much good work in learning to express her anxieties and feelings and developing increased body awareness. Her parents were very cooperative and participated in regular family sessions. The turning point came when I introduced the self-nurturing idea. I asked Julie to bring in a doll or stuffed animal from home. I explained to her that the little girl inside of her had originally begun to wet the bed because she was looking for a way to feel better. Something had happened to make her feel worried and upset and she did not have the words to talk about it, so she wet the bed as a release. "Notice, the next time you go to the bathroom," I said, "how relaxed you feel afterward." I told her that when some children feel tense and anxious, bedwetting is a way to relieve the tension in the body. It starts at a young age and then becomes a habit. We now have to help the little girl find new ways of expressing her feelings and achieving relaxation. "The first thing," I said, "is to help the little girl inside of you feel that she's a good, lovable, OK girl." I asked Julie to talk to the teddy bear who would be her little girl self. I told Julie to tell the bear that it was OK to wet the bed. I explained that if she told her NOT to wet the bed, the little girl would feel tense and worried and would wet the bed! I told Julie to hug her bear every morning and say nice things to it, pretending it was her little girl self, whether she wet the bed or not. Julie followed my instructions and did not wet the bed for three weeks. Then a bedwetting incident occurred after a particularly stressful day at school. At our session we listed everything that happened that day and examined each event carefully. This activity evoked many feelings and Julie appeared to understand the relationship between expressing her feelings and bedwetting and the need to express them in some way. She has completely stopped wetting the bed as of this time.

At this point I would like to summarize some of the salient features of the self-nurturing work. This process can be delineated into several steps:

1. I encourage the child to be very specific. "I hate myself" is converted to specific parts about the self that are hated.
2. We then elaborate, personify these hateful parts.
3. At times we compare them with the ideal polar opposite.
4. The anger that has been retroflected, turned inward against the self, is encouraged to be expressed OUTWARD against those hated parts.
5. We contact and bring forth the accepting, nurturing aspect within the child, sometimes as a projection using the fairy godmother, or some other loving figure.
6. The client is then encouraged to say and own for himself the accepting, loving, nurturing words to the hateful part without the use of a projective aid.
7. At times, we go back to a younger party of self, the self that originally believed, swallowed whole, the flawed ideas of self.
8. We suggest specific self-accepting and self-nurturing experiments for the client to practise outside the session.
9. We encourage the child to consciously and purposefully create a nurturing environment for himself, such as doing nice things for himself each day, and especially when he most needs them.

There are other ways too to help children learn to take care of themselves in loving, healing ways. Allowing the self to experience and express feelings, as anger and sadness is in itself nurturing. Children learn in our sessions together appropriate, safe ways of doing this. Children too seem to find ways of giving themselves self-support when they need it. For example, a child I worked with often came into my office insisting that all she wanted to do was draw or paint rainbows. After she would do this for a while, she would begin to tell me about her particularly difficult frustrating day or event. However, activities that are supposed to make children feel good should not be thrust onto them to protect them and assist them in avoiding painful events. Children, themselves, seem to know when they need support, an inner strength, before they can muster the courage to deal with hurtful feelings. For example, when I asked a young client of mine to draw a picture of her mother who had abandoned her, she insisted on drawing MY picture first. After doing my portrait, she was willing to draw her mother's and deal with the painful feelings this task elicited. Another client, upon my direction, made a clay figure of her step-father who had molested her, and when I asked her to express some of her anger at him by hitting the clay with a rubber mallet (after reassuring her that this was just clay and he would never know), got up and began to examine some toy figures she noticed on the shelf. After talking about these figures with me, she said, "I'm' ready now" and proceeded to smash the clay figure with great energy.

Breathing, relaxation and centring exercises are important tools for self-nurturing. Children learn these exercises and make them their own to use any time they feel the need. A favourite nurturing activity is to fantasize a wonderful place, which we call a safe place. The child will draw this place, or make it in the sand, and can go there in her imagination at any time. We talk about and practise this concept of "nurturing the senses". What kinds of things will soothe your senses? Looking at a beautiful flower or a sunset; listening to the sound of the waves or lovely music; smelling a rose or a box of cinnamon; tasting an ice-cream cone; touching something velvety and soft; running one's hand through sand. Children create their own sensory soothing activities once we bring this idea into their awareness.

One of my goals in the therapeutic process is to give children a feeling of strength, a sense of their own power. Engaging in activities to enhance self-support, express feelings, experience their aggression in positive, acceptable ways does accomplish this goal. When children begin to feel a sense of themselves and feel some of their own power, this in itself is nurturing to the self. In turn, learning tools and techniques for taking care of themselves, for having regard, respect and appreciation for the self, to know how to actively nurture the self, give children the vitality to grow joyfully and meet each developmental task with full capacity. Further, becoming self-nurturing makes it possible for children to develop a loving and caring attitude toward others.

CHAPTER NINE

Working with very young children

When I had just turned 5 years old, I was badly burned when a pot of boiling water fell on me. I was in the hospital for about three or four months and underwent surgical skin grafting. Every "hang-up" that plagued me as an adult seemed to stem from this trauma. This happened before the advent of penicillin and I was kept in isolation. I was not allowed to have any toys and there were no other distractions, as radio or TV in those days. My hands were tied down to keep me from touching myself. I was often admonished by doctors and nurses for crying: "Be a good girl, stop that crying" was a refrain I heard over and over. Covers were raised so as not to touch me, and even though it was summertime, I shivered in cold. To this day I hesitate to admit when I am in pain (to avoid being a bad girl) and need to cuddle in a quilt, even in warm weather. I have no memory of my mother visiting me even though I learned later that my mother came every day. I do remember my beloved grandmother sitting by my bed sometimes and feeding me cherries. My aunt brought me a toy which made me so happy, but the nurse screamed when she saw it and grabbed it. Of course I know now that I was being protected from infection, but no one ever bothered to explain this to me. My parents, Russian Jewish immigrants, had great respect for the doctors and nurses caring for me, and had no idea what I was going through. I do remember, though, hearing my father's voice yelling at the doctor who wanted to amputate my leg because the joint wouldn't heal. (I knew somehow that he was yelling on my behalf.) Because of my father's refusal to let them do that, a big specialist was brought in who did a new procedure: pinch grafting. This saved my leg.

I sometimes imagine what it would have been like to have a therapist like me come and visit me in the hospital to help me through this terrible experience. I imagine she could have used puppets, playing out stories as I watched: a little girl puppet is telling the doctor puppet how mad she is, and then maybe telling the mother puppet how sad she is. I would have loved this, I know. The therapist could read a story to me about another little girl in the hospital and what it was like for her. Maybe we could have sung some songs together. I know that I lay in that bed telling myself stories and singing Yiddish songs my mother had taught me. When I remember this, my eyes fill with tears even now for the resourcefulness of that little girl. Most of all, the therapist could find a way to let me know that I was a good girl, a wonderful girl, not the bad girl who found herself in this predicament. Even though the accident was not at all my fault, due to the normal egocentricity of children, I imagined that it was my fault. I never told anyone about this feeling, and I needed a therapist who understood this phenomenon to reassure me that it was not at all my fault.

It would have been wonderful if I could see this therapist when I finally returned home. She could encourage me to draw pictures about my experience, pound clay to get my angry feelings out so I could know it was fine to have that anger, maybe play out my experiences with a toy hospital set. She could include my whole family sometimes: my two older brothers, mother and father, so we could tell each other our feelings about what had happened.

I wonder sometimes if my hospital experience influenced me to become a therapist. There is no way of knowing for sure, but I often tell people I am training that the best teacher is yourself as a child, and that it is vital to be able to remember what it was like to be a child.

What happens to young children determines so much how they will be in later years, since it is in those early years that the child makes a determination of how to be in the world to best get her needs met. In those early years she absorbs numerous messages about herself—she believes everything she hears about herself since she does not have the cognitive ability to discard what is false and doesn't fit for her. She carries these messages with her emotionally throughout life, even when she later can cognitively know they are wrong.

To begin the therapy encounter we begin with the relationship. A fundamental component of establishing an I/Thou relationship is to meet the client where he or she is, with honour and respect. Understanding the natural development of children facilitates this process. However, we should never underestimate what a young child is capable of doing and responding in the therapeutic encounter. I would like to present some examples to verify this idea.

Alex was a 4-year-old when I met him. His parents lived separately, had never married, had joint custody and were both very devoted to him. Because of his severe stuttering they had taken him to a speech therapist who recommended psychological counselling. I make an assumption, when young children stutter, that either they are unable to say what they really want to say, perhaps holding in angry feelings, or their minds are going faster than they can articulate.

Alex was happy to come into my office without a parent, and we established a relationship quickly, helped, I'm sure, by the many interesting toys around the room. He did not speak, but smiled and nodded. After looking around, he went straight to the doll house, sat in front of it and begin moving furniture around while mumbling to himself.

I sat next to him and asked, "What should I do?" His face registered surprise and he said, severely stuttering, "Get the family." So I retrieved the basket of doll house figures and held up a mother, a father and a boy and a girl for his approval. He then manipulated the figures with the furniture, all the while mumbling to himself. After a while, I said, "I bet you wish you lived in a house with your mother and father like these children!" Alex looked at me, sighed deeply, nodded and moved on to examine other toys in my office. (I do not have a "play room." I have a large office with a couch, pillows, 2 chairs near the couch, coffee table, a large ball one could sit on, a desk in a corner and a large low table with 4 small chairs

around it, strong enough for adults to sit on them. Along the walls
are shelves of toys and games, sand trays with miniatures on shelves
above, a table with a doll house with baskets of furniture and
figures under it. There is a cabinet that holds drawing paper and
pastels, clay and such. A puppet stage leans against a wall. Baskets
of puppets and percussion instruments are nearby, as well as a Bop
bag. Even when I had a very small office, the coffee table served as
a clay or drawing table, and toys and materials were arranged on
shelves. A sand tray slipped under the coffee table. Every bit of
space was used and the room was inviting and attractive. (My adult
clients often made use of some of these materials.)

For the next three sessions Alex went directly to the doll house,
and as soon as I made the statement, "I bet you wished you
lived. . . .", he would leave the doll house and examine other things.
Sometimes we played a game together to finish the session. Suddenly everything changed. Alex picked Superman and Batman off
the shelf and went directly to a sand tray. He moved them around in
the sand mumbling to himself as I sat next to him. I got up and
retrieved a large lion figure with sharp teeth. I said, "I'm going to get
that Superman—I don't care if he's the strongest man in the world!"
Alex yelled, (stuttering), "Put that away! Put that away!" I placed
the lion back on the shelf, sat down again and said remorsefully,
"I'm sorry!" Alex looked at me for a few seconds, and then said,
(stuttering), "Get the lion." And so I did and moved it toward the
figures in the sand tray, "I'm going to get that Superman! He better
not hit me!" and as I got closer to Superman, he hit me slightly. I
screamed, "You hit me! You hit me!" and the lion fell flat into the
sand. Alex gleefully yelled with no stuttering, "Do that again! Do
that again!" And so I did, several times. Then Alex said, with no
stuttering, "I'll be the lion." In this case Superman said, "You can't
get me! But you better not hit me!" And of course the lion hit
Superman who fell flat into the sand. We played this out the whole
session and there was no stuttering at all. But when he walked out to
the waiting room, he told his mother about what had happened,
stuttering as usual.

After doing this for a while at the next session (no stuttering), I
suggested we use clay. As Alex played with the clay and the tools, I
made a clay mother and father and boy. I told Alex he could speak
for the boy and tell the mother and father what he liked and didn't

like. As I manipulated the boy toward each figure, he said (no stuttering) to mother, "I like it when you take me places but I don't like it when you yell at me." To father, "I like it when you play with me but I don't like it when you go away." (His father travelled often on business.) We did this a few times with some suggestions from me: "I don't like it when I have to go back and forth." "I wish we all lived together!" At the next session I asked both parents to come in, and played this game, with each person telling the two others what they liked or didn't like. Alex did not stutter at all during this session much to his parent's amazement.

There was still some stuttering outside the sessions so I suggested several things:

1. That Alex spend some time yelling NO at the top of his lungs.
2. That there be a mad session at bed time.
3. That there be a special Alex time each day.

Alex went to a pre-school and the teachers agreed to allow Alex to yell NO on the playground. So Alex walked around the playground yelling NO, and soon he had a line of other children behind him yelling NO. There was no disruption in the class room and all stuttering had stopped.

At our last session (four months later) Alex told me a dream that had frightened him.

> "I was sleeping in a house and my mother and father were both sleeping there too. It was raining hard. Then my mother and father came into my room and picked me up and threw me out in the rain. A big bird was there and picked me up in its mouth and flew away. And then I woke up. I didn't like that dream!" (He had awakened his mother and crawled into bed with her when he had that dream.)

I said, "Let's make the dream out of clay." So we made a very rough house with indentations for bedrooms. We made a figure of him and his parents and put them in their respective bedrooms.

Me: Here is the boy—you—sleeping. Then what happens?
Alex: My mother and father come in to my room.
Me: Imagine they talked in the dream. What did they say?

Alex: We're going to throw you out!!!
Me: And what do you imagine you said, if you talked in the dream?
Alex: No! No!
Me: But they do throw you out?

Alex nods and I pantomime the parents throwing him out in the rain.

Me: Then what happens?
Alex: Then this big bird takes me away. (We had fashioned a bird.) Then I woke up. I didn't like that dream—it scared me.
Me: Let's change the dream. Here we are back in the house. Your mother and father come into your room yelling, "We're going to throw you out in the rain!" What do you say?
Alex: I say, *"Go back to bed!"*
Me: (*moving the figures back to their bedrooms*). And they do. What about the bird?
Alex: We have to kill the bird. (*He takes a wooden mallet and smashes the bird to a pancake.*)
Me: Now he can't hurt you! Of course we'd never really do that to a real bird. But this is just clay and it's OK. You got a lot of angry feelings out doing that.
Alex: (*Grinning*) Yeah!

As I review these sessions, I am aware of several pertinent points that led to Alex's improvement.

The therapy is like a dance: sometimes I lead and sometimes the child leads. I am alert regarding the appropriate time for me to intervene, as saying, "I bet you wished your mother and father lived in a house like this family." I know that this is every young child's wish.

Connecting with Alex is vital. I was not willing to just sit back and observe.

I decided to try out "aggressive energy" when I picked up the lion. If there was suppressed anger, this kind of energy gives the child support to express his emotions. Again I had made an assumption, and I proved to be correct. If I had been wrong, he would have let me know.

We moved from this play into expressing feelings with clay figures that represented his parents to normalize his feelings.

Then we moved into having Alex express his feelings directly to his parents.

The yelling, "NO" provided an experience with expressing himself appropriately.

Listening

Most children do not feel listened to. I think that is what causes so many problems especially with very young children since they don't have the skills and vocabulary to express what they need to say. I am reminded of a mother and a 4-year-old boy who came to see me some time ago. The mother was at her wits' end because the boy had numerous temper tantrums and she felt that she was losing control. Since it is so difficult for a young child to be involved in an adult-like conversation, I asked them both to draw a picture of what bugged them the most about each other. The mother immediately began to draw a picture of a boy lying on the floor having a temper tantrum. The boy watched her for a while and drew his own picture of a boy having a tantrum and a mother figure standing over him. I asked the mother to tell the boy in the picture what she was mad about. She said, "I don't like it when you have a tantrum. I don't know what to do." I asked the boy to talk to his mother figure, "I don't like it when you stand over me yelling when I'm having a temper tantrum!" As each talked to the pictures, rather than to each other, the boy said, "You don't listen to me." It seems the mother asked him to put his toys, strewn all over, away before dinner. He was trying to tell her that some of the toys were put there by his younger brother. Somehow she didn't get his message and would raise her voice ordering him to clean up, whereupon he would lie on the floor kicking and screaming. This scenario happened many times, for various reasons.

After this session the mother reported that there was a great improvement and was willing to admit that it was because she had learned how to listen.

Basically kids can be pretty reasonable if they feel listened to. I remember when one of my own children would come home from school complaining about some injustice. I would want to do something to fix it or give him advice about how to handle it. I would bite my tongue and just listen, and after telling me his story, he would run out to play, the incident apparently forgotten.

Here are some basic points about listening—good for therapists, teachers and parents:

1. Be present—be in contact. Don't let your mind wander. Block out everything but your contact with the child.
2. Join his rhythm and, if possible, his level. If the child is standing, stand. If the child is on the floor, join him there. If he is fidgety, ignore it. He is probably nervous and anxious. Stay with him.
3. Repeat back softly so she'll know you heard her. "Johnny hit you."
4. Clarify—if you don't understand, don't pretend you do.
5. Use a normal, natural voice, NOT teacher voice or patronizing or teasing or jovial voice.
6. Take the child seriously.
7. Language: Use words the child can understand.
8. Use sound, gesture, facial expressions to show you are listening. Stay present.
9. Do not lecture, explain anything, try to fix anything or give advice at this time. (You can talk to the child about it at a later time. "You know, I was thinking about what you told me, and wonder if it's OK with you if I tell you some thoughts I had about what you said.")
10. Watch the child's eyes, gesture, movement and listen to the voice tones for clues as to how the child is feeling. Articulate this, but if the child denies, accept his denial. "It seems to me that you are really mad about this." "No! I'm not!" "Oh, OK."
11. Articulate for them instead of asking questions. Say instead, "I bet . . ." "I bet that made you really mad." "I bet Daddy made you mad when he didn't take you to the zoo like he said he would." If you are wrong with your assumption, the child will tell you.
12. Use figures to act things out. Or drawings or puppets or clay figures. Or just role play—switching roles.

Alex's father called me a few weeks after our last session to tell me that Alex had started stuttering again. I asked him if anything out of the ordinary had happened. "Well, I had to go out of town but I asked Alex if he was mad about that and he said no." I told Dad to say to Alex, "I bet you didn't like it that I had to go out of town." He did this and reported back that Alex had said a resounding "Yes!!!" and stopped stuttering.

When we ask questions, we put children on the spot and they tend to give the answer they think we want to hear. Making an assumptive statement is very relieving to the child. If the assumption is wrong, they will correct you.

Something else to remember: Children always raise their voices when they want to be heard and they are not aware of this. To admonish them for speaking rudely will only exacerbate a bad situation. They will feel judged and criticized, and definitely not heard. Model the kind of behaviour you would want. Bear in mind that angry expressions are a child's way of expressing the SELF. He does not have the cognitive ability developmentally to be diplomatic nor does he have the words for what he wants to say, so he often uses gross terminology. Also remember that developmentally a child is still egocentric, especially when emotions are involved, and has trouble understanding another's point of view.

Another example

Julie, aged 3½, was brought in by her mother because Julie cried and screamed each time Mom left for her job as a flight attendant. She had not done this before and Carol, the mom, thought that maybe it was a new stage, but it was only getting worse. It happened when her husband was the caretaker or when the baby sitter, whom Julie adored, was taking care of her and her 2 older siblings. I asked Carol to describe in detail what was happening in the household just before she left. We sat on the floor and I made rooms out of blocks and used doll figures to act out the situation.

"Well, everyone gets up and we eat breakfast in the kitchen. (I moved the doll figures into the 'kitchen'). Then the older children get their books and stuff to go to school. They walk because the school is just down the street. Julie hugs them to say good-bye.

"Then we hug and I say good-bye and that's when Julie starts screaming and crying and pulling at me."

I got a car off the shelf and asked if she drove to the airport. Carol nodded. I asked Julie if it was OK for Carol to drive to the airport in the car (as I put the mother figure in the car.) Julie nodded. Then I took an airplane off the shelf, and as I started to put the figure on the plane, Julie started to whimper and said, "It's OK for mommy to go in the car, but not in the airplane." "Oh," I said, "the plane might crash!" "Yes!" Julie said vehemently.

There had been a plane crash some months before, and Julie probably heard her mother and father talking about it. In fact, Carol remembers talking about it with friends on the telephone but she never thought Julie was listening or aware. I told Carol that next time she had to leave for work to say to Julie something like, "I know you are afraid my plane will crash. I'm sorry you have to worry about me. I love you and will always love you no matter what happens." Carol could not tell Julie that the plane would not crash, since she had no way of actually knowing this. Carol did this and within two days, Julie stopped crying when Carol left. By the way, Julie was right in the room when I gave Carol the above instructions. I think that Julie needed to be heard—she felt heard in my office, and now she felt heard when her mother left for work.

Suggestions for parents and therapists

I often give suggestions to parents, though not too many at one time.

1. *Mad session*: This is one of the most successful techniques I know of. Build a "mad session" into the bedtime routine. The child tells you everything that made him mad that day or that he didn't like. There is no discussion—just active listening.

Recently a mother called me up to tell me that after she did a "mad session" with her 3-year-old child, her child threw her arms around her mother and said, "I love you, Mommy!" There actually is no age limit for the mad session.

2. *Give the child experience with some good power*: Allocate 15 or 20 minutes each day (or whatever your schedule will permit) to spend a very specific time with your child. Call it her time: Sara's time. During this time, the child has total power directing you to do something such as lying on the floor and colouring or moving cars around. This is not the same as spending time in other ways—this is a time when your child has total control and you hand over the power to her. If the child goes beyond acceptable boundaries, you come out of your role for the moment to advise her of this, and then go back into the role. It is best to use a kitchen timer to set the time limit.

Giving the child power and control is also a good technique in the therapeutic encounter. I have used this technique with children up to the age of 15 since children often regress in the therapist's office. The young adolescents know you will never tell anyone! (A 14-year-old girl loved to play "store" as soon as she felt sure I would never tell.)

We often plan our time together: "for 20 minutes we'll do something I want us to do and the rest of the time something you want us to do." The kitchen time is called into use.

3. *Don't ask too many questions*: Questions put children on the spot and they worry about giving the right answer. It is far more productive to make statements, as suggested to the father of the boy that stuttered.

Working with young children can be fun and rewarding. I generally don't see a child under four individually, preferring to work with the child and parents.

CHAPTER TEN

Working with groups

A therapy group has the advantage of being a small, insulated world in which present behaviour can be experienced and new behaviours tried out. The child's way of being in the group, and how that behaviour affects others positively or negatively, becomes clearly evident. The group becomes a safe laboratory for experimenting with new behaviours through the support and guidance of the therapist.

The group is an ideal setting for children to enhance their contact skills. Poor contact skills are an indication of a poor sense of self leading to poor social skills. It is natural—as well as being an important developmental task—for children to seek out other children. The group provides an arena for those who have social difficulties to discover and work through whatever is blocking the natural process of connecting and relating well with others. One's process in a group may be much different in a one-to-one therapy setting. When the behaviour becomes foregrounded, we can examine it from all sides, play with it, change it.

Jimmy, aged nine, was extremely disruptive in group meetings. Often group time was spent focusing on his unacceptable behaviour, with the group members offering varied suggestions to no avail.

I began to stop and look at what actually took place: Jimmy received all the attention he could muster—actually it seemed that he was getting exactly what he wanted and needed, regardless of the effect on the group.

At the next meeting I presented a scenario to be acted out by Jimmy and the group. I asked him to imagine that he was a new baby, perhaps the baby Jesus (it was close to Christmas), and the rest of us would be all the people who brought gifts to the baby. So with much giggling Jimmy lay on a mat spread out for him. I modelled bringing him an imaginary gift, talking with great emotion about what a beautiful baby this was and how glad we were that he was born. The other children followed suit, and many imaginary gifts were presented to the baby with much oohing and aahing over this baby. Jimmy lay quietly, with a big smile on his face during that time. Finally I called the group together and asked Jimmy to tell us how he liked our gifts and attention. He said he loved them, and the truth of this was evident from his smiling face and calm demeanour. He commented that he felt that he had been receiving real gifts! I wondered out loud if Jimmy felt a lack of attention in his life. Jimmy spoke with deep feeling about this lack, and there were many thoughtful comments from the other children about their own experiences with attention.

Following this session I made sure that I smiled and spoke to Jimmy as soon as he came into the room, as did the other children. Jimmy no longer created a disturbance at the group meetings. This kind of acting-out scenario allowed Jimmy to experience exaggerated positive attention. Though this was a play situation, the experience was quite real to him. Feeling safe and loved, Jimmy could talk about the polarity represented in his real life. Expressing his feelings and learning how to ask for what he needed in a direct manner were subsequent themes in the sessions. All the children could identify and benefit from these activities.

At another time I brought in a variety of small games—jacks, pick-up sticks, dominoes, *Blockhead, Connect-4*—to a group of eight children, ages eleven and twelve. The children were paired off and each pair was instructed to choose. (This task in itself was interesting to observe.) A kitchen timer was set for ten minutes. At the end of the time the children were asked to switch games and partners. All the games and partners were rotated. When all had had a turn with games and partners, the group talked about the experience. Here are some of the comments:

> "This is the first time I ever played jacks with a boy. I had to teach him how to do it. It was great!"
> "I think I was the first boy who probably ever played jacks. I liked it."
> "Chris cheated, but stopped when I told him I didn't like it."
> "Chris didn't cheat at all with me. He was fun to play with."

The general tone of the children was gentle and tolerant. An air of contentment and calmness permeated the room during and after the game period. There was a lot of noise, the kind of noise one hears when people talk with each other (Oaklander, 1988). It would have been hard to believe that each of these children had been referred to the group because of "poor social skills".

Projections often interfere with the child's ability to relate to other children. For example:

Philip: I don't like the way Allen is looking at me!
Therapist: What do you imagine he is saying to you with that look?
Phillip: He's saying, "You're stupid!"
Therapist: Pretend this monkey puppet is you and you are Allen and say those words to yourself. (*Therapist holds puppet in her hand.*)
Phillip: (*as Allen*): You're stupid!
Therapist: Phillip, do you have a voice inside of you that says this to yourself sometimes?
Phillip: Yeah!

Children need to learn that seeing a facial grimace is not the same as knowing the thoughts behind it. The other child might have a stomach-ache. Of course, projections are most active with children who have a low self-image and a fuzzy boundary. At another session I introduced what I call "self-nurturing" work. I asked the children to think about a part of themselves they don't like and to draw a picture of it. Phillip remembered the "stupid" incident, and drew a picture which he labelled "Mr. Stupid". "This is the part of me," Phillip said, "that is stupid—when I say and do stupid things." I asked Phillip to be Mr. Stupid and tell us about himself.

Phillip: I am so stupid! I do dumb things all the time. I'm really dumb. I don't know anything! I'm just plain stupid. Everyone thinks I'm stupid.

Therapist: How long have you been with Phillip, Mr. Stupid? (*Silence*.)

Therapist: Phillip, was Mr. Stupid with you when you were, say, 3 years old?

Phillip: I don't remember.

Therapist: How about four?

Phillip: Yeah. I remember in pre-school I felt stupid because I couldn't skip like the other kids.

Therapist: If you could go back in a time machine and talk to 4-year-old Phillip, what do you think you would say? (*I held up the picture that Phillip had drawn*.) "Here he is."

Phillip: Well, I guess I would say something like, hey, you're just a little kid. You're not stupid because you can't skip. You'll see, you'll be able to do it soon. Something like that.

Therapist: Phillip, this week, every time you think you said or did something stupid, I want you to remember that you are talking to that 4-year-old who lives inside of you and is the one that thinks you're stupid. See what happens.

All the children in this group seemed mesmerized by this encounter and then began to share their own memories of where the parts of themselves they didn't like came from. Of course these negative self-messages may have had deeper roots, but the children were learning how to be self-accepting and self-nurturing to those younger parts of self, which were so much part of their present lives.

Many activities to strengthen the self are effective in group settings, and actually are more fun and interesting to do with other children. Games involving the use of the eyes as I Spy (a UNICEF game) or the *Where's Waldo* books or listening games, such as Sound Safari, and games involving smelling, tasting and touching are pleasurable and productive.

Here's an example of an exercise that allows children to freely use all of their senses, a necessary prerequisite to owning the self.

Each member of a group was given an orange. They each examined their own oranges thoroughly, put them back in a pile and were able to find their own oranges again easily. We all began to peel the oranges and carefully examine the skin, smelling and tasting it.

Next the white part was peeled, smelled and tasted. After noticing and feeling the glistening layer, the oranges were broken into segments and tasted. Each child then traded segments with other children. They noticed that some were sweeter, some tarter, some juicier and so forth. All agreed that each segment was delicious, no matter what it was like (Brown, 1990). This exercise has been used with many different groups of all ages. One 12-year-old girl said to me, "I can never eat any fruit anymore without thinking of that orange exercise we did!"

Often sensory-type experiences encourage good social conversation in groups. Clay and finger painting are particularly good for this purpose.

A group of children in a special class for severely emotionally disturbed children were given old cafeteria trays on which were dabs of finger paint. Twelve boys, ages eleven to thirteen, made up this group. Their reaction to seeing the finger paint was, predictably enough, "What is this baby stuff?!" I felt that the boys needed to face each other rather than sit at their desks, and tables were set up so that there were six boys on each side facing the other. I hoped that they would find a new way to relate, other than hitting, punching, kicking and name calling. The boys were asked to finger paint in the trays and when ready, I would make a print of each painting by spreading paper over the painting, pressing down and lifting it off. I demonstrated the process, and each boy finished the first painting quickly and was delighted with the block print he had made.

Many of these children had difficulty with both small and large muscle coordination and usually shied away from drawing or brush painting. Finger painting is soothing and flowing, trial designs and figures can be made and quickly smoothed over, and success is guaranteed. During the activity the boys began to converse with each other, first about their designs and then about other things. One boy made something that looked like a bird, and the conversation began to focus on flying and airplanes. Many topics were discussed calmly and amicably. Yes, there was noise—but it was the noise of laughter, happiness and good talking. Not once did anyone hit, kick, or say anything abusive. Contentment permeated the whole group. These children often requested this finger-painting experience, and sometimes the therapist was able to elicit stories about their designs, promoting self-awareness and taking the experience into wider and deeper places. Most of these boys had not had the experience of making a friend, or, for that matter, of being treated or treating others respectfully, so this experience was particularly significant. The atmosphere during the finger paint sessions generalized to the rest of the class time, and although there certainly was occasional acting-out behaviour, the general milieu was one of respect and friendship.

Certain variables are present in this kind of experience. The therapist has set up clear limits and boundaries. She is at all times respectful of each child. The children are dealing with a medium that they soon discover can only lead to success. (The block prints were astounding.) They can experiment and explore colour and design. (They quickly discovered that red, yellow and blue make a murky brown.) There is a soothing quality to the kinaesthetic motions and tactile sensations. The self is strengthened and good contact takes place. And they find that they *like* this kind of contact and want more of it.

A common theme among children in therapy, and probably outside of therapy, is the feeling of being different. The child struggles to establish the self and moves back and forth from confluence to isolation. Confluence involves getting a sense of self from someone else—he must be like everyone else since he does not have a sense of who his is. Since healthy contact involves having a good sense of self and feeling enough support to be able to meet someone without losing the self, the disturbed child must often retreat to a very lonely place to perhaps find something of a self. The group is an ideal setting for helping children maintain their own integrity while relating to others. The group is a safe microcosm of the outside world, and with the guidance of the therapist, and clear boundaries, the child can indeed find himself among others.

A group of children, all with fathers in a military alcoholic treatment centre, were asked to share their dreams. This group of twelve children ranged from eight to sixteen and included several sets of siblings. At the time in question, this unorthodox group had been meeting for most of a year, and the members were quite comfortable with each other in spite of the age differences. They had discovered that they shared many common experiences. One girl, aged 12, described a dream in which she is in a car driven by her father going down a steep hill. At the bottom of the hill there is a lake. The car is going very fast and she is screaming at her father to slow down. She fears the car will go right into the lake. Her father ignores her, and just as the car is about to take its plunge, she wakes up. Generally, following the telling of the dream, I will ask the child to act out the dream as if it is happening and Sally pretended she was in the car screaming, "Daddy, stop! Stop!" The other children listened intently, and as soon as Sally stopped screaming, an 8-year-old boy said, "I have a road in my life just like that."

Discovering that other children have similar thoughts, concerns, worries, fears, ideas, wonders, as well as experiences, is a revelation to most children. The more they feel this linkage, the more support they appear to feel. The outside support strengthens their inner support and a stronger self develops. Paradoxically, they are then more willing and able to present those parts of themselves that are different to the group.

Several young adolescent boys were given clay and asked to make something with their eyes closed. The group had been meeting weekly for about two months and Joe had not participated in any of the activities. He was not disruptive and just sat quietly, appearing to listen and watch. I directed the boys to complete their pieces with their eyes open and each was asked to become the piece and describe themselves.

Joe:	I didn't make anything.
Therapist:	Joe, you have something there so just describe it.
Joe:	(*staring at the clay*) It's just a lump of nothing. (*Joe looked up at me*) And that's what I am! A lump of nothing!
Therapist:	How do you feel right now, Joe, in this group with all of us?
Joe:	I feel like a lump of nothing.
Therapist:	I think that what you're saying is that you feel like you're not worth much.
Joe:	That's right. I'm not.
Therapist:	Joe, I feel very appreciative of you for sharing how you feel with us. It shows that maybe you trust us a little. Thank you.
Joe:	(*slight smile*) That's OK.

What is evident here is Joe's low self-esteem, which he openly shared with the group. In doing so, in telling about his existence in life as he perceives it, he made a giant step toward renewed selfhood. I was tempted to tell Joe about his worthiness, but that would have invalidated his feeling at this moment. I wanted to respectfully accept Joe's self-perception so that he could begin to accept himself. Later I overheard one of the boys telling Joe how he used to feel the same way a lot, and sometimes still does, but not so much anymore.

Group process

A group, though made up of individual children, has a distinctive life of its own. Every group seems to follow more or less the same pattern. The children in the groups described above generally have had some individual experience with me, and a relationship has been established. However, the children do not know each other and come into the group usually feeling very much alone. In the beginning the child is self-conscious and may tend to manifest a variety of negative behaviours to cover up his or her anxieties. I need to make use of this time to help the children feel safe and respected and to get to know each other through non-invasive, non-threatening activities. Limits and boundaries are clarified as needed.

After about four to six weeks with a group that meets weekly, the group begins to gel; children feel comfortable in the setting, and anxieties about sharing themselves below that superficial veneer drop away. There is generally a feeling of companionship with each other and a knowledge that the others will provide support and understanding when needed. Roles emerge: one child becomes the leader, another appears to act out for everyone, one is labelled as the smart one, another the clown and so on. As these roles become evident, I can bring them into the awareness of the group through various techniques. And sometimes the children themselves invent ideas for experimenting with roles.

A group of eight boys and girls, ages eleven and twelve, had been meeting together weekly for several months. They knew each other quite well. Susan clearly emerged as the leader. At one session I presented an exercise that I hoped would promote direct communication called "I like, I don't like." Each child had a turn to make statements to everyone else. One member said to Susan, "I don't like it that you always decide what we should do." At the end of the exercise the discussion was open for reaction. Susan said, "I know what we should do. Let's have each person be the therapist for one meeting and decide everything." The children liked Susan's idea—actually she had many good ones. So each week for a while a child decided whether we should draw pictures relating to a theme of some sort, use puppets or clay, have a discussion about something, or engage in another activity. The child who was the "therapist" not only decided what the group would do but modelled me amazingly accurately. All had turns to be leader, often finding a side of themselves that had never before been presented openly.

Group structure

I have experimented with a variety of group sizes, from pairs to groups of twelve. Generally I find that six or eight children who are over 8 years old is a good size, and three to six children for those under 8. I had an interesting experience with the forming of pairs—two children together. I had finished writing *Windows To Our Children* and went back to work. I had closed my office for the last year to concentrate on writing and when I began to see clients, I took everyone and anyone who wanted to come in since I was at this point deeply in debt. However, I ran out of available times to see children. I remembered a story that Virginia Satir told at a workshop I attended. One day, the story goes, she accidentally double booked two families. When she opened the door to the waiting room and saw them, she was startled. Composing herself, she invited both families to come into her office for what became known as multiple family therapy. So I began to put two children, generally of the same sex and age, together. I remember two 7-year-old boys who had great difficulty getting along with other children in their lives. In the first four sessions, each boy tried very, very hard to be accommodating and friendly. Then these efforts wore thin, and each boy's particular way of relating that generally caused difficulty, became evident. It was now possible for me to stop whatever was happening to focus on the specific behaviour and the feelings underneath it. I had seen each of these boys individually before I "paired" them and had never seen the behaviour that presented itself when they were together. It seemed that this experience was a good prelude to becoming part of a larger group. I know I would not have had the time to give them this kind of attention in a larger group.

It is important to have a co-therapist present in a group if at all possible, since there may be times when a child must have individual attention. The group basically is an ideal setting for children who need connection with other children.

Some groups can be time-limited rather than ongoing, especially groups that are set up for children who have had similar experiences, as victims of child abuse or divorce. Sometimes such groups tend to label the children and set them apart from other children. Children who have been abused, for example, have wider interests and life problems than just the abuse, and these need to be addressed as well.

The groups, which generally meet for one and a half to two hours, depending on the ages of the children, are fairly structured. Each group begins with "rounds"—a time when each child reports anything they choose to share about their week. This in itself becomes a lesson in listening. In the beginning children may be reluctant to say much, but as the weeks go by it becomes necessary to set a time limit for each child. There can be no discussion or questions (except for occasional clarification)—the child has the floor.

Both therapists participate as well. Passing around something that represents a "talking stick" is helpful. Of course, some children cannot help making remarks, poking others, wiggling and so forth. As long as these noises are in the background and the child who is speaking appears not to be disturbed, I have learned to ignore them. It appears that children can tolerate much more commotion than adults can. However, if the hubbub becomes disruptive and disturbing, I will call a halt and the matter is discussed with the group. In effect, this becomes the group's business for a portion of the session. Toward the end of the session, the children clean up and take their seats around the room once more. This is a time for closure: everyone is given the opportunity to say anything they would like to say to me or to anyone else in the room, to critique the activity, to mention something they particularly liked during the time, or something that annoyed them. I must pace the group session to allow time for clean up and closure.

At the closing time of a group 11-year-old Carrie, with much hesitation and caution, told Tommy, "I didn't like it that you always tried to sit next to me today, and when you did, it was too close and I didn't like it." I reinforced Carrie's effort to tell Tommy about her discomfort and said, "Tommy, I'm glad you are listening to Carrie; what she is saying is very important to her." At the next meeting's closure Carrie said, "Tommy, I really appreciate that you didn't try to sit next to me all the time, and when you did, you weren't too close." Tommy smiled as if he had received a great gift.

Group content

The content of the group varies, of course, according to the age range and the specific needs of the children. Unless the purpose is to observe free play, the group is structured. It begins with rounds and ends with closure. In between I plan the experience for the meeting. Although I may have goals and plans, they can be discarded at any time. Sometimes something emerges from the rounds that needs attention; sometimes the children make an alternative decision. Often the session evolves from a prior session.

The activities are varied and generally enjoyable. Basically they facilitate expression of feelings and defining and strengthening the self. Many projective techniques are used, such as drawings, collage, clay, sand tray scenes, puppetry, music, body movement, creative dramatics, metaphorical stories, fantasy and imagery. Often themes of relevance to the children are presented, such as loneliness, teasing, rejection, embarrassment, loss, divorce and so forth. These themes often emerge during group sessions or are suggested by the children themselves. Many games are used as well as projective tests as therapeutic vehicles. At one session the children may draw their safe place and share their efforts with each other. I may at times focus on one particular child's drawing. The children rarely make fun of any-one's drawing—my attitude of respect for each effort sets the tone.

An important theme in almost every group is anger. Children may be asked to draw something that makes them angry, or make a figure out of clay representing someone they are mad at, or play a variety of percussion instruments representing their feelings, or put on a puppet show for the others depicting an angry scene and much more. Gaining skills for expressing angry feelings safely and appropriately is an important aspect of these activities. There is more discussion and examples around the issue of anger in Chapter 5.

One day I brought in a video camera thinking that I would videotape some of the sessions. The children, however, had other ideas, and it became a wonderful therapeutic tool. Sam, aged 14, has a friend his parents do not approve of. Recently Sam invited this boy into his house, ignoring his parents' rule of not having friends in the house when they weren't home. As Sam stood by helplessly, the boy went into the parents' bedroom and threw things around as he examined everything. Sam had been working hard to feel a stronger sense of self and stand up for himself; however, he totally capitulated with this boy. Since he was in great trouble with his parents over this incident, I made it a central theme of one of our group sessions. I suggested that the group act out the event in front of the video camera. Sam selected someone to play the part of the unruly boy while Sam played himself, and with the camera rolling they proceeded to act out the event. I encouraged exaggeration in order to make the situation more obvious. With great energy, the "bad" boy knocked on the door, entered the house, and proceeded to trash the place, describing loudly what he was doing. Sam meekly stood by trying to protest. When the scene ended, I suggested that they try another one in which Sam would act in an opposite way. In this scene Sam loudly admonished the other boy, and forced him to leave the house. At the suggestion of one of the group members, a third scene showed Sam's mother (the children all insisted that I play this role since this was an all-boy group) returning home and showing that she is thrilled and proud that Sam has obeyed the rules. The group immediately viewed the whole enactment on the monitor to much laughter. Sam announced he knew that he could be assertive with that boy if it happened again and, in fact, wondered out loud why he had ever befriended him at all. A lively discussion ensued.

Working with groups is a gratifying, effective way to work with children. The group lends itself to the development of social skills, a feeling of belonging and acceptance, a place to express heretofore unexpressed feelings and a place to experiment with new behaviours. A successful group is one in which each child feels safe to be vulnerable. Group sessions need to be enjoyable for the children, regardless of the subject matter. In fact the enjoyment and nurturing that the children feel in a group actually encourage delving into painful places. As the children feel free to reveal their emotions, thoughts, opinions and ideas, they know that they will find support from and connection with the therapist and the other children. In this way each child makes discoveries about the self that lead to increased self-support and healthy contact in and out of the group.

CHAPTER ELEVEN

Treating children with symptoms of attention deficit hyperactive disorder

A t the numerous workshops that I have given, attention deficit with or without hyperactivity is often the subject of many of the questions I am asked. There is much written and talked about relating to this disorder, but very little of it discusses treatment, other than medication and management of behaviour. Although medication is often prescribed, there is actually no definitive test for this disorder. Judgment is based on a variety of behaviours. The DSM-IV (which is the diagnostic and statistical *Manual of Mental Disorders*, of the American Psychiatric Association and widely used by physicians, psychologists, social workers and counsellors, 1994), lists numerous behaviours, six of which in two categories must be present for at least six months to qualify for this diagnosis. Further, they must be present to a degree that is mal-adaptive and inconsistent with developmental level. The criterion should be considered only if the behaviour is considerably more frequent than that of most people of the same mental age. In other words, all children will show signs of these behaviours at one time or another—therefore, judgment can be fairly subjective. These behaviours are:

Inattention

1. Often fails to give close attention to details or makes careless mistakes in schoolwork, work, or other activities.
2. Often has difficulty sustaining attention in tasks or play activities.
3. Often does not seem to listen when spoken to directly.
4. Often does not follow through on instructions and fails to finish schoolwork, chores or duties.
5. Often has difficulty organizing tasks and activities.
6. Often avoids, dislikes, or is reluctant to engage in tasks that require sustained mental effort.
7. Often loses things necessary for tasks or activities.
8. Is easily distracted by extraneous stimuli.
9. Is often forgetful in daily activities.

Hyperactivity-impulsivity

1. Often fidgets with hands or feet or squirms in seat.
2. Often leaves seat in classroom or in other situations in which remaining seated is expected.
3. Often runs about or climbs excessively in situations in which it is inappropriate.
4. Often has difficulty in playing or engaging in leisure activities quietly.
5. Is often "on the go" or often acts as if "driven by a motor".
6. Often talks excessively.
7. Often blurts out answers before questions have been completed.
8. Often has difficulty awaiting turn.
9. Often interrupts or intrudes on others (e.g., butts into conversations or games).

Research indicates that 4 per cent of all school-age children meet these diagnostic criteria. Since the popularization of this disorder, it seems that a much great percentage of that 4 per cent are granted this label. This disorder was first described in the early 1900s as restlessness and has gone through several name changes such as: Minimal Brain Dysfunction, Hyperactive Child

Syndrome, Attention Deficit Hyperactive Disorder With or Without Hyperactivity and now Attention Deficit Hyperactive Disorder (or ADHD).

There is much controversy over the use of stimulant medication. There is some research being done about this, but still not a lot is known, at least not by the consumer. Some children appear to respond to medication. About 35 years ago, in a class I was teaching of severely emotionally disturbed children, I remember one boy who was unable to sit still long enough to learn to read. He was put on medication (Ritalin) and the results were close to miraculous. I found this to be the exception, however. I think some physicians are too quick to recommend medication. And many teachers push for it. Little is known about the long term results of these drugs.

I recognize two kinds of groups of children who present the symptoms of this disorder.

One group are children who manifest the behaviours early on in life, perhaps from birth. Some research now indicates that true ADHD begins very early—certainly by age 3 or 4—and often at birth. No one as yet has come up with the cause of this disorder. Perhaps it is genetic, or has some neuro-biological basis. Perhaps there is an immature nervous system due to some trauma that may have occurred *in utero* or at birth. Perhaps the child has some sensitivity to food he or she is given. Or consider the fact that environmental toxins may be at fault, or even fluorescent lighting. No one knows as yet.

Another group are those children who begin to show signs of ADHD behaviour later than age 3 or 4, particularly around 5 or 6 when they begin formal schooling. Some children even begin to show some of these behaviours later than that. Although these children are often given the ADHD label, I believe there are emotional and psychological causes for their behaviours.

From a Gestalt Therapy perspective I see this disorder as a contact-boundary problem—that is, an inability to sustain contact with someone or something, as well as an impairment in the sense of self. The ME must be intact for healthy interaction with the environment.

There are great implications for treatment with this view. If a child has a faulty sense of self, much can be done to help the child renew, regain and strengthen that self.

Another aspect to be considered in treatment planning is that the symptoms of ADHD can be seen as deflections, defenses, or avoidances of emotions. In fact there was a time when hyperactivity was regarded as a symptom of childhood depression, and some forms of depression can be seen as withheld feelings, particularly anger.

To further complicate the situation, children who manifest these behaviours, whether they have exhibited them early on or somewhat later in their childhood lives, and regardless of the etiology, receive a great deal of negative reaction. These negative reactions exacerbate the child's bad feeling of self. Since developmentally children are confluent—get their sense of self from the other—and have fuzzy boundaries, the symptoms are often accelerated due to these negative responses from others. Children struggle for separation, a sense of self, a definition of boundaries right from the beginning of their lives in their quest for health and maturity. Since their selves are already repressed, they accelerate their inappropriate behaviours in the service of this quest, not having the cognitive and emotional maturity to understand what's happening. Further, because children are developmentally egocentric and take responsibility for everything that happens, they blame themselves for the negative responses they experience, and feel powerless, helpless to change. Again that thrust for life pushes them on to find ways to feel some power. This is probably why so many of these children—perhaps 40 per cent—exhibit conduct disorder behaviours as well.

Preliminary to treatment comes assessment. In spite of common symptoms, each child is unique with his or her own life experiences and family dynamic. I do take a careful history to get a sense of the child's life. In that first session with child and parent, I direct most of my questions to the child. How do you sleep—do you have bad dreams? What kind of food do you like best? Parents are welcome to give their input to any of the questions (and some, of course, I need to ask the parent directly). I am interested in the child's sleep patterns, diet (I do believe that a child's diet can affect behaviour—it certainly does mine), health history, relationships with peers, family situation, school life, early development, losses, trauma and so forth.

After that first session, I will spend about four evaluative sessions. I don't use formal testing procedures. My evaluation is based on observation and my experience with the child. I am interested in the child's ability to sustain contact and his use of contact skills, as listening, seeing, touching, talking. I assess the child's energy and aliveness level: does there appear to be involvement, interest, animation, excitement—or is there a lack of these? Is the child's voice expressive or flat, audible or whispery? I pay attention to the child's body—how she walks, stands, sits, her posture and how she generally moves in the environment. Does the body appear to be restricted or flexible? I am interested in the child's resistance level and how he manifests it. These are some of the areas I look at along with the child's affect, ability to understand and express emotions, general cognitive abilities and general presentation. I need to know these things in order to determine the kinds of experiences I may need to offer the child in our sessions together.

The relationship between me and the child is the most important element throughout our work together, and in those first few sessions, I am most aware of this. In order to build this relationship I must meet the child wherever he or she is developmentally and behaviourally. I cannot expect the child to be someone he isn't. I have a responsibility to be fully present and contactful, even if the child is not. I will respect and honour this child and I will be my authentic self when I am with him. I respect my own boundaries and do not lose the sense of Myself in our meetings together. I believe that this kind of relationship is the very essence of all therapy. Even though these first few sessions are evaluative, they are therapeutic as well.

Before I discuss some specific treatment approaches, I'd like to say something about the issue of stimulation. When I worked in the schools with very disturbed children, many of whom were extremely hyperactive—literally climbing the walls—the popular conception at that time was that these children functioned best in bland, non-stimulating environments. Children were actually placed in cubicles so that there would be no distractions while they did their school work. This idea went so much against my grain and my life style that it was impossible for me to abide by this rule. And I didn't. My classroom was *filled* with stimulation. There were bright colours everywhere: posters, mobiles, interesting centres of activity. I never had a problem with this, and in fact it seemed to me that all these interesting, wonderful things in the room actually helped the children to focus! If I brought in something new, the twelve children—mostly boys—would gather around with focused involvement as we examined and talked about whatever it was. After that I would often see a child glance up from whatever he was doing to look at it with pleasure, evident by the smile on his face. I noticed, too, that when an airplane flew by, several children would rush to the window, leaving their work, and I would rush to the window too, calling the other children to join us. We would look at the plane, say some things about it and everyone would happily and calmly return to their tasks. I learned that when we focused on the so-called distraction, the children were extremely contactful, and appeared to be calm and satisfied for a time afterwards.

Some research indicates that stimulation actually improves the performance of ADHD children. They need variability, colour, novelty. Distractibility is not a major problem with these children, and in fact, a boring environment, with no distraction, appears to promote problems. Children will find ways to create their own stimulation in these cases. Of course, all children respond best to things that are colourful, interesting, novel—and ADHD children even more so. This discovery sends a strong message to schools. Needless to say, my office is a friendly, comfortable, colourful, interesting place.

I have found, however, that structure is important. ADHD children have very fuzzy boundaries and difficulty following rules. Of course the clearer my own boundaries and limits are to me, the easier it is for me to set these limits with children. Back in the classroom we had structure, though not rigid and inflexible. We had a time for work and time for play and so forth. In my office, we have a set time for our sessions and certain things we can or cannot do. We don't go in and out of the room. All the children help me clean up before they leave, and I pace the sessions to make sure there is time for this. We put one thing away before we start another. We don't flick paint around the room, and my desk is off limits. Of course not everyone abides by these rules at first. I patiently repeat them as necessary and soon they become natural to our sessions. Some of my time is spent encouraging parents to set up structure and limits for children. Children become anxious in an environment where there is no structure and no clear limits, and in a search for relief of this anxiety, tend to act out.

As the relationship develops I pay attention to the contact level of the child. If he has difficulty sustaining contact—being fully present and involved with me for some activity—helping the child sustain contact becomes my focus. Children who are ADHD do not generally sustain contact. At the first session with Billy, age 8 and his parents, Billy did not sit still for a moment. He sometimes answered some of my intake questions, but mostly sat in a chair I have that turns and rocks at the same time. Billy loved this chair. At our first session alone, he ran from one thing to another, picking something up, throwing it down. I followed after him picking each thing up and telling him the rule of putting things back before he went on to something else. Of course he ignored me as I put each item back. He never stayed with anything longer than a few seconds. There was no contact with anything or with me. It was important for me to maintain a stance of genuine acceptability of Billy's behaviour. I smiled, spoke about the rules casually, though firmly, made brief comments about objects he had picked up, even though he had already run off to the next thing. I made every effort to join him but he made none to join with me. At the end of the session, Billy had trouble leaving the room and I gently and firmly moved him into the waiting room where his Mom sat as he yelled and whined the whole time. It would appear that he was the same at the next session, but actually he wasn't. When he picked up a puppet I quickly picked another one and said "hello" to his puppet just as I had attempted to do the previous week. This time, however, there was a slight hesitation on Billy's part before he threw it down and ran off to grab something else. My goal was to make contact with him and to help him maintain contact with something. Sitting back and watching him run around would not have been productive. The involvement and interaction of the therapist with the child, along with a non-judgmental and accepting attitude, is an essential, vital aspect of working with ADHD children. Progress may seem to be very slow, if evident at all. I can't emphasize enough how important it is to be aware of mini seconds of change. Think of it as a sort of *Where's Waldo?* (Handford, 1987) picture where you need to observe with full attention to what is going on. The very slightest change is progress. By the fourth session Billy was able to engage with me, particularly with puppets, for a few moments. I could sense his contact with me and with the puppets.

At the sixth session a most amazing thing happened. Billy went back to the basket of musical instruments, which he had discovered and examined quickly at a previous session. He spent the *entire* session experimenting with the instruments and participated in the basic music process (described in Chapter 12) with me. This music process has been one of the most useful activities in my work with ADHD children. It involves a great deal of contact with me, is enjoyable, interesting, varied and provides a good feeling of mastery for the child. By this time, too, I believe that Billy felt trusting enough of me to stay involved. Billy continued to have difficulty letting go of the room, and sometimes me, at the end of each session. I would firmly and gently tell him that the time was over, and move with my arms around his shoulders to the waiting room and his parent. After two months, this was no longer a problem.

I am well aware that ADHD children do best in one-to-one situations, where they have the total attention of the adult. Some parents and teachers have voiced resentment at this. "Of course he's great with you—all you have to do is be with him." The resentment dissipates when I explain that this is the reason psychotherapy is special. I can take advantage of this kind of interaction to help the child develop healthy boundaries and a strong sense of self that will make it possible for him to function well in the outside world. It is BECAUSE of the kind of time that we have together that this can happen. The experiences the child can have with me are unlike any he may have elsewhere. Experience is everything in work with children. We must never minimize this.

Sensory work in an important aspect in building the self. I want to help children own their own senses: looking, listening, touching, tasting, smelling. Back in the classroom those many years ago, twelve extremely disturbed and hyperactive boys, ages 11, 12 and 13, spent many an hour standing calmly around a table finger painting. The slippery feel of the paint was delightful to the children, and as we painted (yes, I did too), the children held wonderful conversations with each other, shared thoughts, opinions, ideas and expressed locked up feelings of anger and sadness. Wet pottery clay was a big favourite too. Many of these children had not had much opportunity to experience activities natural to the development of young children. It is never too late to provide these experiences. Various sensory activities can be found in activity books for very young children, and some are described in my book, *Windows To Our*

Children. Billy did not like clay, but he did finger paint; he loved smelling, touching, tasting the orange segments in the orange exercise described earlier; painted while listening to music; and spent one whole session gazing at various things in my office through a kaleidoscope with great excitement. The kaleidoscope was sitting on the small table in front of the couch when he came in. Quick to notice anything different, he grabbed it and yelled, "What's this?" I suggested he look through it and see. The best thing that happened was that he wanted me to look through it too at every new thing he discovered. There was real contact here.

Hyperactive children may seem to use their bodies a great deal, but it is done in aimless, abandoned ways. They have a poor body image, a lack of control of body movements, an unclear sense of their body boundaries. So providing various body experiences is essential. The therapist must be creative, depending on the space available. I have asked a child to show me the different ways he can fall onto several pillows. Sometimes I have tried some of the easier ways to see what it feels like. Lots of body control is needed to do this, I found. Creative dramatics, particularly pantomime, is an excellent way to use the body. Acting out things we can do with fingers (and guessing what they are), arms, heads, feet and so forth. Acting out sports and games, various animals and specific situations, are fun. I can assure you, from my own experience with these exercises, that one becomes very much attuned to the body, *aware* of the body when attempting to get a message across without words. Billy loved to act out entire scenarios (with words) that he would develop and direct. Sometimes I would bring in some objects: a felt hat, a belt and anything else that struck my fancy, and present them to him and say, "Let's do a play." Billy loved making up a play using these objects. He would often include something from the office—a pair of play handcuffs were his favourite. I would be the robber and he would capture me, or sometimes he would direct me to be the capturer. In any case there was purposeful, controlled movement just as there would be on a real stage. He would, for example, say, "No, your stand there and I'll hide here and you won't know it, and then I'll jump out and capture you." Sometimes we would have a fight with Batacas, which are sturdy foam bats, within a small space with very specific rules (start and stop when I make a bell sound, no head or front of the body hitting). Sometimes we would fight pretending to be uncooked spaghetti, and then cooked spaghetti, or two 100-year-old people, or a king and a queen, etc.

The breath is important too. Blowing up balloons, keeping them in the air with our breath, having a contest when doing this is a popular activity. It is my belief that ADHD children, as well as children who are anxious and fearful, do not breathe well. Full, healthy breathing is calming and soothing. Relaxation exercises that use imagery are very helpful as well. Most of these children are not very relaxed. Their muscles are tense and tight and much restriction is taking place within the body. Many of the ADHD children I have worked with love the martial arts and I certainly recommend such classes if at all possible. There are some interesting Aikido exercises I have used with children right in my office.

I have recently become interested in the Feldenkrais Method (Shafarman, 1997), developed by the late Moshe Feldenkrais, an Israeli neurophysiologist. This is a gentle, hands-on method of helping people with a variety of physical pain and disorders, as well as body reactions to life stresses, to feel healthy and whole and comfortable. Many Feldenkrais practitioners work with children with impressive results. I believe that ADHD children would greatly benefit from this experience.

There are many mind/body therapies that can benefit these children as well which parents can learn such as Energy Field Therapy (Arenson, 2001), which involves tapping certain acupressure points, and brushing, a sensory activity developed by Jean Ayres (Ayres, 1995). Both of these therapies are easy to do and very effective.

Biofeedback has been used by some practitioners with ADHD children with impressive results.

As the child begins to know herself through sensory and body experiences, her very being begins to strengthen. We continue to find approaches to give the child ways to define her boundaries and feel her own self-support.

I want to emphasize the importance of giving children the opportunity to make choices. All children need this experience and ADHD children even more so. In our enthusiasm to create limits and structure and routine and order in the lives of these children, we often neglect to give them enough practice with the strengthening process of making choices. To make a choice is to exercise one's will and judgment. It requires one to tune into the feeling and thinking functions, and even the intuitive sense. Taking responsibility for one's choice is a learning experience. I have watched the most fidgety, restless, spaced out child stand forever, it seems, in front of a pile of construction paper of varied colours making her choice of the three colours she has been told to choose. One can almost see the brain moving and churning within this child's head as she contemplates the papers, becoming stronger through this exercise. Often she may be worried that she will make the wrong choice, that she will be sorry for her choice. She may rather that I hand her three colours so that she can blame me if they turn out to be wrong for her project. As she develops a stronger self in our work together, choices become easier to make. She can begin to say internally, "I want this one. I like this one. No, I don't want that one." To be able to make these statements implies security of self, a strength of being. I give children choices whenever possible, and encourage parents to do so. I put out various art materials to choose from: crayons, markers, pastels, coloured pencils, ordinary pencils, as well as varying sizes of paper. I may say, "Do you want to work with clay today or would you rather make a scene in the sand with these miniature objects?" Sometimes a child will stand still, quietly for several minutes before deciding. If he is very insecure and unsure, he may say, "I don't know" or "whatever you want me to do." If his energy is fading, I will make a suggestion. If he says, "I don't want to do any of those" I will certainly reinforce this direct statement. I may say, "OK, choose something you would like to do."

We sometimes play a game that involves making a statement about the self, followed by signifying if it is true or false. I can give the child the statement and she can then give me one, for example, "You like the colour grey". The child must repeat the statement as "I like the colour grey. Mmmm. False" and so forth. We talk about how she knew that it was false—where was the clue in her body. Sometimes we use objects real or imaginary: "I would like to have a big, colour TV for my very own. (*Pause*) True!" The rule is that we have to close our eyes and wait a few seconds before answering. "I would like to go to bed early every night and never watch TV. (*Pause*) False!" This exercise has many variations and can help children to tune into that "intuitive" part of the self, messages given by one's body. Try it yourself. Imagine you had to divide up everything in your house with someone else. Imagine picking up each object and saying, "I want this—true or false." It's amazing how the body will send messages to let us know what to choose. Remember to pay attention to the body signal and not to use rational and argumentative thinking.

To repeat, experiences in making choices reinforce the child's selfhood. Many of the things we do together strengthen the sense of self—an important requirement for ADHD children. It bears repeating that the relationship itself is a factor.

I do not play a role (except within the context of our games)—I am my authentic self. I do not manipulate. I meet the child with honour and respect. I maintain my own integrity. I enforce rules and limits natural to the setting in which we are working in a gentle, clear, firm manner. As the child improves in contact skills, the self is enhanced. Looking, listening, touching, smelling, tasting, moving, making statements, expressing emotions, are all functions of contact. Most ADHD children are cut off, restricted, inhibited, blocked, interrupted in one, more, or all of these functions. As the child feels more of herself through experiences with her contact functions, as she feels the trust and strength to stay present and involved with me and whatever we are doing, her self is strengthened.

Providing opportunities for children to make many statements about the self, sharing thoughts, opinions, ideas, imaginings—are self-supporting. There are numerous games available to make this easy and fun to do. Helping children feel mastery is important. Most ADHD children, as well as those who have experienced trauma or have lived in dysfunctional families, often do not have the opportunity to gain the mastery they need at each developmental level. When we think of mastery, we often think of great accomplishments. This is not the kind of mastery I mean. Each small achievement is a building block for the child's sense of self. When the baby feeds himself or drinks from a glass by himself, this is mastery. When he figures out which cube fits into the other cube, this is mastery. Each developmental level has its own areas of mastery. Sometimes we need to go back and give children the experiences they may have missed—as playing we're babies and crawling around, for example. Billy, mentioned previously, spent time at a few sessions, washing the clay tools and dishes we had used, with energy and delight. Another child worked at cleaning the clay table and made it cleaner than it had ever been. Others like to figure out a new game, or how to make a bird look like it's flying in the sand tray. The mastery experiences are often inherent in whatever activities we are engaged in and sometimes I need to introduce them.

Feeling some power and control gives a child a feeling of mastery. When children are so contactful that they begin to organize the session and take control, I know we are making great progress. This control is important and of course always must be within the limits and boundaries of what is appropriate.

Another way of helping children gain a strong feeling of self is through experiences with their own aggressive energy in safe, positive ways. ADHD children are confused by this energy, since it so often is manifested by acts of aggression, which only gets them into trouble. Those children who are timid, fearful and withdrawn have little access to this energy and that wonderful feeling of power within is either repressed or lost. This kind of energy needs to be celebrated. I provide a variety of experiences for children to feel and express their power in safe, permissive, fun ways. Pounding clay as hard as we can with a rubber mallet, having Bataca fights with each other, developing a story in which the puppets attack each other, serve this purpose. I have a number of games that involve hitting or smashing something. What is important in these activities is our interaction. The child needs to know that I enter into this play with him and that it is permissible. Boundaries and limits are clearly set. Repressed children gradually find their power, and out-of-bounds children can revel in this energy that can be controlled and used safely. In both cases there is a strong feeling of self. There are four requirements for the therapeutic use of aggressive energy:

1. it must be experienced in contact with the therapist;
2. it must take place in a safe container (the therapist's office) with clear boundaries;
3. the aggressive energy is exaggerated; and
4. it must be fun.

Ten-year-old Julie's process was to space out, showing marked attention deficit. This is quite typical of a child, as Julie, who had been severely sexually abused for several years by her stepfather.

Spacing out was her *modus operandi* in life, particularly in situations she found stressful, as school. Julie was diagnosed with ADHD though medication had no effect. This does not surprise me since there were clear emotional reasons for Julie to be inattentive. I think the turning point in our work together came when we began to focus on accessing aggressive energy. Julie was timid and fearful of this kind of activity, but in the arena of imaginary fun was soon able to allow herself to become involved. I remember asking her to pick up a puppet she liked, and characteristically she chose a cute little kitten. I picked a large alligator with a big mouth and sharp-looking teeth. She was a bit taken aback by this. I said in my most growly voice, "Hello kitten. I am very hungry and you look good enough to eat." Julie began to back away with her kitten. "You can't get away from me," the alligator said, "I'm going to eat you up. But *you better not hit me!*" The alligator yelled this several times as it came very close to the kitten. Julie then had her kitten tentatively touch the alligator with a paw. "Oh! You hit me! You hit me! I told you not to hit me!" yelled the alligator as it fell to the floor. Julie responded with "Do that again! Do that again!" This is a phrase I hear over and over from many children when I use a similar scenario. We re-enacted the scene several times at her request—all tentativeness gone. In fact a whole story developed out of this beginning, with other bad puppets slain by the kitten. This kind of support helped Julie confront a clay figure of her stepfather—something she had never been willing to do before. As her feelings emerged, Julie's ADHD symptoms disappeared.

I have had this kind of experience with children many times. As indicated previously, many children, particularly those who manifest ADHD symptoms after the age of 4, are sometimes simply avoiding feelings that are painful, or too overwhelming and confusing to face. A child who is unable (or unwilling) to express held-in feelings certainly may have trouble sitting still, paying attention, focusing. I know that when I am upset or angry about something, and not dealing with whatever it is, not even always knowing what it is, I become hyper, have trouble settling down, forget things, lose things. Finally, at some point, I will force myself to focus on whatever I'm feeling. Sometimes tears come. Sometimes I need to pound a pillow. Sometimes I write what comes up for me. Sometimes I talk to someone about whatever it is. In any case, clarity comes and I feel much better. Children do not have the cognitive and emotional ability to engage in this kind of self-reflection. Anxious children will have a fear of getting involved in any kind of activity—making real contact. They will constantly move from one thing to another, and are unable to give their full attention to anything. Children who are fearful, angry, grieved, or anxious will often have all or many of the symptoms of ADHD.

Some years ago a 12-year-old boy was brought into my office because of his severely hyperactive behaviour. His parents felt that he had been that way as long as they could remember and that it was accelerating. They had tried medication but it hadn't helped. All of his teachers were upset; the parents were upset. Bringing him into therapy was not to their liking but they thought they would try it as a last resort. While taking the history, I learned that Jeff, at age 7, had been in a serious automobile accident along with his mother, who was killed. Jeff recovered and after some hospitalization time, went to live with his father and step-mother. (His parents had divorced when he was very young.) When I asked his parents how they handled the situation, the exclaimed, "We wanted him to forget it as much as possible and start a new life. No use looking back." Jeff's father thought that Jeff had shown hyperactive symptoms well before the accident, but wasn't too sure. "He was always an active kid," he said. Even though Jeff was definitely evidencing hyperactive behaviour after the accident, his parents never connected it to the trauma.

When I asked Jeff to tell me about the automobile accident he told me that he had no memory of it. Nor could he remember much of his life with his mother. In fact, he hardly remembered what his mother looked like.

Jeff and I spent many sessions devoted to sensory and body awareness. He drew some pictures, worked with clay, made scenes in the sand. He enjoyed these activities and actually was never hyperactive in my office. His work was fairly superficial. I don't mean this as a judgment; I merely want to point out the fact that we never went very deep into Jeff's inner self and feelings. He would only go so far, and then he would shut down. Then, one day, after nine months together, Jeff had a dream about his mother. (I encourage children to try and remember their dreams.) Jeff drew a picture of the dream (sometimes I have the child make a scene from the dream out of clay), and we worked with it. After this work, the floodgates of his memory opened. He remembered everything. He drew pictures of the accident. He painted the blood at the accident scene. He drew pictures of the hospital and his house before going to live with his father. He drew pictures of his mother and some of the things he remembered that they did together. He talked to a clay figure of his mother, expressing his grief and also his anger that she had left him. This did not happen all at once, but over a series of sessions. Sometimes we just played some games together. Children do not have enough support to keep the momentum going in a situation like this, and need time to hang back and assimilate what has emerged. This is not resistance in the sense of closing down. After a while I would gently and casually bring the subject back to his trauma. Of course there were many other issues to deal with, some with his family. Jeff felt, deep down, that he was a very bad kid. First of all, he blamed himself for the accident and his mother's death, as children will. Secondly, he had received much negative reaction to his hyperactivity. And his step-mother was not, at first, too eager to have a new son full time. She had two other children of her own that complicated matters.

As Jeff opened himself to the deeper places within himself, his behaviour totally changed. He no longer showed ADHD symptoms, began to do well in school and at home. Occasionally he would space out or become hyper once more, and he learned that he did this to cover his feelings about something happening in his life. Knowing this, he could choose a safe mode of expressing those feelings.

An 11-year-old girl was referred to therapy because of severe "spacing out" behaviour. Cathy was inattentive in class at school, she often forgot to bring home her homework and she frequently lost things. Since she was falling behind in her schoolwork, the child's teacher recommended that she be taken to a physician so that she could receive medication. The parents decided to consult with me first. Certainly it was advisable to make sure Cathy was in good health, but I urged the parents to hold off giving her any medication at this time. The history of the child pointed to the fact that she was probably reacting to the stresses of her life. Her parents divorced when she was around 5 years old. Her mother and father each remarried. Her mother gave birth to another child. She spent one week with her Mom and one week with her Dad in a joint custody arrangement. Both parents were caring and involved. Although there was no major trauma in Cathy's life, there were enough changes and stresses to have an effect on her. Every child develops a process in life, a way of being, in order to cope, survive, get needs met, grow up. Why one child chooses one way of being and another something else is a matter of speculation. Cathy's process was to "space out" in order to protect herself from unpleasant situations and feelings. As children grow the coping behaviours do not disappear without intervention—they only become accelerated. Cathy might, as she grew older, find more adolescent ways of "spacing out" such as taking drugs and as an adult, drinking alcohol. Life rarely gets easier for people—only more complicated. Life changes affect children. We live in a very stressful, changeable society, more so than ever, and we need to be alert to the ways children are affected. Parents need skills to help children through these changes and life occurrences. Children often blame themselves for whatever negative things happen, such as divorce, and have difficulty talking about this, or even understanding what that vague, uncomfortable feeling is all about. Further, children will have mixed feelings about events as a remarriage, the birth of a baby, or going back and forth to spend alternate weeks with each parent. They may feel happy, excited and relieved but they also may feel angry, jealous, sad, frightened and worried.

Mixed feelings confuse children and they will attempt to avoid and push them away. They may show the good ones since those bring approval. But the negative feelings simmer inside of them and cause a variety of inappropriate behaviours and symptoms. Parents need to know that they need to find ways to help their children express those negative, bad, ugly feelings without making the child feel bad or guilty for expressing them. Asking, "Do you feel upset about this?" does not help. Questions cause children to close down or feel put on the spot. They will say "no" or "I don't know" or shrug their shoulders. Sometimes just making a statement to the child such as, "I bet you didn't like it when Mommy and Daddy divorced," or "I bet you get tired of going back and forth to be with Mommy and Daddy" is extremely effective. The child will often nod with great relief to have his feelings articulated.

I make assumptions that many of these negative feelings exist and then find ways that are interesting and fun to help children through them. I may be wrong sometimes, and if I am, children let me know in ways that I know are genuine. Usually I am right. We need to provide ways of making the expressions fun and interesting because children are frightened of the weight and seriousness of the situations and their feeling. So we exaggerate many of the feelings in ways that make kids laugh. For example, I did a puppet show for Cathy depicting two animal puppet parents arguing loudly about ordinary things. The scene ends with the parents deciding to divorce. The next scene shows a child (animal puppet again—I very rarely use real-looking people puppets, unless they are caricatures) talking to the audience (Cathy) about how she feels about the divorce in an exaggerated manner. "I hate this! I don't *want* them to get a divorce. What will happen to me? Oh dear, oh dear. What should I do? It must be my fault! If I had been a better girl, this would not have happened." In the next scene, the child puppet confronts her parents with all of her feelings. They say they are sorry and hug her and tell her they love her and that she didn't do anything to make the divorce happen. She yells back, "I still don't like it!" The show ends at this point. The purpose here is not to make thing better or find a solution or pacify the situation, but to bring out the feelings I assume that Cathy is feeling, and that many, many children feel in situations like this. Cathy loved this show and did a similar one for me. At one point I said, "I bet sometimes *you* feel the way that puppet felt." Not a question, just a statement that Cathy could accept or reject. Her response was a heartfelt "Yeah!" I have actually had children say when watching a similar show, "That's just like my life!"

Similar techniques were used with other events in her life using drawings, clay, the sand tray, creative dramatics, music, games. The possibilities are endless. I asked her to make a scene in the sand representing the divorce in her life and she made a graveyard with a toy gravestone I once bought in New Orleans (it originally had candy in it) and a Mom figure at one end of the sand tray and a Dad figure at the other. A girl figure stood in front of the gravestone. "Divorce is like someone dying," she said. I asked her to have the girl figure talk to the Mom and Dad figures. Much feeling emerged, particularly anger. Cathy was very pleased with this activity and the pleasure of making the sand scene gave much support for her expression of negative feelings.

It is very difficult for children to express the anger that is kept hidden. It sometimes comes out in uncontrolled ways, which only makes things worse. If the child feels at fault for the divorce, for example, how can she express her anger? She loves both of her parents—how can she be mad at them? She hates it when they are mad at her. They are moving into separate houses—maybe she'll be abandoned and left without a place to live. She'd better keep her feelings to herself. The child may not articulate these thoughts to herself. Often they are visceral feelings. The organism, in its everlasting quest for health, seeks to rid itself of the blocked energy, causing, I believe, the child to behave in troubling ways. In Cathy's case the organism's thrust for equilibrium pushing against her blocked feelings resulted in ADHD symptoms. Cathy was able to express many of her feelings in our work together and to her parents in family sessions. Her "spacing out" behaviour disappeared. All of this took about nine months of weekly, 45-minute sessions.

It feels important for me to add here that though I have plans and goals for my sessions with children based on the issues involved and my assessment of the child's therapeutic needs, I have no expectations. Whatever happens in the session, in my meeting with the child, or with the child and her parents, is what happens. It is important for me to have this kind of stance—one of acceptance of whatever takes place—since I believe that having expectations is likely to breed failure. This does not mean that I don't evaluate the session and review what *did* happen. There is much to learn from doing this.

Working with parents is an ongoing, vital part of my work. When parents are interested and involved, progress takes place faster. It is important that parents understand the process of therapy and that I spend time explaining it to them. Most parents are grateful for this information. I see the parents with the child every four to six weeks. Sometimes we use this time to discuss issues, how the child is faring at home and at school, concerns the parents have and sometimes the parents participate with the child is some expressive technique, as a drawing, a clay exercise, a game. If there are other children in the family I will engage the whole family as necessary. One of the most important issues that I bring up with families involves anger—how each family expresses anger, what happens when they do, what kinds of things make them angry, what the anger feels like in their bodies. Sometimes I will ask each person to draw a picture of something that makes them angry. A successful exercise is to ask each person to say to every other family member, "One thing I like about you is . . ." And then, "One thing that makes me mad (or I don't like, or bugs me sometimes) is . . ." There is no discussion during the game—this can happen later. This exercise helps children to see that anger is natural and permissible and can be stated calmly without explosion. Sometimes I ask each person in the family to rate the family on a scale of one to ten or 1 per cent to 100 per cent, the highest number being perfect. For example, in one family Dad gave a rating of 80 per cent, Mom a rating of 60 per cent and Allen, the 12-year-old, a rating of 40 per cent. I asked each to discuss what was missing in the family to make it 100 per cent and to talk about the good part too. This was one of the most illuminating sessions we had.

Often I will assign "homework" to the parents. Such homework is presented as an experiment, to be tried for a limited time—one or two weeks and the task to be broken down into small, do-able, practical items. For example, I might ask the parent or parents to practise limit setting, deciding on a specific limit and sticking to it. Many parents of ADHD children have difficulty setting and enforcing limits, causing, I believe, much anxiety in their children, which further exacerbates their ADHD behaviours and symptoms. I help parents understand that it takes some time for a child to respond to limit setting, and that patient, firm, consistent rule setting is necessary. We talk about "natural consequences" fitting the developmental level of the child. I am totally against violence directed toward children, even slapping. There are kinder, more effective, longer lasting methods, and I have only seen negative results come from hitting children for ANY reason. The child, of course, will rebel at first against limits. This is completely natural and to be expected. Children have a right to be angry, sullen, or grumpy about them. Some parents want their children to abide by the limits and be happy and cheerful about them, probably because it makes the parent feel better.

One of the most important parts of the therapeutic process has to do with helping children learn how to be self-nurturing. As mentioned earlier, ADHD children absorb many negative messages about themselves. No only do young children blame themselves for all the bad things that happen to them, but because of their unpleasant symptomatology, receive a great deal of unfavourable response, which further reinforces the self-blame and bad feelings of self. Without therapeutic intervention, these negative introjects remain with the children throughout their lives. Much of the work that we do involves helping the child regain and strengthen the self that has been cut off, inhibited and restricted. However, as the child makes gains, there is that part of the self, generally a younger part, that still retains those negative messages. And so we must help the child make contact with and nurture that part. Changed parental attitudes are wonderful, but do not as a rule change those damaging beliefs of self. It seems to be a task for the child himself, a task that becomes most feasible when self-support is present.

I might ask the child to draw a picture, or choose a puppet, or make a form out of clay to represent a part of himself he doesn't like. (These parts generally represent the negative self message, or negative introject.) For example, 8-year-old Billy, mentioned early on in this chapter, chose a puppet that reminded him of the "part of myself that gets me into trouble." My puppet—I generally choose a fairly neutral one—talked to Billy's puppet who told me all the ways he got Billy into trouble. "How do you feel about this part of you?" I asked Billy directly. "I hate him!" he replied vehemently. I encouraged Billy to talk to the Getting Him Into Trouble puppet and tell him. Billy yelled at the puppet, "I *hate* you! I wish you would go away!" I cheered Billy on because I knew that, although he appeared to be yelling at himself, experientially he was actually expressing a lot of his repressed anger outward rather than allowing it to be turned back onto himself. In this way Billy was giving himself the support he needed to contact his nurturing self. I asked Billy how long this part had been with him. He responded, "All my life." I said, "Do you remember him when he was four?" Billy shook his head. "How about five, when you started kindergarten." Billy nodded. I said, "Let's pretend he's 5 years old—just a little boy. Pick a puppet that could be his fairy godmother." He did. "What would his fairy godmother say to him?"

Billy was able to say things, with a little help from me, like, "You're a nice kid. I like you. You don't do things so you'll be bad. You're really a nice, good boy. Sometimes you just want people to listen to you, to play with you." I asked Billy to put the fairy godmother puppet down, and say these things as himself to the puppet that gets him into trouble. He did. "How does it feel to say these things to yourself?" I asked. Billy responded, "Good!" I told Billy to choose something at home to be that 5-year-old part of himself, a teddy bear perhaps, and to say those nice things to it every night for a week. In this way Billy began to integrate those negative parts of himself with his stronger, healthier self. See the chapter on Self-Nurturing for further information about this process.

As you can see, treatment of children diagnosed as having Attention Deficit Hyperactive Disorder is not much different than treatment of any other child who comes into therapy.

The therapeutic process is natural to the development of every child. The therapist merely gears this process to the child's needs, taking into consideration each child's uniqueness and particular life experiences. Every child has the inherent right to develop, strengthen and express every aspect of his or her organism: the body, the senses, the emotions and the intellect. As the child begins to know all of herself and is able to connect with her world in fulfilling, healthful ways, her path of life and growth will be a joyful one.

CHAPTER TWELVE

An innovative way to use music in therapy

everal years ago I had the privilege of attending a week-long
workshop with the renowned musician Paul Winter at his
music village on his farm in Connecticut. I was deeply moved
by the experience, I thought that if this experience so affected me in
the way that it did, perhaps I could adapt this method to my work
with children. The response was even better than I had ever antici-
pated. I would like to describe to you some of the experiences I had
with the children, the various formats that I used and, of most importance, the therapeutic effects. Bear in mind that it is always difficult
to put into words something that actually needs to be experienced.

Preliminary to getting started is an assortment of instruments
such as drums of various sizes, tambourines, clackers, clickers,
whistles, gongs, shakers, xylophones and any other sound-making
gismo. All of these items can be stored in a large basket. No matter
whom I'm working with—individual child, family and group of
children, adolescents or adults—everyone needs to have some time
to experiment with the instruments. So I generally empty the con-
tents of the basket on the floor (an event in itself) and each item
is picked up and examined for its sound quality. (Floor sitting is
recommended for this experience.)

Description of basic process

This exercise is usually experienced with one person, although I have used it with success with two, or even three others. Each person chooses an instrument from the pile to start with. The client begins to play the instrument in any way desired. After a few moments, I will begin to play along. After a few moments of playing together, the client will stop and I will play alone. The client then chooses another instrument and joins with me. After a few moments I stop playing and the client plays alone. I choose a new instrument and join with my client. After a moment the client stops and I play alone. The client then chooses a new instrument and plays with me, and so on. It may take a few rounds to "get it" but it generally happens quickly. We do not speak. At times I may need to give hand signals for stopping, playing alone, joining.

What exactly is happening here? The experience and benefits vary with different children. For example, James, aged 11, is stiff and rigid in his body, controlling in his relationships with peers, siblings and parents. His emotions are locked deep within him. During the time that we did the above music experience, his body obviously relaxed and he appeared loose and fluid. He liked the structure of the process and began to give me hand signals for stopping and starting, taking some appropriate control. We did this process often and gradually his body response carried over into other areas of his life and he began to express some of his buried feelings in our sessions.

Another client, Steven, aged 8, is constantly in motion. He is diagnosed with ADHD and even medication does not calm him. When we do the music, he becomes focused and relaxed and stays with the activity the entire session by his own choice. Lately, in our sessions, he has become interested in many other activities and his new sense of self is carrying over into his home and school life.

I, myself, experience a wonderful feeling of aliveness when I participate in this process. I feel myself—a sense of myself. I am aware of my breath, my body, my boundaries. It's difficult to put this feeling into words—one must experience it. As the child and I make music together I look at the child and imagine that he or she feels the self as I do.

Writing about this experience is difficult for me. What we are doing is basically "right-brained," non-linear and non-verbal. I am trying to describe an experience with words even though I say over and over that it is difficult to express in words. I hope I can convey at least the essence of this most valuable experience.

In Gestalt Therapy terminology we could say that contact in its best sense is taking place. Contact requires having a sense of the self when meeting the other. It involves having good use of the functions of contact: listening, looking, touching, tasting, smelling, moving. Contact requires awareness of the various aspects of the organism: the senses, the body, the emotions, the intellect. Children who make poor contact with others—peers, siblings, parents, teachers—are cut off, restricted in some or all aspects of the organism. These troubled children engage in inappropriate defenses, or manifest detrimental physical symptoms. The healthy flow of organismic self-regulation is interrupted. Not only do these children have difficulty engaging in satisfying and healthy contact, they usually have a poor sense of self and low self-esteem.

The experiences of this music process enhance and strengthen the self and the contact functions. The child experiences a feeling of mastery. Joining with the child's rhythm as we play our music is probably the most significant part of this process.

Johan, my apprentice from Germany, observed the musical experience described above with me and 8-year-old Steven. He states, "When you were doing the rhythms with Steven, pacing and matching his rhythm, I was watching him. He was so involved with it—his face—he just had this look of being so satisfied to feel that you were with him. He would change his rhythm and then you would change yours to match his, and he would take a very deep breath. It was as if he were testing you to see if you were really with him. The colour of his face changed—he just glowed. I could see that he really enjoyed doing this—that it gave him something. It's so hard to put this into words." There's that statement again. It IS difficult to describe this experience in words. It is definitely an adventure into a non-verbal realm.

This basic form has endless possibilities. Often at some point after we have been playing together, I will ask the child how she feels. The typical response is "good" or "happy". And so I suggest that we play "good" or "happy" using any of the instruments in front of us. I may then ask for another feeling. "How about sad? Think of something that makes you feel sad." "I felt really sad when my cat disappeared." "What is your sad feeling about? You don't have to tell me if you don't want to. Now let's play sad."

We think of other feelings or states of being: afraid, crazy, bored, angry, silly.

Often when we go through the feelings I experience a sort of spiral of expressing more and more of the feeling until I feel that I've had enough; I'm satisfied. I'm finished for now. I've made some closure. Making the feeling sounds together gives me a feeling of support; I'm not alone with my feeling. There is a friend with me, looking at me, smiling at me even as I'm sad or angry or crazy. It feels as if someone understands me—someone accepts me. No matter what the sounds are like to your ears, I am feeling something deep and wordless inside me. Since it would be so difficult for the child to articulate what she is experiencing, I can only project my own experience and imagine that she feels the same way that I do.

Variations

Melissa, aged 10, is a silent child, diagnosed as an elective mute. When I'm with her I am fairly quiet *myself*—meeting her as much as I can where she is. She does some drawings, makes scenes in the sand, forms objects out of clay and will nod yes or shake her head no to my enquiries. Her energy level is generally fairly low. When we did the music process, there was a decided change in her demeanour: I could see the excitement and energy well up in her. We spoke to each other through the musical sounds. When we moved on to the feeling portion, Melissa's excitement heightened. Her eyes shone as we played happy and crazy. Her lips pursed tightly as we played mad. Her eyes filled with tears, as did mine watching her, when we played sad. And at the end when I softly asked her how she felt inside right now, she whispered, "Good"—the first word I had ever heard her speak. Melissa's feelings were overwhelming to her due to severe trauma in her life. The music playing appeared to provide a way for her to express some of her feelings non-verbally with more power and congruency than any of the other media we had used, and gradually helped her to feel enough support to express herself in words.

Sometimes I make up a story about different feelings—a metaphorical story, about a dog, perhaps, who has lost his way and feels very sad, and we play the music to this story. "Once there was a little dog who lived with a family he loved very much. One day he decided it would be great to surprise the boy in the family by meeting him at school. When no one was looking the dog made a run for it. He was sure he knew the way but somehow the streets looked different. He ran up one street and down another. It started to rain and it was cold and windy. The little dog huddled in a doorway and didn't know what to do. What do you think happened next?" Each child comes up with a different scenario and we play our music to each one. Of course often the child's story is a projection of something in his or her life that we can talk about if we want to. My story, I realize, is a projection too of course! When I was in Kindergarten in Cambridge, Massachusetts, I was supposed to wait at a certain spot at school for an older child to meet me and walk me home each day. One day I decided to assert my independence and walk home alone. I got hopelessly lost. Each street looked like the other but none led to home. I began to cry when I realized the world was just too big for me. A man stopped and asked if he could help me and I told him I was lost. I told him where I lived (actually the address of my father's tailor shop since I spent a lot of time playing there). I trustingly went with the man who took me to my father's store (just around the corner). My father was totally surprised to see me and I was so infused with joy to see him that he couldn't bring himself to reprimand me. He didn't need to since I learned from this experience to accept who I was—a very little girl in a big world.

Sometimes I tell a story about a girl who heard her parents fighting one night when she was trying to go to sleep. The fighting sounded like this (loud drums and shaker noise). She got scared when she heard them fight because maybe they were going to get a divorce. Let's play how she must have felt. Knowing something about the child is helpful for creating stories—though there are many universal feelings and situations that we can all relate to.

Sometimes I use imagery. "Close your eyes and imagine that you are at the beach. Feel the sun on your back. Listen to the sound of the waves. Bend down and let your fingers run through the sand. Smell the ocean. Taste the salt on your hand. You notice that someone is flying a kite. What colour is it?" (Wait for response from child.)

"What shape is it? You can feel a gentle breeze on your skin—the same one that's moving the kite around. Open your eyes and let's play music for the kite." This image is particularly good to help children wind down, centre the self, become more grounded, before they leave my office to go out into the world.

The children come up with many creative ideas to add to the experience. One child, only 6 years old, suggested that we do a continuation story and play music for each other. I began a story about a little girl lost in the forest and Lisa played lost in the forest music. "Once upon a time there was a little girl who went for a walk in the forest. Suddenly she realized that she was lost! She didn't know the way back at all! (There's a lost child story again!) Suddenly she heard a cackling sound. She looked all around and out from behind a tree came a wicked witch. What happened next?" As I began to play wicked witch music, Lisa pointed to one of the instruments, telling me with her eyes that she felt IT would be more appropriate for witch music. And so on we went.

It is important to mention that all of the variations I have mentioned—expressing feelings, imagery, storytelling—came about *after* we did the basic format described in the beginning. I think the experience of contact that comes with the process—playing alone, joining together, withdrawing, coming together again—is an essential prerequisite to further nuances of the process. It provides the self-support the child needs for further expression.

I have used this music-making process with siblings and with families. Nine-year-old Susan loved this music process and wanted her mother to participate. Susan's mother was a recovering alcoholic, in AA for only a few months. Susan had been a victim of physical abuse by both her parents, who were now divorced. She rarely saw her father. Susan literally fought for control of her life at home and school with her peers. The three of us sat down on the floor with the instruments and I explained the process to Susan's mother. The format we used was the same as described previously except that now we were three instead of two. Suddenly Susan said, "Mom, just watch my hands—I'll give you signals when to come in and when to stop. One finger means 'join in' and two fingers mean 'stop'. You watch my fingers too, Violet." Susan took control of the whole session within the structure and framework of the music format. Her mother understood. Instead of engaging in their usual power struggle, Susan's mother gave the control to Susan in this acceptable, appropriate setting that had clear boundaries. I had asked Susan's mother previously to provide times together when Susan could feel some power and control in a safe way. After this music experience she realized the value of my assignment.

As mentioned previously, children invent many ways to use the music. Susan asked me and her Mom at another session to play music to her puppet show. Again she took on the persona of a true conductor, moving her arms and fingers to let us know when to play, when to stop and even which instruments to play.

I would like to describe another kind of format that I use with groups. The group can be a family as well as the more traditional kind of group. The technique works well with a group of four, five, or even six. If the group is large, the rest of the members make up the listening audience and later the listeners become the players. Originally this chapter was written as a script for an audio tape, and present in the studio, when I recorded the tape, were three children (siblings) and their mother. Here are my instructions to them:

I'd like you to sit around the instruments (piled on the floor), one on each side, forming a sort of circle. You have a few minutes now to experiment with the instruments to see what sounds they can make.

OK, now I would like each of you to pick one or two instruments that you will use. We will all close our eyes for a few moments. The listeners will keep your eyes closed but after a few moments those of you in the centre may open your eyes if you need to. As soon as any one of you feels ready you will begin to make a sound with your instruments. I would like to emphasize that we are not interested in melody or any sustained rhythm, just sounds. You might want to experiment with different kinds of sounds and different ways to make sounds, as playing soft sometimes, or loud. You might want to play fast or slow. You might want to be quiet for a few moments to listen to the other sounds. You might want to make contact with one of the others and communicate with your sounds. If you feel a particular urge to pick up another instrument from the centre pile to make a special sound, as with a bell or a gong or a drum, go ahead and do it! After a while you will feel that it's time to stop and you need to pay attention to that stopping place. If necessary I will let you know when to stop since we have a time limit here today.

So let's all close our eyes now and all take some deep breaths. Go inside yourself for a few moments. Listen to the silence. Let the quiet surround you. When anyone feels ready, just begin. The rest of us, me and the crew here in the studio, will keep our eyes closed and listen. We might see some pictures in our head as you play, or the sounds might remind us of something.

The group does this exercise for about eight minutes and comes to a stop without needing a signal from me. I asked the children and their mother to share their experience, and then the listeners to share theirs. Whenever I am listening to one of these exercises, it's like a meditation for me. Sometimes I imagine that I'm in the woods hearing all kinds of nature sounds.

Not long ago I introduced this process to a family who were in therapy with me. The parents had complained that both children, aged 8 and 11, did not listen or cooperate with anything. The parents had very little awareness of their own responsibility for their sons' behaviour. "What was it like for you?" I asked the boys after their experience with the music. Both agreed that it was fun. "Tell me what you noticed other people doing," I said. One answered, "Well, I was very conscious of Jimmy (the 8-year-old) playing very loud."

Jimmy: I had to so you would hear me.
Me: Do you feel that your parents don't hear you a lot?
Jimmy: Yeah, they never hear me.
Me: Did any of you find yourself talking with your sounds to anyone else?
Jason: (*the 11-year-old*) I was doing this thing with the drum with Mom and I think she was answering me with her sticks.
Mom: That's right I was. That was nice.
Me: Does that remind you of anything in your everyday life?
Mom: Well, sometimes I think Jason is more like me.
Jimmy: Yeah, you love him more than me.
Mom: Jimmy, that's not true. I love you so much! (*Jimmy sits on his mother's lap.*)

I turn to the father. "What was your experience like with the music?"

Dad: I don't know. I was just playing the instruments. I wasn't paying attention to what the others were doing.

Mom: That's what he always does! He goes off on his own and I'm
         left to do everything with the kids.
Me: You sound mad.
Mom: Well I am! I hate it when he does that. I guess I take it out on
         the kids, especially Jimmy.

I asked the family to do the music process again and make some
changes. "I want you, Dad, to be more involved with what the
others are doing. And Jimmy, you try to play a little softer, and the
rest of you make an effort to hear him."

After the second try everyone, except Jimmy, agreed that there
was a big difference. Dad smiled broadly. Jimmy still felt that no one
was listening to him.

Me: Pick someone in your family, Jimmy, who doesn't listen to
         you the most.

Jimmy chose Dad. They tried the process once more and this time
Dad, without any prompting, smiled at Jimmy and joined his
rhythm. Jimmy was delighted.

Both parents agreed that they had learned more from this music
session than from any other session we had had. Some of the
dynamics that caused difficulties were symbolically presented to
them through this enjoyable experience. They reported to me that
the metaphor of the music experience became part of their in-family
communication, and very positive changes were made. Further,
there was much motivation to work in our subsequent sessions on
the various issues that had emerged in the music-making.

Whenever families engage in some kind of exercises together,
the dynamics of the family, that is, how they relate and react to
each other, are often crystallized. Issues that need exploration come
to the fore.

In examining what happened at this session, what is most striking
for me is the realizations these parents had coming out of a pleasant
and enjoyable experience. I think the pleasure of experience provided a very positive resource to deal with some negative, painful
aspects of this family's interactions. Further, I think the non-verbal
experience of the music making enhances awareness, and makes it
possible for people to be more receptive and less defensive. I have

seen the same kind of thing happen when I have used clay exercises with families. Not all families are willing to "play" with music, or clay or other creative media. They want to get down to the serious business at hand. It DOES take a certain amount of convincing on my part regarding the value of the experience. It is true, though, that those families who are willing to participate in these creative, expressive adventures are more likely to respond and effect positive change. One thing that does impress parents the most is that they see clearly how much more their children listen during and after the experience. Since "not listening" is a big complaint of both parents and children, this alone is a big selling point. The children in the families are *always* willing to do something that precludes talking.

The music-making was a turning point in my work with 13-year-old Jeff. He had much to be angry about in his life, but denied that there was anything to be angry about. He lived with his father who had brought Jeff in for therapy because he was failing all his subjects in school and not pulling his weight at home. In a session with his father, I asked Jeff to tell his Dad some things that his Dad did that made him mad. (Jeff's Dad always spoke freely about what angered him about Jeff.) Jeff replied, "Nothing." His body stiffened, he looked away and his energy faded. His contact was broken. His father said, "This is what always happens when I try to talk to him." I suggested we try something new and different—the music experience. The three of us sat on the floor and participated in the first process described above. Jeff said, "This is silly" as he played the instruments vigorously. Eventually I moved aside and asked father and son to "talk" to each other with the instruments. Then I suggested they play "mad" music to each other. Jeff and his father did this with great energy and laughter. Finally I asked if they had anything to say to each other with words. Jeff responded, "I'm really mad that you never spend any time with me that's fun!" The lines of communication were now open.

I'd like to describe a format that is wonderful to use with groups, the larger the better. Each person chooses one instrument. Someone is designated to begin playing his or her instrument, making a continuous sound. The second person, after a few moments, joins in. Then the third person joins the other two, and so on. Finally everyone is making their sound at the same time. Generally the sounds are consistent, that is, no one goes off into a new rhythm (although actually there is always room for trying this out to see what would happen). The cumulative sounds are very satisfying, particularly when the group is made up of ten or more people. Often people add voice sounds or get up in the middle and move as they play. After a while the person who started, stops. Then the next and so on until the last person is playing alone.

Whenever I have participated in this experience I have felt as if I were part of a wonderful orchestra. I feel connected to everyone else. I feel joyful and relaxed. I feel a sense of mastery. I feel accomplished and gifted.

There are other ways of making sounds besides through the use of instruments. By the way, *any* instrument can be used. One does not need to know how to play the saxophone, piano, guitar, etc. One need only know how to make the tone of the instrument. (This can be tricky with some instruments, as with a flute.) We can make sounds with our bodies: slapping various parts of our own bodies makes different sounds. We can make mouth sounds using tongue and lips to blow and click. We can make all kinds of voice sounds. We can hit the floor with hands and feet. It's fun to experiment with al of these sounds and to use them alone or in conjunction with the instruments.

I have written about my model of the therapeutic process in previous chapters. I would like to explore with you the many ways that these music-making techniques blend with this process.

In the beginning we focus on establishing a relationship with the child. In Gestalt Therapy we talk about the I/Thou relationship, one in which two people come together with respect and honour for the other. This kind of relationship is an important prerequisite for any therapeutic work, and actually is in itself therapeutic. As we meet together as two entitled beings, the child can experience her own *self*, her own boundaries. The very nature of this music experience meets the requirements for an authentic I/Thou relationship, and as we play together, the relationship flourishes.

The next step involves the issue of contact. I've discussed this earlier and I'd like to reiterate some of what I've written since this is such an important step. If a child is unable to sustain contact, not much therapy can take place. Contact involves the ability to be fully present in the moment, and making use of one's contact functions to make this possible. If I find myself spacey and out of contact, I need only bring myself to the awareness of what my eyes see around me, the sounds I hear with my ears, what I might smell or taste and what my hands can touch. I bring myself into the here and now. Contact is further enhanced when I acknowledge the sensations present in my body, such as tingling, aches and pains, tightness, relaxation. Recognizing my emotions, whether I choose to share them or not, further strengthens my ability to be present. And finally, being able to communicate the self—my thoughts, opinions, needs, wants, wishes, likes and dislikes and so forth—amplifies my contact abilities. Good contact also involves the ability to withdraw appropriately, rather than to become rigidified in a presumably contactful space. Contact is a fluid phenomenon—coming together and moving apart, coming together and moving apart.

The music experiences promote contact and the enhancement of the contact functions. The first format described is particularly excellent for contact enhancement through the process of playing alone, joining together in rhythm and listening to each other. Certainly the senses are in operation, particularly the auditory one. And in our storytelling and imagery the other senses are purposefully brought into play.

I will often direct the child's awareness to his body in these experiences. For example, "What do we have to do to play the tambourine? What parts of our bodies do we use and what happens to the rest of the body as we play?" Everything is connected, we discover. Making sounds with the body creates new body awareness as well. Children tense and relax throughout the process, become fluid where before they may have been stiff and rigid. Breath plays an important role in these experiences. Sometimes breath changes are clearly visible. Tense and anxious children (and adults) will hold the breath periodically and breathe in a very shallow manner. As children participate in the music experience, they begin to take full, deep, healthful breaths.

The next step in the therapy process involves what I call self work, or helping the child develop a strong sense of self, find self-support within, experience mastery and power, define and strengthen the boundaries of self and make use of the aggressive energy that precludes sound self-expression and emotional expression. All of the work we do involving the strengthening of the contact functions and increased body awareness, is part of the enhancement of the self. Learning to express the self kinesthetically and verbally provides further self-support. Every time a child makes a statement about herself, she gains self-support. I see the music experiences as a forum for self-expression. When I participate I feel that I am making a statement about myself each time. As described earlier, I feel myself in an intense way. One's process becomes clear in the music exercise, as evidenced by the description of one family's experience. Further, the exercise gave members of the family the opportunity to experiment with new kinds of self-expression.

I believe that energy plays an important role in enhancement of the self. I speak often of helping children find their aggressive energy. I do not mean that kind of aggression that hurts or harms people in any way. I am referring to an energy that allows the child to feel the full force of her power, herself and makes it possible to present herself to the world with entitlement. Many children who have been traumatized, particularly through sexual abuse, present themselves in timid, fearful, passive ways. Louise was just such a girl. She had been sexually abused by her step-father for several years before the disclosure. Louise handled her trauma by being a very good girl, remaining unnoticed as much as she could. In our work together I hoped to restore to Louise that lively self that she had once had as a baby. Though willing to do almost anything I suggested (it was always difficult for her to make any decisions on her own), she passively resisted anything to do with the expression of anger. She preferred to make cookies and pizza out of clay rather than pound it; she could never think of anything at all in her life that made her mad; she professed to like everything, even cauliflower and broccoli; she selected the cute kitten puppet and wouldn't even look at monsters or anything with teeth; and she would *never* agree to have a Bataca fight with me. During the time I worked with Louise, the music process came into my life. Louise loved it and actually requested that we do it many times. Each time I noticed that her body posture, facial colouring and energy level changed. She sat up straighter, her face glowed with healthy colour and her energy was high. Her mother, who often participated, noticed these phenomena too. One day as we were playing various feelings with the instruments, I suggested that we play feeling mad (I had suggested this before but Louise's mad playing had been listless and lethargic). This time Louise said, "Yeah!" as if she'd never heard the suggestion before and began to pound on the drums with great vigour. "Can you think of things that make you mad?" I asked. She grinned and nodded. "Me too!" I said as I pounded energetically along with her. Louise had found her aggressive energy, and from that point on our therapeutic journey together took a new turn. All the heretofore-suppressed aspects of herself came flooding through. It was as if she had broken the dam that had blocked the spontaneous, alive, energetic child within herself.

With Louise's new-found self-support, she was able to work through many of her withheld emotions, the next step in the therapeutic process. The music was one of her favourite ways to express her previously buried emotions of rage and grief, though she made good use too of drawings, clay, imagery and fantasy exercises, puppets, creative dramatics and the sand tray. All of these techniques are powerful in helping children express deep, blocked emotions. It is interesting to me that certain techniques are more effective with some children than others. Generally I'm not aware that the music, for instance, will be a turning point for emotional expression for a particular child. Sometimes I intuitively sense that the music will be right for a particular child. Or I'm just reaching for straws. Or I'm excited about wanting to try the process. When I first began experimenting with the music process, my own interest and motivation in using it was so high that it was difficult for any client to resist it! I used it with everybody. One child would have a tremendous breakthrough while another just thought it was fun. (I must say that no one as yet has ever disliked it.)

Sometimes the music is the catalyst that allows the child to express her emotions. Sometimes it is the support that the experiences with the music give her. The music is a vehicle for safe expression. Often when a child plays a particular feeling, we go deeper into that feeling. After one child, Elise, played sad feelings to a story we made up, I asked her if the story reminded her of her own sad feelings. She told me about her sadness when her parents leave her with a sitter. I asked her to draw a picture of herself being sad in such a situation. She drew a girl standing in a house with tears coming down her face. I asked her to actually BE that girl and speak for her. "What would she be saying?" I asked. Elise responded, "I'm crying because my Mom and Dad aren't here. I like my sitter but I want my Mom and Dad. I don't like it when they leave." "What's the worst thing that could happen?" I gently asked. "They won't come back," Elise whispered. Elise had been abandoned by her birth mother when she was 7 years old. She had never known her birth father. She was now, at the age of 10, after living in two foster homes, adopted into a new family. No wonder she was sad when her parents left for the evening. However, she had never been able to articulate the feeling before this time. Elise's fear of abandonment was debilitating for her. Bringing her feelings out into the open was a vital prerequisite for her healing journey.

An important step in Elise's healing excursion was to learn how to be nurturing to the little girl inside of herself who had suffered so much trauma. Self-Nurturing Work, as I call it, is one of the final steps in the therapy process. In essence, my goal here is not only to help children nurture the younger child within themselves, but to help them know how to be accepting, caring and nurturing to themselves in their present lives. Children are certainly often given a double message about enjoying themselves. Although we expect children to play and have fun, we often give them the message that fun is all they think about, they are lazy and not being responsible. Children become very confused. They feel guilty about feeling good. Children who are troubled and disturbed, children who have experienced trauma, feel that they are responsible in some way for the bad things that have happened. Somehow they did something wrong. They have introjected, swallowed whole, taken in, many faulty messages about themselves from a very early age, and these messages can remain with them through life and interfere with their leading happy, productive lives. I find that even if parents change their manner of relating to their children, attempt to give them new positive messages, the children are still harbouring the old messages and a faulty belief system about the self. Teaching children to forgive, love and nurture themselves is vital work. Finding joy in aspects of their lives, having fun, laughing, doing things they like, are interested in, have pleasure from—are essential elements in leading healthy, productive, caring lives.

The music experience is a nurturing experience. Each time I participate with a child, I feel joy and happiness within myself. The child's delight is unmistakable. There is a calmness and serenity present for both of us. Even when we are banging on the drums to express anger, we do so with pleasure.

The music experience can be used as a vehicle for communicating with and nurturing the younger child within. Elise used the music to show me how that little girl felt at various times of her life when words were not accessible to her. Some of her experiences were actually pre-verbal. Elise developed her own way of talking to her inner child through the music with a private language of her own.

As you try out the various music formats with your clients, your experiences may be different than mine. You may discover therapeutic aspects that are not mentioned here. You and your clients will invent new, creative ways to use this approach. In any case, I know that you will have a rich, exceptional experience.

Just remember, there is no such thing as a wrong note.

Addendum

Here is a story someone sent to me on the internet some time ago:

On 18 November 1995, Itzhak Perlman, the violinist, came on stage to give a concert at Avery Fisher Hall at Lincoln Center in New York City. If you have ever been to a Perlman concert you know that getting on stage is no small achievement for him. He was stricken with polio as a child, and so he has braces on both legs and walks with the aid of two crutches. To see him walk across the stage one step at a time, painfully and slowly, is a sight. He walks painfully, yet majestically, until he reaches his chair. Then he sits down, slowly, puts his crutches on the floor, undoes the clasps on his legs, tucks one foot back and extends the other foot forward. The he bends down and picks up the violin, puts it under his chin, nods to the conductor and proceeds to play.

By now the audience are used to this ritual. They sit quietly while he makes his way across the stage to his chair. They remain reverently silent while he undoes the clasps on his legs. They wait until he is ready to play. But this time, something went wrong. Just as he finished the first few bars, one of the strings on his violin broke. You could hear it snap—it went off like gunfire across the room. There was no mistaking what that sound meant. There was no mistaking what he had to do. People who were there that night thought to themselves, "We figured that he would have to get up, put on the clasps again, pick up the crutches and limp his way off stage—to either find another violin or else find another string for this one."

But he didn't. Instead, he waited a moment, closed his eyes and signalled the conductor to begin again. The orchestra began, and he played from where he had left off. And he played with such passion and such power and such purity as they had never heard before. Of course, anyone knows that it is impossible to play a symphonic work with just three strings. I know that and you know that, but that night Itzhak Perlman refused to know that. You could see him modulating, changing, recomposing the piece in his head. At one point it sounded like he was de-tuning the strings to get new sounds from them that they had never made before. When he finished, there was an awesome silence in the room. And then people rose and cheered. There was an extraordinary outburst of applause from every corner of the auditorium. We were all on our feet, screaming and cheering, doing everything we could do to show how much we appreciated what he had done. He smiled, wiped the sweat from his brow, raised his bow to quiet us and then he said, not boastfully, but in a quiet, pensive, reverent tone, "You know, sometimes it is the artist's task to find out how much music you can still make with what you have left."

So perhaps our task in this shaky, fast-changing, bewildering world in which we live is to make music, at first with all that we have and then, when that is no longer possible, to make music with whatever we do have.

EPILOGUE

There is much more I could have written, but I had to stop somewhere. As I have always said in workshops I give, I just can't meet everybody's need. I hope that you will find enough of what you need in the chapters I did write. I have given workshops over the years on some topics that are not included here: divorce, child abuse, using the media in the service of therapy. I did not write about using puppets, therapeutic metaphors, or other specific techniques. Nor did I write about working with parents and families or what happens at the first session. I did not include five original children's stories that I wrote a long time ago that I still love. I have a large envelope filled with questions people have submitted at workshops and thought a chapter (or book) on "The Questions People Ask Me" would be useful. I did not include a case from beginning to end, as some have requested. (See my chapter "From Meek to Bold" in *Play Therapy in Action*.)

It is probably not a good thing to focus on the negative, except that it does help me to realize that there is a wealth of material in my heart and mind about working with children and adolescents that might take more years than I have left to share and write about. This kind of realization is actually a good thing since it makes me feel very alive.

When I do my annual two-week training programme, I emphasize that I do not want people to imitate me, but to find their own way to make use of what they learn in the trainings. We have had many wonderful discussions on this topic. To find your own way opens you to incredible creative possibilities and frees you to become a vital therapist. So I hope you will take whatever information seems useful to you in this book, and allow it to become assimilated in the wonderful you that you already are.

Good luck and best wishes.

REFERENCES

American Psychiatric Association (1994). *Diagnostic and Statistical Manual of Mental Disorders (DSM-IV)*. Washington, DC: American Psychiatric Association.

Arenson, Gloria (2001). *Five Simple Steps To Emotional Healing*. New York: Fireside.

Ayres, J. (1995). *Sensory Integration and the Child*. Los Angeles, CA: Western Psychological Services.

Beiser, A. (1970). The Paradoxical Theory of Change. In J. Fagan and I. L. Shepherd, (Eds.), *Gestalt Therapy Now* (pp. 77–80). New York: Harper.

Bowlby, J. (1973–1983). *Attachment, Separation and Loss*. New York: Basic Books.

Brown, G. I. (1972 and 1990). *Human Teaching for Human Learning*. New York: The Gestalt Journal.

Buber, M. (1958). *I and Thou*. New York: Scribner.

Eos Interactive Cards. (Unknown date). *Oh Cards*. Victoria, BC, Canada: Eos Interactive Cards.

Goodman, L. (1971). *Linda Goodman's Sun Signs*. New York: Bantam.

Handford, M. (1987). *Where's Waldo?* Boston, MA: Little Brown and Co.

Jolles, I. (1986). *A Catalog for the Qualitative Interpretation of the House-Tree-Person (H-T-P)*. Los Angeles, CA: Western Psychological Services.

Kubler-Ross, E. (1973). *On Death and Dying*. New York: Macmillan.

Luscher, M. (1971). *The Luscher Color Test*. New York: Pocket Books.

Mayer, M. (1968). *There's A Nightmare In My Closet*. New York: Dial Books.

McConville, M. (1995). *Adolescence: Psychotherapy and the Emergent Self*. San Francisco, CA: Jossey Bass.

Mooney, R. L. (1950). *Mooney Problem Checklist*. New York: The Psychological Corporation.

Murray, H. A. (1943). *Thematic Apperception Test*. Lutz, FL: Psychological Assessment Resource, Inc.

Oaklander, V. (1978). *Windows To Our Children*. Moab, UT: Real People Press.

Oaklander, V. (1988). *Windows To Our Children*. New York: The Gestalt Journal Press.

Perls, F. (1969, 1947). *Ego, Hunger And Aggression*. New York: Vintage Books.

Phillips, J. Jr. (1969). *The Origins of Intellect, Piaget's Theory*. San Francisco, CA.: W.H. Freeman and Co.

Polster, E. & Polster, M. (1973). *Gestalt Theory Integrated*. New York: Brunner-Mazel.

Rubenfeld, I. (1992). Gestalt Therapy and the BodyMind. In Nevis, E. C. (Ed.), *Gestalt Therapy: Perspectives and Applications*, pp. 147–178. New York: Gardner Press.

Sams, J. and Carson, D. (1951, 1988). *Medicine Cards*. Santa Fe, NM: Bear and Co.

Segalove, I. & Velick P. B. (1996). *List Your Self*. Kansas City, MO: A Universal Press Syndicate Co.

Sendak, M. (1963, 1970). *Where the Wild Things Are*. New York: Penguin Books.

Shafarman, S. (1997). *Awareness Heels: The Feldenkrais Method for Dynamic Health*. Reading, MA: Addison-Wesley Publishing Co.

Silverton, L. (1991) *Problem Experiences Checklist, Adolescent Version*. Los Angeles, CA.: Western Psychological Services.

Smith, R., Joanne, R., & Campbell, H. J. (1996). *I Can't Live With Mum and Dad Anymore*. New South Wales, Australia: Burnside Press.

Terr, L. (1990). *Too Scared To Cry*. New York: Basic Books.

Viorst, J. (1972). *Alexander and the Terrible, Horrible, No Good, Very Bad Day*. New York: Aladdin Books.

Wagner, E. (1969). *The Hand Test*. Los Angeles, CA: Western Psychological Services.

INDEX